CAMBRIDGE LIBRARY COLLECTION

Books of enduring scholarly value

History

The books reissued in this series include accounts of historical events and movements by eye-witnesses and contemporaries, as well as landmark studies that assembled significant source materials or developed new historiographical methods. The series includes work in social, political and military history on a wide range of periods and regions, giving modern scholars ready access to influential publications of the past.

Two Letters to Sir Charles Forbes

Originally published between 1824 and 1853, these four pieces by James Silk Buckingham (1786–1855) illuminate the concerns of a broad-minded traveller and the problems of governing an empire. A newspaperman, social reformer and fierce critic of the East India Company, Buckingham published the *Calcutta Journal* until his expulsion from India in 1823 for attacking vested interests. The first and second pieces reissued here are his open letters, written anonymously in 1824, to the M.P. Sir Charles Forbes regarding press freedom and the expulsion, without trial, of himself and another editor. These are followed by an 1830 account of the reception of his public lecture tour on the East India Company's monopoly, and an 1853 outline for the future government of India. Together, these polemical texts provide great insight into contemporary colonial debates surrounding British rule in India.

Cambridge University Press has long been a pioneer in the reissuing of out-of-print titles from its own backlist, producing digital reprints of books that are still sought after by scholars and students but could not be reprinted economically using traditional technology. The Cambridge Library Collection extends this activity to a wider range of books which are still of importance to researchers and professionals, either for the source material they contain, or as landmarks in the history of their academic discipline.

Drawing from the world-renowned collections in the Cambridge University Library and other partner libraries, and guided by the advice of experts in each subject area, Cambridge University Press is using state-of-the-art scanning machines in its own Printing House to capture the content of each book selected for inclusion. The files are processed to give a consistently clear, crisp image, and the books finished to the high quality standard for which the Press is recognised around the world. The latest print-on-demand technology ensures that the books will remain available indefinitely, and that orders for single or multiple copies can quickly be supplied.

The Cambridge Library Collection brings back to life books of enduring scholarly value (including out-of-copyright works originally issued by other publishers) across a wide range of disciplines in the humanities and social sciences and in science and technology.

Two Letters to Sir Charles Forbes

*And Other Short Writings
on the East India Company
and the Freedom of the Press*

JAMES SILK BUCKINGHAM

CAMBRIDGE
UNIVERSITY PRESS

CAMBRIDGE UNIVERSITY PRESS

Cambridge, New York, Melbourne, Madrid, Cape Town,
Singapore, São Paolo, Delhi, Mexico City

Published in the United States of America by Cambridge University Press, New York

www.cambridge.org
Information on this title: www.cambridge.org/9781108046459

© in this compilation Cambridge University Press 2013

This edition first published 1824–53
This digitally printed version 2013

ISBN 978-1-108-04645-9 Paperback

A

LETTER

TO

SIR CHARLES FORBES, BART. M.P.

ON THE

SUPPRESSION

OF

PUBLIC DISCUSSION IN INDIA,

AND THE

BANISHMENT, WITHOUT TRIAL,

OF

TWO BRITISH EDITORS

FROM

THAT COUNTRY

BY THE

ACTING GOVERNOR-GENERAL, MR. ADAM.

BY A

PROPRIETOR OF INDIA-STOCK.

LONDON:

PRINTED FOR J. M. RICHARDSON, 23, CORNHILL.

1824.

MARCHANT, PRINTER, INGRAM-COURT, LONDON.

A LETTER,

&c. &c.

SIR,

I ADDRESS this letter to you because you are said to have declared publicly, in the House of Commons and the India-House, that if any man would satisfy you that freedom of discussion in India would be beneficial TO THE NATIVES, you would assist in establishing that freedom by all the means in your power. In saying this, you put the question on its true and just footing, for the natives compose the infinite mass and majority of the governed in that country; but they are too commonly left out of view by the English debaters of the Press-question, who seem to treat it chiefly with reference to its bearings on commercial and political parties, or on family connexions, and matters of patronage.

It is the object of the following pages to convince you that the good of the Natives, including, of course, the mixed races, cannot possibly be ensured under the East-India Company's distant and doubly-delegated rule, without establishing among them a *local* check, by public scrutiny through the Press. If I should succeed in convincing you, you are too honest and independent, I am told and I believe it, not to shrink from avowing that conviction, and redeeming, to the uttermost, your pledge in favour of a people and country to whom you are indebted for much of the consideration you justly enjoy, with men who are not the zealots of party, or bigots of any caste or complexion.

In the following examination of the question under discussion, regarding the Indian Press, it is proposed—

First.—To give a brief view of the past and present condition of the Press in the British territories in India, which are entrusted to the temporary management of the East-India-Company.

Secondly.—To state the arguments that seem to bear on the general question of a Free Press in India.

SECTION I.

Historical Sketch of the Indian Press.

1. Before commencing on the historical sketch proposed, it seems expedient to prepare the way by shortly defining the nature and limits of the *restraints* usually considered applicable to the dissemination of opinions through the Press.

2. In every nation, each individual is free to *think* unrestrained. No human contrivance can reach or prevent the fullest freedom of thought.

3. Thought may be communicated by spoken or by written language ; and this intercommunication of thought between man and man *is* susceptible of human restraint.

4. That restraint is more or less effectual, according as the intercommunication takes place between the greater or smaller numbers of thinkers, at the same moment.

5. It is difficult to restrain conversations between two persons, or prevent their corresponding by writings. But it is easy to restrain men

from addressing large assemblages, or from circulating multiplied copies of the same written
address.

6. Printing is such a multiplication of copies.
He who harangues a hundred men at once
communicates his opinions one hundred times
more rapidly than they could be spread from
man to man. He who distributes one hundred
copies of his opinions, enables one hundred men
to harangue each his hundred; therefore, intercommunication by the Press *may* be ten thousand
times more rapidly effectual than ordinary communication between man and man; and the copies being permanent in form, and exactly alike,
may serve over and over again for successive assemblages of hearers.

7. The Press is, therefore, much more dangerous, if it be dangerous that men should intercommunicate thoughts, and much more beneficial, if intercommunication be beneficial, than
any other mode of spreading opinions; it is also
more susceptible of restraint from those who have
the wish and the power to restrain intercommunication, by reason of its machinery.

8. The restraint may be *direct*, that is, may be applied in the form of prohibition, total or partial, against free intercommunication of thought: or it may be *indirect*, in the form of subsequent threatened punishment, the fear of which shall deter and intimidate those who print.

9. Previous censure of writings proposed to be printed, and systems of revocable licensing, are both modifications of *direct* restraint in its partial form. No nation has ever practised a total and absolute direct restraint; for tyrannical rulers always encourage the Press while it only praises them, and spreads agreeable or scientific intelligence. No nation has altogether dispensed with *indirect* restraint. Even in the United States of America, it exists in the cases of individuals who have civil remedy for false and malicious injury through the Press, as through any other vehicle of wrong. In England, the *indirect* restraint prevails by law in a very strong degree.

10. In the East-India Company's dominions, up to April, 1823, no special legal enactment, touching the liberty of printing, existed. The power of making *laws* for India, generally, rests

with the British Legislature, and has no other
limit than their discretion. The power of making
local laws for the Company's territories, except
within the cities of Calcutta, Madras, and Bombay, is vested in the governments of the three
Presidencies above named. The power of making
local or bye-laws for those three great cities is
vested concurrently in the Governments and the
King's Supreme Court of Judicature at each,—
the former *proposing*, the latter *sanctioning*.

11. The local laws enacted by the Governments and King's Courts, *conjointly*, must not be
repugnant to the laws of England, and may be
appealed against by individuals, to the Privy
Council, acting *judicially*, not ministerially. The
laws enacted by the Governments *solely*, are not
required to be consonant to English law, and
may only be repealed by the Governments themselves, by the Court of Directors of the Company,
or by the Board of Control.

12. Printing was first introduced into India by
the English in their great cities; but the custom
of circulating manuscript newspapers in multiplied copies is of considerable antiquity among

the Natives, the Mahomedans particularly:
and these Ukhbars (as they are called) have
always contained political rumours and intelligence, often mixed up with satirical and personal
remarks.

13. The English Governments have never,
until 1823, restrained printing in the provinces
under their *separate* legislative jurisdiction. That
it was, therefore, lawful to print without restraint
up to that period, may be inferred from the very
step of passing a law, in 1823, which constitutes
into a crime, punishable by heavy fine and long
imprisonment, the having or using any press,
materials, &c. without special license; or any
book, or printed paper, of which the circulation
shall be prohibited by Government in their Gazette: such fines or imprisonment to be summarily inflicted by a single justice, (appointed, paid,
and removable by Government,) who is also
vested with power of domiciliary visitation, and
of seizing all such books or implements of printing, simply on his own belief that such obnoxious
articles are concealed on any man's premises.
Such has been the law since April, 1823, in the

provinces of Bengal, without the ditch of Calcutta.

14. Within the metropolitan jurisdictions of the Supreme King's Courts, reside almost all the Europeans in India not in the service of the Company; most of the numerous mixed races of Anglo-Indians and Indo-Portuguese; most of the Armenians, Parsees, Chinese, and other Asiatic foreigners, together with a vast population of indigenous Mahomedans and Hindoos. No accurate census exists in India; but writers have supposed Calcutta, and its immediate suburbs, to contain 600,000 souls. Madras and Bombay, together with Calcutta, may perhaps reckon a million of inhabitants in all.

15. These cities and all their population, from the earliest charters of the Kings of England, have been governed by English criminal law alone; while the Mahomedan code has been the law of the provinces, excepting only where British-born subjects, or Native servants of the Company, are concerned; in which case, the King's Court at the metropolis had exclusive jurisdiction. Justice has always been administered in the name

of the King, in the Courts of Calcutta, Madras, and Bombay. In 1773, the Old King's Court of the Mayor and Aldermen of Calcutta being thought by Parliament not sufficiently powerful and venerable in the eyes of the Company's servants, a new and independent Court was created expressly to protect the subject against the notorious despotism of the Government, and abuses of power by its servants.

16. To this Court, the jurisdiction of which, at first pervading the entire dominions of the Company, was subsequently limited to Englishmen and public employers without, and to *all* men within the City of Calcutta, whether Native or English, the power was confided of a negative upon all legislative measures of the supreme Government. No regulation could have the force of law within Calcutta, until approved by the King's Court, as consonant to British law. In April, 1823, this Court (one judge only present) passed a law, proposed by the Government, prohibiting the printing or publication of any periodical work, without previous license, *revocable at pleasure*, under heavy pecuniary penalties, to be inflicted by

justices summarily; such justices being paid, appointed, and removeable by Government. From this local law, an appeal has been made to the King in Council, and various protests and reclamations were presented by Natives and Indo-Britons: all upon the ground that this licensing of the Press at will was repugnant to the principles of English law.

17. Until April, 1823, therefore, no *law* existed in Calcutta to restrain free printing: but an indirect method of influencing the Press did exist before, and was effectual so long as none but Europeans possessed skill and capital sufficient to conduct the business of printing.

18. This indirect method arose out of a power vested in the Company from the very beginning of its monopoly, and inherent in a strict monopoly, of preventing any British-born subject of England from resorting to or residing in India, but such as were in its employ, or had its license to remain there, as private merchants, sailors, planters, and the like. This power has been continued in every successive renewal of the Company's charter, and in the last, 1813, was put

in a particularly strong and distinct shape, although the *commercial* monopoly of the India Company was taken away, or so altered as to hold out a *free trade* to British subjects with the East, China alone excepted. The Government having the power of sending any British-born subject to England· a prisoner, without reason assigned, it is evident this terrible engine, though created for purposes of monopoly, and continued for other purposes not avowed, might be used effectually to intimidate any individual within its scope from doing, or leaving undone, any thing whatsoever that might not be agreeable to authority.

19. On the first establishment of the Parliamentary-Government-General, and of an independent Council, and independent King's Court, in 1773, the Press in India was actually, as well as legally, free: that is, responsible only to the English libel law and a jury; but this freedom virtually ceased as the powers of the Court were curtailed and those of the Governor-General enlarged, while the privileges of the Council were at the same time cut down, and civil servants re-

sumed the exclusive right of filling seats at that board. In fact, from the epoch of Lord Cornwallis's administration, it may be said, British-born publishers have been intimidated from printing any thing unpleasant to persons in authority, or those protected by them, more or less effectually, according to their opinion of the irritability or mildness of the individual Governor who holds the undivided prerogative of transportation at pleasure; but, in 1798, Lord Wellesley made use of this same power, in a more sweeping form, to compel *white* printers, through fear of banishment, to submit to the previous censorship of a Government Secretary. Still there was no *law* to restrain the Press ; and, in 1818, when Indo-British editors began to start up, they refused to submit to the censorship, which they were professionally advised was a thing unknown and repugnant to law.

20. Lord Hastings, on that occasion, abolished the censorship, and circulated anew certain rules prohibitory of topics unpleasing to authority, which had been established by Lord Wellesley to guide censors and editors in his day. These

prohibitory rules, however, were not *law*, not having been formally passed in the Supreme Court. They were, accordingly, in point of fact, never enforced, although the indirect power of fully enforcing them by intimidation on English editors still existed, and Lord Hastings publicly announced, in a speech to the assembled community, his intention and meaning that the intercommunication of thought by printing ought to be unrestrained for the sake of the governed, and should be so under his administration.

21. Mr. Adam, in 1823, succeeded temporarily to the Governor General's fearful prerogative, and found the influential press chiefly in the hands of Englishmen. Having all along disapproved of Lord Hastings's notion of unrestrained intercommunication by printing, he re-established the system of restraint by intimidation; and immediately, on his accession, transported one editor, Mr. Buckingham, without trial or further notice, under the powers given him by the act to withdraw at pleasure the license of any British-born man to remain in India.

22. The Press, in consequence, began to fall

into the hands of Indo-Britons and Natives, who
were beyond the reach of any power except that
of the King's Court, administering English law.
But Mr. Adam prevailed on the single judge
(Macnaghten) then remaining on that bench, to
let him enact a regular *bye-law*, in point of form,
which should put down all free printing by *direct*
restraint, and should constrain Natives and Indo-
Britons equally with Englishmen. This novel
contrivance appears to have been readily agreed
to by that single judge, and became law, as
stated in par. 20.

23. At Madras and Bombay, previous censorship, enforced upon British-born residents, by terror of summary banishment, has existed, in imitation of Lord Wellesley's system, since his day,
and is still in force. But no law for licensing has
yet been solicited by those governments of their
supreme courts ; or if solicited, the King's judges
have refused to lend themselves to such purposes,
so that the Indo-British, or Native inhabitants,who
cannot be got rid of in a summary way, are free
to print without restraint, subject to the English
law of libel only, and to a jury of English-born

men, whose individual votes in a verdict cannot be known so as to expose them to intimidation for acting conscientiously.

24. To understand thoroughly the state of the Calcutta press, after the censorship was removed and free discussion was publicly invited by Lord Hastings, it must be remembered that the power of summary transportation is *not* vested in the majority of the government, but personally in the Governor-General alone. The circular " *regulations*" to editors, substantially the same as Lord Wellesley's, were the work of the collective government—namely Governor-General and three councillors; but as these regulations were not in any respect *law*, they could only become operative to the extent that the Governor-General, individually, should choose to give them indirect penal effect, by backing them with his *personal* and special warrants for transporting such as should disregard the missive of the government.

25. When the Governor-General, therefore, openly challenged that scrutiny of the public press, which the Government had previously forbidden by its circular, the only means of giving

c

efficacy to the vague denunciations of that missive being in *his* hands, the inference naturally followed, from this gloss of the Governor-General, that the regulations were not according to his taste, and should remain as a dead letter. In point of fact, they did so remain for several years, notwithstanding the unceasing exertions of the minority in council.

26. This then is the actual state of things with regard to the press in India. 1st. All intercommunication of thought by printing, or circulating of things printed, is prohibited by law, save under revocable license, within the Bengal provincial jurisdiction.—2. All periodical printing or circulating is prohibited by law, save under revocable license, within the jurisdiction of the King's Court at Calcutta.—3d. Printing in the Madras and Bombay provincial jurisdictions is not yet restrained by any known law.—4th. Within the cities of Madras and Bombay there is no legal restraint, and the King's Courts affect knowledge of none other than the libel laws of England. Nevertheless a previous censorship is enforced on British-born subjects only,

through the fear of summary banishment. But natives, foreigners of whatever country, Indo-Britons, are all, in short, except British-born subjects, free from other restraint than that of the English law : they are really as well as legally free.

27. The Indo-Briton and various classes of Native inhabitants of Calcutta complain, that the revocable License-Act deprives them of the most valuable of their privileges and *birth-rights*, secured by repeated royal and parliamentary charters, since the first settling of Fort William, and, therefore, inherited from the remote ancestors of existing generations. They maintain, that they cannot lawfully be deprived, through the machinations of an unconstitutional judge and arbitrary governor, of their privilege to be governed, in all things, by English law, and bye-laws strictly consonant thereunto. They affirm, that if any political or other expediency requires that the law be changed to their detriment, such change can only be judged of and determined by the British Legislature; before which they can safely plead, and be fully

heard in defence of liberties, immunities, and properties, without fear of offending or of being intimidated into silence and submission to arbitrary power. They expect that the King in Council will be advised, by his servants, to use his power in quashing an irregular or improper Indian bye-law, without putting the aggrieved to the charges and risk of a judicial appeal in so flagrant a case.

28. The unfortunate natives in the provinces of Bengal have no channels of judicial form through which to appeal against the more sweeping new law of prohibition and confiscation, to which their intercommunication of thought and opinions is subjected. They have no *right* to assemble or petition collectively, and individuals are afraid to offend power, unprotected as they are by any institutions, or even by any tribunals essentially independent of a Government which pays, appoints, and removes at pleasure. They try to hope that the Directors of the Company, or the Board of Control, who have the power in their hands, will annul a regulation that destroys their privilege of intercommunicating,

and bars all speedy and substantial improvement of their minds or condition.

29. The British-born inhabitants of Calcutta join in the protest of their non-British fellow-citizens against the licensing system, which deprives them, also, of their right, even more undoubted, to be governed by English law only. They further expect, in common with Englishmen at Madras and Bombay, that their *property* and persons will be protected, in future, by the abolition or narrowing of the arbitrary power of discretionary banishment; since without this, no real freedom or equal justice can be secured, however much the semblance of administering equal English laws may be kept up in vain forms. The same intimidation that silences a printer, or forces him to submit to censorial restraints not acknowledged by the laws of England, might be employed in any other injustice which those in power chose to enforce by this omnipotent means. Crimes might be shielded as easily as legal innocence punished. Men might be intimidated from prosecuting just but unwelcome claims, or resisting wrongs and

demands productive of collision with those in authority. The very institution itself of a supreme King's Court—they maintain—set up, though it be declaredly, to do equal justice between high and low, may be thus virtually defeated and nullified, or reduced to an expensive mockery, by a system of unavowed, but well understood intimidation, at the mere pleasure of an intemperate or unwise ruler, with courage to incur local odium or reliance on powerful protection at home.

SECTION II.

Arguments bearing on the Question of the Indian Press.

The argument on the expediency of allowing free intercommunication of thought [see par. 3 and 4] among the inhabitants of British India, may be thus stated, setting out as a basis from certain points upon which all men profess to be agreed.

31. England has publicly declared, by the organ of her Parliament, in 1813, her resolution to forward the intellectual, moral, and religious improvement of India as a primary and bounden duty. From this national pledge few will be found to dissent avowedly, however much they may practically act in contravention of a praiseworthy sentiment that virtually binds the governing power to consider the good of the governed as its primary object.

32. The enemies of free intercommunication

either *do* or *do not* desire the good of the governed as the primary end of our Indian Government.

33. FIRST. If they *do not,* then they must consider some *other* good as primary, and that can only be the good of the governors ; for every man who has attended to the science and history of government is aware that there can be no honest compromise of *goods,* no middle course between pursuing the separate good of the governing and that of the governed: one or other must be primary; the true benefit of the governors, in an enlarged sense, will surely follow the good of the governed; but not the converse: for no separate good can be wrought to the governors that is not at the expense of the governed. Hence it follows, that if the opponents of free intercommunication declare their primary desire to be the good of the governing power, they must hold that the English Company having conquered India, maintain it as a pure conquest; that the chief object of England is to extract all the profit or tribute in its power from that conquest; and only to do so much good to the

conquered as shall be prompted by the fear of losing or rendering less productive this profitable milch-cow.

34. If such sentiments be confessed, and they have been often hinted at second-hand, as an argument against the improvement of India—the avowal should at least be made openly, and the policy, which undeniably follows from the premised seeking of the good of the governors, defended. All Europe would then know, that what has so often been said of our Indian policy, by Napoleon and other foreign rivals, is unblushingly admitted and openly justified. There would be an end of canting about our Indian administration, our humanity, beneficent sway, love of civilization, pure religion, morals, &c. &c. &c. All these complacent self-attributions are wholly incompatible with the idea of our holding India as a profitable despotism; such gratulations only serve to betray great ignorance or greater hypocrisy.

35. SECONDLY, but few men will boldly avow this doctrine with its unavoidable sequences. If then, the opponents of free discussion in India

D

profess that they *do* desire the greatest good of the greatest number, then they are agreed with the friends of the Press, as to the object of our Indian domination, differing only as to the means of best attaining what is the sum and end of all good government; namely, the most perfect administration of cheap justice, and the lightest possible taxation, compatible with complete security to person and property from foreign or domestic danger.

36. Even as to the means of compassing this common object, both parties are *so far* of one mind as to agree that free public scrutiny and the control of public opinion (to be exercised *somewhere*) are legitimate and necessary means towards keeping the Indian Government, like every other, in the right path of duty. Even Mr. Adam fairly admits this, in a printed Indian appeal to his countrymen at home; and no one has yet denied that in the Indian Government, *as in all other polities*, there must be a constant struggle between the general interest and the particular interests of individuals and classes of the rulers.

37. But the two parties professing this same

end of good government, and agreeing as to the means of influencing its attainment, differ utterly as to the time when, and *place* where, this control of public opinion can be best exercised; one party would only have it exercised in England, the other (approving, likewise, of its employment in England) is of opinion that it can only be exercised with the greatest vigour and benefit on the spot where its effects are to operate, and near the time when the evils may be supposed to happen, which it is proposed to correct by this influence. One party would limit this avowedly desirable control to the authorities in the mother-country—the English Parliament—the English Press—in short, the Public in England; the other party would place reliance on those authorities also, but only as auxiliary to the best and *proximate* check of this description; namely, the public voice in India itself.

38. Whether this control be exercised in India, or in England, it is evident to all, that two essential conditions are implied in a right notion of such a check.—SAFETY and EFFICACY are those conditions. An efficient check attended with

danger—or one that, being safe, should be without efficiency, are equally unsuitable to the desired purpose of promoting the interests and happiness of the body of the governed.

39. By SAFETY is understood reasonable secureness of the general interests (in this case represented by the Government) against external violence and unjustifiable internal convulsion. By EFFICACY, of course, is meant the power of stimulating the Government to good, and deterring it from evil, to such a degree as may balance the natural proclivity of all men entrusted with authority to prefer particular before the general interests.

40. If the control of public opinion through the Press on our Indian government takes place in England only, such control will indeed be, in one sense, quite SAFE, precisely *because* it will be INEFFICACIOUS. This impotence arises, first, from remoteness of time; second, from remoteness of place; third, from the slender degree of interest which the British public takes in Indian affairs; fourth, from the inveterate *party* habits of English statesmen; fifth, from the peculiar cir-

cumstance that India is leased to an exclusive Company. The affairs of, and events occurring in, that country, do not, therefore, become generally known, *in course*, as heretofore, to individuals at home; especially since the annual budget has been discontinued, and party destinies no longer hang on India bills and the mockeries of impeachment; nor are Indian occurrences *necessarily* known in any detail to the Ministers or Parliament, except where special occasions arise to call forth party attention.

41. Any control, hampered with so many clogs and disadvantages, must be quite inefficacious for purposes of general usefulness, and therefore no doubt SAFE enough in one sense, and in the direct ratio of its impotence; but how long will this SAFETY continue? Only a limited time; and for this reason; that if the supposed control (exercised only in England) be, for the five reasons here assigned, inefficient to correct the evil tendencies admitted to exist, [par. 36,] then it follows that the Government in India will go on acting precisely as if no such popular check or

corrective at all existed. The tendency to misrule, common to every human Government, will
be aggravated by distance and feebleness of responsibility; our Indian system of governing will
not ameliorate. Surplus revenue, beyond all the
wants and expenses of the State, will continue to
be exacted, till the country becomes more and
more prostrate, and every day less able to take
English products, because less able to give any
in exchange. Justice will be taxed higher and
higher, and become less accessible, and dearer,
too, inversely with the means of paying; old monopolies of necessaries and luxuries will extend and
become daily more rigorous and penal, as in proportion poverty and temptation to violate become
more powerful; new monopolies and extortions,
in different shapes, will be devised; confiscations
and sales will multiply, until property shall almost completely shift hands, and the old extruded
landholders, poor and ignorant, but proud and
influential, inflamed with rage against their official
despoilers, are ready to head the general revolt,
which must, *sooner or later*, follow this national

course and progress of misrule in a dependency, the administration of which is relieved from apprehension of vigilant and hourly scrutiny.

42. This picture is not imaginary: such a course and progress of internal misrule, followed by such revolt, did occur in a province at no great distance from the seat of Government, only a very few years ago : and although it cost so much blood and treasure, at a most critical period of general war, to subdue the rebellion which was not *thoroughly* got under for years, the story has scarcely ever transpired to the notice of that English public, in which some profess to see a fit and sufficient organ for controlling and guiding the Indian governments! How such remarkable events as this, and other recent affairs of a like nature, came to be kept from public notice, from the newspapers, from Parliament, even from the Court of Proprietors, does indeed seem a mystery. Such, however, is the fact, and it speaks volumes as to the utter inefficacy of the English Press and English public, (unaided by those on the spot,) as checks on men or measures in India.

The censorship was then in full vigour, and this very Mr. ADAM was the censor.

43. Experience, however, was not needed to prove this utter worthlessness of such checks; that was sufficiently evident, *a priori*. (See par. 40.) But some who disapprove of public discussion in India, whether from dislike or fear, and who also admit the proved inadequacy of the English public press, will nevertheless say that the check exercised by the East-India Company and Board of Control would still continue to be sufficient, *as it has been heretofore,* for watching and checking misrule abroad, without the aid of *any* public or press, here or there. This merits examination.

44. As to the Board of Control, its share in the expected operations of watching and checking may be speedily discussed and easily measured. Whatever may have been the wishes of the political parents of that Board, it is notorious, and scarcely denied in Parliament, that the only Member of the Board, permitted to work at all, is the Cabinet Minister at its head. But it is not less notorious that the Presidentship

is looked on as one of the lowest in rank and consequence of the ministerial ladder, and as a mere stepping stone to a higher position in the Cabinet, or not unfrequently to the place of Governor-General, that very functionary, whom, by our hypothesis (par. 43), the President of the Board is supposed to watch so vigilantly, and to curb in his undue tendencies to stretch authority! At all events, the Presidentship is deemed a se-cond-rate and temporary office. He who obtains it, applies himself unwillingly or not at all, to acquire knowledge and discharge duties of a strange, new, and painful sort; he languishes to escape from the office by translation to some other; if abroad, more lucrative and influencial; if at home, more congenial and elevated. In the weary interim he virtually resigns his impor-tant functions (save only in the *vital* concerns of patronage) into the hands of some officious and shrewd leading member of those whom it should be his proper and jealous office to control. Is this an exaggerated delineation? Is it little war-ranted by the experience of twenty-three years since LORD MELVILLE resigned the President-

E

ship? How then should such an Indian Zero, as a President, with all his attendant cyphers, ever acquire political integrity sufficient to qualify him for figuring as representative substitute for free public discussion in overawing Indian misrule? *Ex nihilo nil.*

45. But are the East India Company able and willing to discharge efficiently this great duty, in substitution for the public press in England or India, or both? Who are to undertake the office? The Proprietors or the Directors? Not the former; for they cannot practically stir a step, they cannot know any thing, or see any paper, if the Directors choose to keep them in the dark, and—by juggles with the governments abroad, the committees of secrecy and correspondence, and the Board of Control—to baffle their inquiries, or lay their jealousy asleep. Neither can it be justly said, that the Proprietors, generally, are very well fitted, whether from previous habits and actual pursuits, from the constitution of their body, or the nature of their prescribed forms—for meddling often, or with effect, in the details of administrative business abroad. Thus, then, we

have only the Court of Directors, or rather its efficient Council of Nine, and more efficient Council of Three, left us to represent the Company, and to perform the part of a jealous, vigilant, and disinterested Public, eager to detect and make known delinquency—directing public and general scrutiny to every abuse in a system, or fault in those who administer it,—having no interest in public exactions — deeply penetrated with sympathy for the poor, distant, and unrepresented native Indian, when suffering under the pillage of extortion, or the hard gripe of fiscal and monopolizing rapacity;—in fine, free from all fellow-feeling or undue bias towards servants abroad, whether arising from *esprit du corps*, the love we all bear to our own creations, or reluctance, as the coarse Napoleon expressed it, to let our neighbours see us wash our dirty linen! Alas! for India ; if she have no more zealous and effective guardians than such substitutes for public opinion,—*quis custodiet ipsos custodes?* The Court of Directors have essentially and naturally an interest distinct from that of their unfortunate subjects,—a particular interest, counter

to the general interest. It is not their *fault*, but
their *fate*. They cannot sincerely seek the
greatest good of the greatest number, if they
would. They are urged on by an incessant cra-
ving for " surplus revenue,"—for taking without
giving in return; and the financial annals of
India, for some years back, show how perseve-
ringly such a ruinous system may be acted on for
a time. What its *end* will be time must show.

46. But if there were no other reasons that
effectually and, *à priori*, prove the Court of Directors to be peculiarly disqualified from acting
alone and unchecked in that task of controlling
their governments abroad, which some men
would assign to a Free Press, one reason, sufficient in itself, remains to be noticed; it is their
hostility, as a body, to the existence of an un-
shackled Press in India. If they had no interests to follow out, distinct on the one hand from
the general interest of the Proprietors, on the
other hand from that of their subjects in India,
how could it possibly have happened that so un-
heard of an unanimity should have taken place
among thirty or forty gentlemen, (OUTS and INS.

during several years,) who are apt enough to split into parties on all other questions? In this case of the Press, it is said, they have all been of one mind for the first time on record! But the Proprietors are not so unanimous on the question; and it might be supposed the Directors were a faithful extract enough from the constituent body, —a tolerably exact image and representative of the shades of opinion prevailing in the " Lower House!" Not so. On this single question of the Press, all differences appear to be sacrificed at the approach of danger snuffed from afar, and all come forward, like so many life-and-fortune addressers in other epidemic times, to devote themselves to the sacred duty of keeping down, if even for a time only, the monster Free Discussion,—of stifling, while yet in his cradle, the infant Hercules, who is prophesied to go forth at maturity purging the world of beasts of prey in every shape!

47. Whence, then, arises this sort of instinctive and universal feeling among all Directors, past and present? If their interest coincided with the

general interest, they would naturally desire to obtain all the information they could, from every available source, as to the proceedings of all their Masters' (the Proprietors) servants abroad, high and low. The Press of India would certainly seem, at first sight, to have a claim naturally to the particular favour of the Directors; and one would have expected to see them supporting it with almost intemperate zeal *against* the very natural efforts of the servants of every class abroad, to put down an obnoxious tell-tale. The unanimity against the Press, of which the Directors boast, does seem, to the eye of unprejudiced reason, the very reverse of a *merit*, at least, as far as the Proprietors and English nation are concerned, and is altogether a circumstance so suspicious, as at least to bar their claim to be thought competent to watch over Indian government, *unwatched themselves* by a jealous Public here and in India. It must not be forgotten, that if a Free Press had existed in India, the revolts in Cuttack, Rohilkund, Bundelkund, and elsewhere, could not have happened so completely without the knowledge of Government in India, nor could the Proprietors and Public of England have been kept in ignorance of them to this day.

48. But even if the unchecked tendency to misrule should *not* produce among the Natives the dangerous effects here supposed, or if the danger shall appear so distant as not to be an object of dread with those small-minded persons who live only for their own times, another *alternative* subject of uneasiness presents itself in the half-European population, who are not likely to submit much longer to be kept down in a state of political Helotism. Experience has abundantly shown the convulsions to which European dependencies are every where subject, from the just pretensions of this race, and the arrogant claims of the whites to the privileges of a superior order of beings.

49. But it is proverbial that governments never profit by the lessons of history, and experience has taught no wisdom in this matter: the Indo-Britons are multiplying to a degree unknown to indolence in a country where no accurate census of any considerable portion of the population

exists. They are rising in talent, education, and
wealth; yet they all labour under a greater or
less degree of tacit social and moral proscription.
The males, at least, are scarcely associated with
by the proud European; are hunted out of all
high and honourable public employment by the
Directors at home; denied important civil rights
by the Judges abroad; shut out, by Government
in India, from beneficial and coveted stations in
the judicial and other administrative branches of
the public service; yet often treated as Natives
where that distinction is felt as invidious; in fine,
these men have been lately defrauded, through a
political collusion of the protector with the oppressor of their BIRTH-RIGHT of free printing; heretofore the only counterbalancing privilege in their
favour against the otherwise overwhelming superiority of their white fellow-citizens.

50. From the evils to be apprehended, sooner
or later, if unchecked misrule be allowed to
bear down the natives, or half-castes, the *English*
Press alone affords no real safeguard; nor is it
easy to see how that engine is to be brought to
bear on Indian misgovernment, for want of

information as to passing events and measures of authorities abroad. The whole frame of our governments in India seems contrived as if their subjects abroad, and. fellow-citizens at home, were intended to have no knowledge whatever of any thing that is going on, save when the Councils choose to speak their oracles in proclamations and general orders. Their despatches to their superiors at home *may* abound in garblings and glossings, suppressions and misrepresentations : no one can contradict them in England, for no one can know what is true and what is not, if the liberty to those on the spot to speak freely be taken away. But even those despatches, such as they are, the Directors habitually keep to themselves, and communicate them to the British public on rare occasions, and in a cooked-up state. The English Press, therefore, unassisted by a Press abroad, to collect facts and opinions, is utterly worthless for any primary purposes of giving publicity to Indian affairs.

51. In this INEFFICIENCY those only will imagine they see SAFETY who delude themselves into the belief that all must be well within when

F

all looks smooth without, and that it is less dangerous to govern the Natives badly than to let them suppose any one thinks they might be governed better. *That* SAFETY *is only immediate, not durable.* To ensure PERMANENT SAFETY the very reverse of the favourite hood-winking policy must be followed up in the present advanced and *progressing* condition of society in British India : namely, a system of internal rule, that is honest, fearless, open as light, " having nothing to conceal."—No people so governed ever yet revolted, for no people ever yet rose, as one man, against their rulers without good cause.

A PROPRIETOR OF
INDIA STOCK.

MARCHANT, PRINTER, INGRAM-COURT, FENCHURCH-STREET.

A

SECOND LETTER

TO

SIR CHARLES FORBES, BART. M.P.

ON THE

SUPPRESSION

OF

PUBLIC DISCUSSION IN INDIA,

AND THE

BANISHMENT, WITHOUT TRIAL,

OF

TWO BRITISH EDITORS

FROM

THAT COUNTRY

BY THE

ACTING GOVERNOR-GENERAL, MR. ADAM.

BY A
PROPRIETOR OF INDIA-STOCK.

LONDON:

PRINTED FOR J. M. RICHARDSON, 23, CORNHILL.

1824

MARCHANT, PRINTER, INGRAM-COURT, LONDON.

A

SECOND LETTER,

&c. &c.

---◆---

Sir,

As I perceive by the papers that the subject
of the Press in India is to undergo another discussion at the India-House at an early day, I am
desirous of following up, without loss of time,
the observations I had the honour to address to
you in my former letter, by making the application of the arguments therein stated, and offering
some illustrations on the great value of a Free
Press, as it regards the good government and
happiness of the natives of India.

SECTION III.

Safety of the Press in India, as it regards the Permanence of our Empire.

53. The conclusion being obtained that the exercise of scrutiny and indirect control over the Indian governments by the press and public of England *only* would be without EFFICACY, although SAFE *for a time*, till misrule should ripen, and the proscribed races feel their growing strength,—let us proceed to inquire whether free discussion through the Press IN INDIA would be SAFE and EFFICACIOUS for the desired purpose of influencing the government to pursue good and avoid evil.

54. The ablest philosophers, and best writers on legislation and historical politics, are agreed that there is never any strong tendency among the governed of mankind to rise against their governors; but, on the contrary, a disposition to bear misrule long beyond the point when resistance to oppression would be justifiable in the eyes of God and man, at least, of all men, *except those concerned in the oppressions resisted.* Revolt

is hazardous in its issue,—destructive to person and property during its progress, even should it succeed, but still more should it not,—it is further aggravative of the evils resisted if it fail. Men will bear very much before they become all of one mind to " rise and be doing;" and it is only when they are almost all of one way of thinking that rebellion has any tolerable chance of success against the fearful odds of disciplined and organized authority. No presses, no harangues, no examples will be of the smallest power in persuading poor and peaceful peasants that they are ill used, if they do not really feel the scourge of oppression at their backs : if they *do* feel it to be beyond endurance, no one is needed to tell them so. Writers and haranguers against abuses starve or thrive in proportion only as rulers furnish them with texts. If the good considerably preponderates over the bad in any government, there cannot be unfeigned apprehension of revolt, (see par. 42). The public, I repeat, *never* rise in general resistance without good cause.

55. But there are those who sincerely think, and those who affect to think, (from whatsoever motives,) that some special exception exists, in

respect to India, to these great truths, collected
by wisdom from the lessons of history, and admitted to the rank of political axioms, on the
subject of revolt, long before the days of Mon-
tesquieu. The first of the above classes of
thinkers deserves every patience and attention,
for it consists of men sincere and worth convert-
ing ; but, unhappily, none are so hard to be persuaded by reason as those who are under the dominion of fear.

56. It is truly of the utmost consequence to
the cause of civilization, of sound religion, and
of humanity, that the thinking and sincere portion of the English public should be undeceived
in this fatal idea, imbibed by many, because so
sedulously and earnestly inculcated, that there
is a disposition in India to revolt, an aptness in
the Indians to throw off our " foreign yoke," as
it is vulgarly called, which proneness does not
depend, as every where else it does, on the
goodness or badness of the system of government, but on causes altogether extrinsic to any
notion of merit or demerit on the part of those
who rule over our Indian fellow-subjects. If this
position were true, it would, indeed, be fatal to

the happiness and melioration of more than
sixty millions of human beings, for it would
afford the tyrant's ever-ready plea, *necessity*, in
one of its most plausible shapes, as a prompt defence of every positive act of violent misrule, and
every negation of improvement. If the people
of India are not to be acted on by means of those
ordinary feelings, or of those balancings of motives and chances, that actuate other men, in de-
termining the great *home-questions* of resistance
or submission, they must be scarcely better than
brute animals, and it signifies but little, indeed,
who is the driver of such cattle, or by what method they are kept to work and food.

57. But, happily for an unfortunate and undefended people, there is no truth in the position,—
not even the shadow of truth. It is incumbent,
in the first place, on those who take that distorted
view of our Indian subjects to burden themselves
with the proof of a position so unnatural and
contrary to all experience. But let us sift this
matter somewhat closer.

58. Who are " *the people*" of India that are so
prone to learn, as the first result of their lessons
from us, that they are bound, by their own interest

and duty, to throw off a foreign yoke? The Indo-Britons?—their hour is not yet come! The other insulated small bodies of Portuguese, Parsees, Armenians, and so forth?—they are not as a drop in the sea of our Indian population. The Mahomedans?—they are no pupils of ours: they have " learnt nothing," if they have " forgotten nothing," in the course of the eventful revolution that has cast them down for ever in the extreme East, and stripped them of the conquests of seven centuries. Doubtless, the dreaming and arrogant remnant of their Hidalgo chiefs (if any such remnant there be under a politico-religious system, that is essentially hostile every where to the establishment of an aristocracy, or the perpetuation of great families) would gladly recover, if they could, so bright a gem as India in the trophies of Islam. But have they needed *us*, and our presses, and instructions, to teach them this? Have they profited aught, or is it in the genius of their *sept* to profit, by enlightenment so readily? Admitting, then, that *their* desire to throw off our " foreign yoke" be as strong as the *advocate* for darkness and retrogradation assures us it is among all the Indian people, generally, does it follow that their *hopes* are as lively as their desires? or that they are not tolerably capable of calculating their chances of success in a struggle against the united mental superiority of the English and physical outnumbering of the Hindoos? With such a tremendous struggle before them, and against such fearful odds, will they not weigh well the inducements to remain tranquil? and will they reckon for nothing in the balance of inducements and motives, that the English, who thrust their Indian Colossus off its *political* base, have not trampled in pieces the scattered members, but, besides conferring on all ranks equal rights of property and person with other subjects of the state, have preserved to their middling and better classes the monopoly of office in their criminal law, and a full proportion of public employment, and promotion in the army of the conquerors?

59. But the Hindoos, the infinite majority of the population,—will the first-fruits of their eating of our tree of knowledge lead them to discover that it is their duty and their interest to rise against their instructors, and throw off a " foreign

B

yoke ?" So far from it, that they only learn, from intercourse with us, their own nakedness, and cling the closer to a protection which, whatever lesser evils it may involve, and however defective in comparison with what it might be, and should have been, at this time of day, is still for the Hindoos a substantial benefit, when placed by the side of any one in the infinite series of foreign dominations, to which the Hindoo nations, or tribes, appear to have been successively subjected, almost from the days of ALEXANDER of Macedon.

60. The body of the Hindoos are likely to quarrel with us, when the sheep shall disclaim connexion with the protecting shepherd's dog in presence of the wolf! We are their natural allies against their old enemies the Mussulmans, who have not abated one jot of their pretensions to recover their empire, if any turn of the cards should chance to put an end to the English supremacy, and leave the field free to Mahomedan energy and unity of effort. In such a strife the Hindoos, excepting, perhaps, a very few of the ruder warlike septs, thinly scattered in the north and west, would have no chance. A long course

of passive submission to successive conquerors,
and the debilitating influence of a superstition, at
once the most barbarous and abject the world
ever saw, have politically, if not physically, ener-
vated almost all the Hindoo nations : to the influence, indeed, of their contemptible system of a
religion without morality, resting its monstrous
fabric mainly on the division into castes, may be
ascribed, without much hesitation, the remarkable
circumstance, that they have been unceasingly a
prey to less civilized nations. This fatal authority of their priests, and all the destructive divisions of castes, still prevail in unshaken strength;
and it may be doubted, notwithstanding the
strange rise and fall of a solitary Hindoo power
(the Mahrattas), within little more than a century,
whether any Hindoo kingdom could possibly
stand, in the present day, against the superior
energy of the Mussulmans, who are all as one
nation and one faith, while the Hindoos are split
into innumerable sections of tribe, caste, and
country, united by no common bond. In the
extravagant case of a successful revolt of the
Hindoos being supposed to clear the field of the

English, there is no doubt that a Mahomedan power would rise on their ruins; and, however distracted by civil wars and successive contests, still the crescent, backed by shoals of needy recruits from the northern and western hives of Islam, would keep its hold, till some second invasion should take place from sea, under extraordinary circumstances of desperate courage, talent, and good fortune, such as distinguished our early efforts in India, and once more push the faithful from their stools.

61. The more intelligent and cultivated of the Hindoos are perfectly aware of the common interest subsisting between them and us; they feel and admit that their Mogul conquerors have been the only real losers in the tremendous revolution which we have effected in India, within the last seventy or eighty years. Our toleration has won over to us the priesthood, habituated to Mahomedan brutality: our good faith with the army, (eleven-twelfths of whom are Hindoos,) in regard to pay, clothing, pensioning, promotion, and distribution of justice by the verdict of themselves, has ensured us the strenuous attachment of the

warlike classes of the north. The banker and merchant classes enjoy comparative immunity from irregular pillage, unknown in the days of our Mahomedan predecessors ; and if the condition of the ryots and manufacturers is, unfortunately, in *statu quo* nearly, because we have too exactly followed our predecessors' track, things are, at least, no worse than they were.

62. It has been remarked, that, exactly in proportion as a Hindoo, by dint of the knowledge and independence of thought which we teach him, begins to purge the film from his eyes, so does he see in a stronger light the *comparative* merits of the English rule, without being blind to its grave defects ;—so does he descry and admit that our cause is his cause, and that the only hope of political regeneration, and of religious emancipation to his people, rests upon their connexion with the English. This prospect he allows to be *infinitely* remote, owing to the exceeding prostration of the Hindoo mind; but still it *is* looked to, in the fullness of time, even if not anticipated by the approximation, or even amalgamation of the races in the course of that

Colonization and intermixture which must, sooner or later, take place, in spite of all endeavours to prevent them.

63. Let it not be supposed that these speculations are unreal, and of European fabric. Those who have seen the writings and correspondence of that patriotic and learned Brahmin, RAM-MOHUN-ROY, the real apostle of Christianity among the Hindoos, are well aware that the sentiments and opinions here described are those held and zealously inculcated by that excellent person, and his small but increasing school of European-minded Hindoos. The British Government has no such true friends among its Native subjects, for it has none besides, that are Native, attached to it from reason and deep reflection. Painful it is to think that such men should have been obliged to protest in the Supreme Court of Calcutta, and before the whole world, against the gagging and licensing system, by which Governor Adam and Judge Macnaghten have deprived them of their Presses, of a birth-right which they had used for the noblest, and purest, and most peaceable purposes! Painful to think

that RAM-MOHUN-ROY, who had descended to edit a Native periodical paper, with a view to contribute his great influence in that mode to enlighten his benighted fellows, should have found himself obliged *publicly* to abdicate so honourable an employment, environed as it became, under the new restrictions, with difficulty, degradation, and suspicion.

64. It is hoped that enough has been said to show that the general disposition to throw off " a foreign yoke," of which so much has been said, even to nausea, by superficial and timid men, is not only unlikely to *increase* with the progress of political improvement and instruction, but also not likely to have any existence at all, unless we drive men to such recourse, by perseverance in misrule, and by refusing to let our own eyes and ears be open to the evil of our ways. No chimera that ever haunted the imaginations of the weak and ignorant was more devoid of reality than this absurd idea of proneness to rebel in India; it might have been left to be dissipated by time and returning reason, were it not unhappily a mischievous as well as stupid phantasy, afford-

ing pretext for bringing into play restrictions, tests, penalties, expurgatory indexes, and all the wicked and contemptible machinery of persecution for opinions' sake, which was thought to be pretty well exploded every where, but is now again revived almost simultaneously by the Pope, the beloved King of Spain, and Governor Adam. Each of these individuals, no doubt, conscientiously plumes himself on the validity of his special reasons for playing such fantastic tricks in his own particular dominions, and each by his friends is, of course, considered the best intentioned of rulers, and kindest of men; as if the possession of power had no tendency to transform and corrupt! as if the private virtues of public men might safely for mankind be admitted in qualification or extenuation of their public measures! as if, indeed, the personal good qualities of an arbitrary ruler were not a positive enhancement of the evils he inflicts, by blinding many to the true quality of his acts, and disposing them to greater forbearance! Yet of such puling stuff is the invariable defence compounded of every public man whose measures are attacked, and whose ready host of friends and connexions instantly start up with a plea of character.

65. If we desire to retain India for England, from a conviction that in the present state of that country we do thereby really seek the greatest good of the greatest number in both countries, our policy is plain and simple. Honesty is that policy ; and all suppressions of opinion, puttings down of intercommunication of thought among the governed, forbidding of books, gagging of the press, and ruining, fining, banishing, or imprisoning individuals who speak out and are our *truest* friends ; all such pernicious vagaries of wanton power should be put an end to as soon as may be. This done, there will be no real cause for apprehending any thing like a general discontent or revolt ; but even if there is such a tendency, the friends of free discussion and good government triumphantly ask of the reasonable and reflecting among their countrymen, whether is it *most* likely to have been created by the fomentings of a press, or by real and grievous misrule, considering how passive and long-suffering a people the Hindoos

have always shown themselves to be? Or if such disposition to rebel exists, will expurgatory indexes or muzzles on the press keep men from thinking and conversing? Will they hinder the secret ferment from working and heaving? The opponents of publicity would do well to avoid sounding too loudly this alarm of danger from likelihood of revolt, lest the English public should indignantly demand, of what nature their administration must be in that country, since more than sixty years' undisturbed possession of the greater and richer part have not yet secured for them the affections of the governed beyond the reach of disturbance from " paper shot !"

66. The question how far indirect control over public measures by the Press would be SAFE if exercised *in India*, may be considered as set at rest in so far as concerns any danger of general revolt arising therefrom, or any *special* disposition to resistance in that country. There *is*, however, a danger of particular and provincial revolts to which our Government in India is greatly liable—not because there is too much license, but too little!—not because there is too much

freedom of discussion, but because there is none!—not because there are too many residents in India, independent of the Company " factious," " interested" " would-be-reformists," &c. &c. but because there are too few !

67. Assume, if only for argument's sake, that an impolitic impost is laid on, which bears particularly hard upon this town or that city—on a cloth, sugar, or silk district—on an opium, or salt province; or let us assume, what may be equally improbable, that a European chief functionary of justice, revenue, police, commerce, opium, salt, or the like, oppresses a distant province, whether from bad temper, from *positive* corruption, or from *negative* malversation in not preventing his swarms of officers and defendants from fleecing the helpless natives. In any of these cases, the Government has no means of coming at the facts of wrong suffered or imagined, except through official channels. No one likes to report that this tax or that monopoly will excite discontent or resistance in *his* district, for such reporters are not looked on kindly by the counsellor or secretary who

patronized the tax. The spirit of discontent is not represented in strong enough colours. The Government remains in ignorance of the impending resistance until a positive revolt breaks out, being the only *constitutional* mode of resistance known from time immemorial in the East, whether before or since our time.

68. Then in regard to delinquencies of public officers, the Government in India is more overwhelmed with minute forms and tedious paper proceedings than any on earth. Give it *regular* knowledge through " regular channels" that any thing is going wrong, and such wrong, in most cases that are flagrant, and do not too nearly touch on matters of revenue, will be fairly inquired into, and probably redressed. But suppose the official channels are themselves shut or polluted? Suppose a less flagrant case— namely, that the provincial " channels," being utterly dependent for their very subsistence on the good pleasure of Government, should not show any great alacrity to bear bad news or disagreeable representations to the supreme authority? Suppose some governor-commander, or

counsellor, or even some secretary, should have happened to play the projector, and should view with parental fondness particular measures, and eye with coldness such as reported evil of his projects? Or, imagine cases of provincial malversation in a judge or collector, is the *oppressor* expected to be the ready organ of accusation against himself? Is the suffering party, a poor, ignorant, helpless Native, to put himself courageously forward in the breach, and to persevere in the unequal strife against power, riches, ingenuity, and prejudice, until he prevail in getting the Government to listen to him, and tumble his oppressor from his seat? Such expectations are truly preposterous, and it may be doubted if any one can be sincere, who professes to put faith in them, knowing the state of society in the East Indies.

69. Even in the Mahomedan days, it was the duty and the practice of the King in his capital, and of his deputies elsewhere, to sit " at his gate," and listen to the complaints of the meanest of his subjects. Doubtless, the duty was often neglected, and the practice as often reduced to

a vain form ; but the meaning was good, and the customs and tongues of every nation in the East show how deep-rooted and universal is the feeling that the wrongs of the subject were to be freely and publicly heard. What substitute has the English system provided for this and other rude customs of appeal? A series of official complaints, through ascending " channels," to be conducted under forms that utterly overwhelm the poor suppliant by their magnitude, their intricacy, expense of time and money, and more than doubtful issue.

70. One would think that for such a frame of government and state of society, the application of free discussion through the Press—anonymous (otherwise a mockery), but subject to severest penalties in case of falsehood—is the very one thing ; the desideratum for India ; that expedient which cannot fail to be of the clearest benefit both to governers and governed. Let us look at this more closely.

71. In India there are two grand divisions of inhabitants, connected in public relation, but mutually abhorrent of social connexion. One

of these is the dominating race; the few, certainly, but the able, the opulent, the powerful, *White*. The other is the subjected class; the
ignorant, the poor, the weak, the *Black*. Of the
dominating race, a more select few monopolize
all power and place in the state, from seats in
the Supreme Legislative and Executive Council,
down to the lowest deputyship of revenue or
police. These select few are educated in England by the Company, at a separate seminary,
as if to keep them a distinct caste from other
English gentlemen; they go to India as candidates for public employment, (of which their
order has a rigorous monopoly,) they are there
entirely dependant on the goodwill and favour of
the Government; appointed and removed at pleasure; extremely well paid when in office, in the
greatest poverty and want if out of employment.
They compose, as it is evident they cannot but
do—a potent aristocracy of place, the only body
in India answering to an aristocracy of any
kind, since, by the Mahomedan system, which
we found in play, no power, no property, could
stand up between the one king and the many

people; all of these were on a level, compared with him, and were kept down nearly to that condition, by the legal and illegal rapacity of their system.

72. The provinces of India are parcelled out into districts, or circles, that may be likened to large English counties; in each of these, many of which are from five hundred to a thousand miles from the seats of Government, one or two of these Company's European servants reside, to administer justice of the first instance, to superintend the police, to collect the revenue, and so forth; they are, in general, free from any of the restraints which the irksome vicinity of gentlemen, their equals in talent, wealth, and *complexion*, must necessarily impose on persons in power: they are, in truth, without any *moral* control, but their own consciences, for each chief stands alone in his proconsulate, erect amid thousands that lie prostrate. The *constitutional* controls and checks provided are, theoretically viewed, not inconsiderable, in respect of steps and gradations of appeal and complaint; but all labour under one common and radical defect—namely,

that all are exercised by the same class of men ; the same aristocracy of *place*, of *origin*, of *complexion*. The head of the Government and the chief of the Army are the only individuals in authority to whom this disqualification does not *always* apply : of these, one is not likely to engage actively in matters foreign to his habits, and particular sphere of duty, while the other, in general, occupies himself with the department of foreign policy, naturally leaving local and ministerial details to those of his colleagues, whom he presumes to be more experienced than himself, although, in reality, they are the worst fitted to sit in judgement on any part of a system, in the midst of which they have grown grey.

73. To this view of the state of society and frame of government in India, we may add, by way of finish to a very singular and original picture—*First.*—That the legislative and executive powers are both in the same hands—those of the Council, consisting only of four men, of whom two or three are from the civil service of the Company, and one almost always a military man fresh from England. *Secondly.*—That this Coun-

cil is in the habit of corresponding with the judges of its provincial courts on matters more or less connected with their judicial duties ; and employs them in commissions of inquiry, political offices, and other matters not strictly judicial, while the highest Company's Judge, in the country, is removable by the local Government, without cause assigned, or by the Court of Directors at pleasure. *Thirdly.*—That the Judges of the Supreme King's Court, ostensibly set up to protect the people against the Government, are not themselves protected against the effects of that Government's displeasure as they ought to be by being made irremovable by his Majesty's Ministers, at the intance of the Company's Government, or of the Company of the Board of Control, who are, practically, one and the same. *Fourthly.*—That, in all the Company's dominions, there is not an *institution* independent of the ruling power, nor any admitted right of petition, or of meeting to petition. No corporations—no colleges—no privileged orders—no constituted bodies —in short, of any description, who have the *right* of addressing the Government in the collective form of " *we !* " The system of *centraliza-tion*, over which Bonaparte boasted, as comple-ting the *beau ideal* of despotism, is thoroughly realized in India ; where the shadow of political or municipal privilege is not to be found in any individual under the Government.

74. All this machinery is perfectly well under-stood among the parties concerned, actual and expectant holders of high office. Is it then very surprising, *First.* — That distant *Pro-Consuls* should occasionally fall into malversation and in-justice themselves, or slide into indolent, if not corrupt, connivance in the crimes of their *locusts* of native dependents. *Secondly.*—That a fellow-feeling should prevail among the superior grades of the same order of men, if not to screen actual delinquency, at least to create as little public scandal as possible, for the reputation's sake of the Government itself; and still more for that of the order to which *all* in common belong. Parties interested may, and, doubtless, *will*, attempt to raise a cry of libel and calumny in this matter; but it will not be the less undeniably true, *First.* —That any men, or order of men, similarly cir-

cumstanced, are likely, in all human probability, to yield to similar temptations, and to err exactly as the present civil servants of the Company are supposed liable to err. *Secondly.*—That no imputation against all its individuals is necessarily contained in general remarks on viciously constituted public bodies ; there always have been and always will be great exceptions—greater, because of the difficulty to resist temptation—to ordinary cases and maxims. *Thirdly.*—That no body of men ought to be entrusted with vast powers, under circumstances that virtually take away, or infinitely enfeeble, responsibility.

75. But the Press seems to be expressly devised for coming into play in such a case as this of remote *lieutenants*, each clothed with almost unlimited happiness or misery, in respect to men under his sway, with whom he has few or no sympathies. If the Central Government wished it ever so much, if it were ever so free from bias towards its servants, and desire of giving the authorities at home an impression that all goes on well and smoothly abroad—it would not be in its power to exert an efficient and minute super-

intendance over those remote *lieutenancies*. Distance, intimidation, and fear of odium, too often
hinder the truth from reaching the metropolis;
and, if it *could* arrive there, its quantity and
magnitude would exceed the powers of any *general* government to go into in detail. *But there
is a method* by which distance may be made to
vanish—a moral vicinage of talent and keenness
be created, where none physically exists, to
overawe idleness, injustice, favouritism, or pecu-
lation—by which the arm of Government may be
nerved and elongated—its dim sight strengthened
—its dull tympanum quickened. That method
is the Press; and there is none other in the wit of
man to devise, which shall effectually and for
any length of time answer the desired purpose.
It is for want of that engine which, when free,
cannot be cajoled or silenced, that the Government, in India, is kept utterly in the dark on the
very eve of those sudden and violent revolts of
provinces, which every now and then arise from
the oppressions of the " official channels," and
the absence of all modes of constitutionally opposing men in power. In no country might the

Press be *such* a powerful SAFETY-VALVE as in India. It is folly, or hypocrisy, to say that the denunciations of a free Press should not be *anonymous;* if its operations are *not* so far concealed it loses all its real utility, and becomes only another mode of preferring accusations under attestations which expose the oppressed man, who turns the accuser, to all the persecutions of the accused, or of his brethren; the very evil which, by hypothesis, the Press should be set up to remedy. Is it then to be inferred, that any one of the friends of publicity, and to anonymous discussion, (the only shape in which it can be truly free,) desire to free the Press from responsibility for falsehood or proved malice?—Far from it: but it is a favourite mode of arguing this subject —the motives sufficiently obvious—to beg that part of the question, to assume a Free Press to mean the printing of *any thing* without liability to punishment, however false, slanderous, or malicious; as if any offence against society ought to escape the visitation of law, because committed through one or another instrumentality, whether of Press, or speech, or action, &c. &c.

76. Few will deny that the Libel-law of England, as explained by modern Judges, is severe enough; so much so, that it would extinguish all public writing whatever, but for the attempering given by our Juries, even our special ones. Fewer will deny that one of those statutes, which are usually called the Six Acts, (1819,) makes the old law still more severe, by inflicting banishment for a second offence. Yet this severe body of law would be received with thanks and rejoicings, as the Press-Code of India, because administered by a Jury, even a special one. In exchange for the late illegal violence of revocable licenses, and for the terrible Star-Chamber mode of arbitrary banishment by a Council of Government, but without the trial and defence allowed even in that abhorred tribunal, any code which ensured a public trial would be a blessing. Suppose the power of summary banishment for presumed state-offences, of great danger and urgency, were taken from the Government, and vested in a full bench of the King's Court under the same forms of public hearing, concurrence or rejection which are at present in use to pass a bye-law on

the proposition of Government? This would be virtually enabling the authorities in India to take out of the hands of a Jury, and vest in those of the Judges, all such *extreme cases* as both executive and judicial power should concur in considering of imminent hazard, to the welfare of the State. Such a change would be no small departure from constitutional principles, yet even this would be a blessing, compared with a state of law, or rather lawlessness, where the property and person of every Englishman are placed in the wanton, because irresponsible, hands of Government.

77. Fenced in by such powers as those of the English Libel-law, of 1819, and even (if it must be) with power of moving the King's Court to banish summarily, will not the Indian Government, the Civil Service, and the Company, consider themselves secure against the terrors of the Press? What can be the meaning of this extrordinary panic of terror? What the extent and nature of the evil apprehended through the Press, a word which means no more than free intercommunication of thought between man and man? It has been shown [par. 58 to 61] that in the divided state of

society, population and interests in India, all idea of *general* revolt, under reasonably good government, is out of the question. If then a Government were actuated solely by the adherence to the general interest of the greatest number, and not by any particular interests of individuals or classes in the State, it is rigidly demonstrable that it would naturally form the strictest alliance with the Press, as a firm and fast friend, as the most powerful auxiliary conceivable, in the common cause of promoting good government. It is, indeed, true, that, in the first instance, individual writers and printers set up in order to their own advantage, in like manner as men pursue any other avocation that benefits the public secondarily, themselves primarily; such being the order of nature and society, that, in the struggle of individuals, each for his particular profit, the general profit is best wrought out. Hence, if an editor should depart from truth, frequently and wilfully to appearance, or should seemingly give way to private hatred of himself or others, under colour of public good, or otherwise dissatisfy the society in which and by which he lives, it would

E

be a signal to others to invest capital and labour in rival publications: self-interest would keep each alive to the falsehoods and faults of the other, and the *general* interest and advantage could not but profit by the detection of error and the promulgation of truth.

78. But it is said it would not be SAFE to allow the subjects of a government to print matters " tending to bring it into hatred and contempt." To this may be *asked*, by way of reply, if the government justly deserves hatred and contempt, ought it not to suffer such treatment? If I am told it ought not, then it will follow that crime should be protected, not merely from punishment by positive infliction, but from punishment by loss of good name; it will follow that a false impression is to be given of such a government, which is thus to derive support in its misconduct from falsehood, instead of being forced to cease meriting " hatred and contempt," that it may by such reformation avoid reproach. Evil is to be done that good may come of it: end sanctifies means! But where is a government to stop—a Christian government planted among immoral Hindoos

and talking largely of reforming them—where is it to stop if once it begins a career of falsehood and vice, as part of its ordinary ways and means? Did ever any government derive durable strength from such confusion of right and wrong, of truth and falsehood? You cannot hinder every individual from judging of the government as he thinks its acts deserve. You cannot hinder them all from *speaking* of it to one another; what then is gained by hindering the intercommunication of those evil opinions which, by supposition, (vide supra,) every body entertains? And in whose eyes is the gain obtained, of passing for what you are not? Not in the eyes of those who already think the evil, and know what you are; it must be in the eyes of others, foreigners, that you try to raise a false impression of respectability by keeping back the truth from being written. This, perhaps, is the real explanation of the extraordinary uneasiness testified on the subject of the Press. The Indian Government and the Company want to deceive England, America, and Europe, as to the true state of their dominions in the East. It is a remarkable fact that nothing offends a Press-censor, in all countries, more than any public allusion to his censorial erasures, and to the suppressions of truths and impressions of falsehood, which it is his occupation to create. This is, at least, a consolatory homage which political vice pays to virtue : the false impressions would fail in their effect, if readers were fully apprised of the arts of censorial cookery employed to produce effect. In the last years of Bengal Censorship, it was considered the height of contumacy—a " *lese Majesté*" of the deepest dye, if an unfortunate editor, at a loss for matter to fill the chasms suddenly caused by the censorial pen, studded the gap with eloquent stars. Such are the caprices of despotic power ; its objects must not only bear with its inflictions, but pretend as if they felt them not !

78. But if the Government does *not* merit hatred and contempt, and knows that it does not, why should it wince, like the galled jade, under every severe thing that any one may say of it. No good government ever was brought into lasting " contempt or hatred," unless it well deserved to be so ; and a ruler, who is strong in conscious integrity, and in the knowledge that he

always pursues the greatest good of the greatest number, will smile at the puny efforts of malignity to misrepresent him, assured that the delusion cannot last. But why suppose that the Press would be likely to try to bring into hatred and contempt rulers who did not merit such obloquy? He who prints what is *not* according to the opinions and tastes of a large class of readers, will not be read, nor, in a country like India, where there are no struggles of parties as in England, to obtain the conduct of public affairs, and a monopoly of loaves and fishes, will he long pursue the expensive amusement of printing for gratification of private malice. He whose abusive strictures find continued encouragement and patronage from a considerable class, shows by that unquestionable proof, that his censures are not devoid of foundation. The former should be beneath the notice of a good government, the latter only so far worthy of notice as to draw attention to those evils of which the presence is indicated in the system, by the angry inflammation on the surface.

79. It is in vain, however, to argue on the

reasons assigned by the Indian Governments for
wishing to stop every Press but their own paid
one, and to suppress every thing like freedom of
judgement or discussion on their measures.
They will go on for ever assigning any reason but
the true one for their unnatural hostility to that
best friend which they and their masters at home
can have. They know, too well, that there is
no likelihood of any general revolt in India.
They know that if there is danger of *partial*
risings, in consequence of sheer despair and
resistance to oppression, such insurrections have
not a chance of ultimate success, while our
general government is tolerably good ; and, at all
events, the Press has never had any thing to do
with such revolts, not one of which has occurred
since the Press was free. They know, besides,
that not a score of Natives in all India are yet
capable of reading, *to understand*, discussions in
an English newspaper, and that the minds of a
very inconsiderable number are yet matured to
comprehend political discussion, even in the
Native languages, fewer still being capable of
translating such from English, and not a dozen,

perhaps, of writing original matter on such topics. They know, finally, that if a Native or European journalist were to blow the trumpet of sedition, and summon the Blacks to rise against the Whites, the European editor, if he escaped the lunatic asylum, would have very little chance of escaping from the furious hands of the Whites, who must form the jury to try him for treason or sedition,—about as little chance as one similarly situated in Jamaica would have from a jury of slave-drivers and planters. As to a *Native* editor, if in Calcutta, he must pass through the hands of a similar jury of Whites; if in the provinces, through the hands of a single White judge. All these pretended alarms for the " consequences" of a Press (subject to the English Libel-law) are miserable pretexts, the real object being to escape the shame of having faults and jobs exposed: they deceive nobody on the spot, however effective in Leadenhall-street and on the Stock Exchange. The Press has always been entirely free in our slave colonies, and the slave states of America: but who has ever yet been mad enough to employ it to rouse the

Blacks to a servile war? In like manner the Press was virtually and practically free in India for several years posterior to 1818. Yet no man ventures, agreeable as it would be to those in power, to point out *any* injury that it did to the country or its rulers. If a free Press had been likely to produce danger, that danger *must* have been greatest at first starting from a state of thraldom. Yet never was India in profounder tranquillity—never, certainly, better governed! never so progressive!

80. The secret cause of hostility to the Press arises, most probably, on the part of the Directors of the Company, from an extreme unwillingness to draw more public attention than they can avoid towards India. They are egregiously deceiving themselves, if it be so—in supposing that any such policy will avail them in the approaching day of their utmost need; when their present victories and triumphant votes will be remembered bitterly against the petitioners, who will then be humbly soliciting a renewal of lease, and showing cause (against the merchants, manufacturers, and ship-owners, of the

land) why they ought to have the confidence of the liberal and the pious continued to them. Times are greatly changed since 1813, when England had her hands too full to think much of the Company. There are *some* redeeming, and even constitutional points in the system of governing India through an organ of patronage not *directly* at the beck of the Minister of the day; and if the Directors wish to come before the public of England with a good case in 1833, they would do well to think of showing what they have done for the country entrusted to their management—what improvements, " intellectual, moral, and religious," they have encouraged, rather than come forward to make a merit of having quenched utterly the spark of Free Discussion that had been kindled by the most liberal of their Governors, and of having bound the intercommunication of thought among their subjects in India with stricter chains than had ever before been devised.

81. The irritation on the part of the local governments against free discussion, through the Press, appears to arise from none of the motives

F

of alarm and so forth, which they have alleged through shame of confessing the littleness of the real motive. This seems neither more nor less than the love of undivided power—in other words, the preference of particular before the general interest common to all governments under the sun, and which should always be studiously counteracted in every good system of civil polity. It may almost be doubted if even the best earthly governments *heartily* love and cherish, perfectly, free discussion. In India, to these ordinary feelings aud motives are superadded others peculiar to the situation of that government, to its long enjoyment of undisturbed absolute power, and to the nature and composition of the civil body. All these circumstances united produce, in the Indian authorities, a degree of arrogant conceit, of ludicrous bursting indignation, at the bare idea of any one not of the privileged order, or constituted authorities, presuming to have any opinion on public questions, or daring to obtrude it; to which Cervantes or Swift, perhaps, might have done justice. But the contiguous sublimity and burlesque are forgotten in the melancholy spectacle of free-born Englishmen thus de-nationalized and de-moralized by long residence under a debasing system of arbitrary rule on one hand, and slavish submission on the other. Still more distressing is the recollection that, for a time, at least, and until this indignant country shall recall powers that have been so abused, these men have it in their power to do very much evil, and to defeat the national wishes and schemes for the intellectual improvement and civilization of millions.

SECTION IV.

Efficiency of the Press in India as a local Check against Misrule.

82. The positions being established,—*First*, That the exercise of scrutiny and indirect control through the Press *in India* is perfectly compatible with the SAFETY of our empire. *Secondly*, That such control is essential to the PERMANENT SAFETY of the country, however uncomfortable to rulers who desire not, *primarily*, the greatest good of the greatest number; it remains to prove

the EFFICIENCY of such a local check. On this part of the argument it is unnecessary to dilate,— *First,* because most of the considerations affecting the questions of EFFICACY have been touched on incidentally, in the proof of SAFETY, in which they are necessarily involved. *Secondly,* Because to the EFFICACY of a Local Press, the Governments abroad bear the strongest of all testimonies in their extreme alarm at the establishment of so unwelcome an intruder among the monopolists of office.

83. The favourite position put forth in all shapes and phrases by the enemies of free discussion, to catch unthinking people in England, is this—" There is no Public in India—therefore, " no public opinion—therefore, no use for an organ " to express it—therefore, a free Press can do no " good, and may do harm, &c."—This is the language of Mr. Adam.—It may be doubted if a more contemptible sophism ever before disgraced the manifesto of any ruler, or trusted in the weakness of those to whom it was addressed. But the Press in India was first silenced, and dared not expose the sophistry; it was hoped, therefore, that any bold begging of the whole questions

at issue would suffice for people in England, when India was the subject.

84 " There is no Public in India," that is, no public capable of forming opinions worth attending to. No? Not even when they *praise* the political, military, financial, or judicial conduct of their rulers? Why, then, are they allowed to assemble and offer their incense? But we must examine this assertion a little more in detail.

85. *First, as to the public of India, generally.* It may suffice, perhaps, to ask who lent the State the forty millions sterling of which the Public Debt consisted but the other day? Unless it dropped from the clouds, perhaps, it may be conceded that they who lend such sums, in any state in all the world, would not be thought very unreasonable in pretending to have *some* political existence, not to say influence, in public affairs!

It may also be asked, without exceeding arrogance, who were they that formed a large European, Portuguese, Armenian, and Native militia, at the several Presidencies, in the times of Lord Wellesley, when danger was apprehended from French and Mysorean hostility? That militia, horse and foot, was indeed afterwards put down, with many other obnoxious measures of the Noble Lord ; but because it *is* not, does it follow that it *was* not? or that there was not then a Public, and is not now one, infinitely greater in numbers and in moral force?

Finally, it may be demanded, and not without some claim to a grateful reply from the people of this country,—Did not the Indian Public, or *No-public*, of all classes and *colours*, come forward lately to subscribe between £30 and £40,000 to the relief of the distressed Irish ? Yet we are told they are as a negative quantity in the political arithmetic of the Honourable East-India Company and their honourable servants abroad!

It may suffice after this to enumerate a few institutions and employments in Bengal, in which Natives and Europeans are indiscriminately engaged, as Directors, Contributors, Managers, or Capitalists. Such are the Society with a large capital for clearing Saugor Island.

The Banks of Bengal, Hindostan, and the Commercial Company.

The Native Hospital.

The School-Book Society.

The Society for Native Education.

The Agricultural Society.

86. *Secondly, as to the non-existent Native public.* It is quite true that the Natives have not, and ought not, to have political weight according to their mere *numerical* strength ; but it is not less true that those of them who reach to a certain degree in the scale of property, intelligence, education, and integrity, ought to carry with them the same weight which the like attributions would obtain for them in any other modern community.

87. This granted, it may suffice to notice that the Natives are creditors of the state to a vast amount, as RAM-MOHUN-RAY and his brethren assert in their unavailing Memorial, and Protest against the purposed Restrictions of Governor Adam and Judge Macnaghten, a document which will be admired in more unprejudiced times, as a masterpiece of reasoning and eloquence. The Natives are directly concerned in the various undertakings and societies mentioned (par. 85) under the head of the *general* public. Many of them, at the Presidencies particularly, are individuals of prodigious wealth, acquired in external commerce and interior traffic,—Hindoos,

Mussulmauns, Parsees, Portuguese, Armenian, and Indo-British, deeply concerned in shipping, ship-building, indigo planting, coffee planting, rum distilling, &c. &c. They have assembled and voted addresses of praise, pictures, statues, &c. to several of their Governors, and particularly to many retiring Judges of the Supreme Court, with whose distribution of justice they were satisfied. They lately voted addresses of praise to a Chief Judge of the Company's principal Court, on his leaving India, and again on his returning to fill a temporary seat in Council. On the death of Warren Hastings many of them joined the European community, who assembled to applaud that Governor-General's conduct, and subscribed for a public monument to his memory, censured though he had been by repeated resolutions of the Commons of England, and subjected to impeachment.

88. Is it not then the most contemptible of drivelling, to say, that such men as these are to be considered as political non-entities? Every day brings them, in some relation of their multifarious and busy occupation, into official contact with the King's Judges—the Company's Courts—the Ma-

gistracy—the Officers of Revenue; nay, in appeals, with His Majesty in Council, himself. Shall it then be boldly said by Englishmen, and to Englishmen, that men so situated have *not* a direct interest in the purity and efficiency of all those, and all other public establishments under the government?—that they have not a just and lawful right, under responsibility, to scrutinize the conduct of such judges and officers, and so by shame intimidate them into doing their duty, if they think it is not done well? We may, perhaps, for some time longer, terrify the less advanced, and more timorous Hindoos into submission to demands so extremely unreasonable as this; that they shall not meddle with the conduct of any of their superiors, however injurious to themselves. But how long can it be supposed that we shall be enabled to intimidate the HALF-CASTE population into such absurd acquiescence? Examples enough might be cited of the vanity of such human wishes, if examples were ever of any use to mother countries, urged on blindly to their fate. Our own America, St. Domingo, the Spanish and Portuguese colonies, all might be

G

quoted, but would be quoted in vain. Each nation in turn flatters itself *it* is in the right, and that there is something different in the particular relations of its remote dependencies than those of other nations that have gone before ! Every state having colonies forgets that the growth of new and prosperous dependencies, and the increase of Creole population, are not to be measured by the same *time-standard* that marks the improvements of older people, and increase of population in advanced periods of human society. British India is now moving on in its course with considerable rapidity, nor will the puny efforts of the Company, or its servants, be able to stop, or materially retard, a career which, on the other hand, is accelerated even now, and will become much more so, presently, by the *overdone condition* of universal England—the redundancy of capital—redundancy of population—redundancy of public burdens and public unredeemable debts. In a thriving colony, twenty or thirty years do as much work as a century in an old country. He that has been absent from India for thirty years is probably about as ill qualified to form an accurate

notion of its present political and statistical position, its administration, the habits of public men
and of society, or the *feelings* of the various classes
of inhabitants, as " THE SPECTATOR" would be,
if he had to rise, and write, at this day, a " Her-
mit in London." If we apply this observation to
our Indian system, it will not be difficult to find
a clue to much of the strange matter that is put
forth from time to time, about India. The remark
that there is no Public in India, was felt—bitterly felt to be without foundation ; but it was
believed to be of a *sort* still current in Leadenhall-street.

89. *In the third place,* we come to the *European part of the non-existent Public of India.* It
is composed, we are told, of soldiers, officers,
King's and Company's, and of Civil servants, besides a scum of inferior persons engaged in the
law, in trade, shipping, or handicrafts, only resid_
ing in India by sufferance (the badge it seems of
all this tribe). It is asked, with a sort of triumph,
silly enough, considering the unlooked-for answer that *may* be given—Whether a greater ab-

surdity can be imagined, than that of a government being controlled by its own servants, or those whose existence almost depends on its favour?

90. Now, in the first place, we might well deny much of the premises in this formidable looking argument; we might deny that a gentleman or nobleman, holding a commission in His Majesty's service, and stationed in this or that particular part of the King's dominions, forfeits the smallest tittle of his right to have and to deliver opinions (under responsibility) touching the conduct of the colonial government. If he can do this at home; if he can sit in Parliament, and oppose the King's domestic administration, can he not do so of a subordinate government? In like manner we deny that the liability to be tyrannically seized and transported, however it may intimidate, can be said to take away the legal *right* of a lawyer, a trader, nay of a Company's servant of any class, to judge, speak, or write as he thinks fit (under responsibility to law) of the local government.— But, waving all these important doubts, let us

grapple with the main position, that it is absurd to suppose a government " *controlled*" by its servants and dependents.

91. The sophism involved in this question lies altogether in the significant meaning artfully given to " CONTROL." If, indeed, by that were necessarily meant a PUBLIC and formal power, exercised by the servants of out-voting their master, or an authority vested in avowed dependents of OPENLY censuring or putting their *veto* on the acts of their benefactor, unquestionably this would be quite as absurd, as it is meant to be thought by those to whom it is thus adroitly put, in the hope that they will not detect the trick. But there is a wide difference, indeed, between DIRECT and INDIRECT control ; as between *power* and *influence;* or between *force* and *persuasion.* The Press every where does undoubtedly CONTROL in one sense, because it influences the measures of Governments, either by shaming or convincing ; but does the Press—*can it* CONTROL the operations of Governments in the same sense that Parliaments or Courts control Executive Authority ? Yet in this unworthy confusion of

terms—this affecting to employ the same word used by an adversary, but employing it in a sense that was not, and could not possibly be meant, lies the entire force of this stupidly-triumphant question, and of the reasoning derived from it! So we are told with affectation of philosophical phraseology, that we should not apply the institutions of a highly civilized state to a less advanced state of society, as if there was question about FORCING the uncivilized to use the Press, to print, or write, or even read! or as if it were any good reason why those who are *sufficiently* advanced should not use the Press if they choose—that numbers of their countrymen are still unable to profit by or use it!

92. The very essence of a free Press in all countries consists in the liberty of *anonymous* writing in matters of opinion or reasoning, and also in statements of fact, subject always to rigourous *legal* responsibility for every thing that is published. Take away the privilege of writing anonymously, and things will be no better than under the favourite system of " *official channels*" of complaint, although, therefore, it would be

absurd to suppose a servant should *publicly* and avowedly arraign the measures of Government, or the (assumed) delinquency of a superior; yet so far from being preposterous or inexpedient that public servants should censure *anonymously* the measures or actions of any, whether above or below themselves, it is, in fact, a thing extremely to be desired, *first*, because the DIGNITY of *Government*, which might be thought compromised if it were arraigned by its own servants, is effectually saved by the anonymousness : *secondly*, because all it has to think of in this case is not who wrote? but what is written ? *thirdly*, because none can be so fit and qualified to judge of public measures and public men as that very class who are solely employed in public affairs from their infancy, and who are eulogized in the strongest terms by Governor Adam (himself one of their number) for their capacity and distinguished qualities. But, at any rate, we should think the Directors at home ought to be very glad to get servants of so much experience and ability to write (anonymously) in the public prints, seeing that in no other conceivable way could the Directors so well discover what *was* doing—what was *not* doing—and what *ought* to be doing by their stewards and servants abroad.

93. But if it is proved to be innocent and even expedient that the Company's civil servants should apply themselves to influence the acts of Government, and their fellow servants, through the Press, (provided always they do so under the decorous garb of anonymousness,) it is needless to go further and prove that the *servum pecus,*—the *canaille*, of Men of Traffic,—Law,—Handricraft, &c. may use the Press with still more propriety than the Company's own servants, (provided always they do it in a respectfully anonymous way, as in duty bound towards those who claim to be as the breath of their nostrils). Probably, however, communications of this inferior class will not be likely to prove very useful to a Government of such high pretensions to infallibility.

94. And is there then, no European " Public" in the great Presidential cities of India? It was not thought so of old, when they assembled in their Town Halls, or their Churches, built by subscription, to lend their weight *in support* of

measures or men favoured by the government.—
There they petitioned the Crown, in despite of *Sir
Elijah Impey* and his brethren; unsuccessfully
petitioned indeed to have their Juries restored in
civil suits; when they voted addresses and money
to Warren Hastings, though under the ban of Parliament; when they subscribed to Loyalty loans
and contributions in 1798; when they addressed
the late King on Hatfield's attempting his life,
and other occasions; when they complimented
every possible Governor or Commander, in coming
and going; formally approved Lord Wellesley's
political plans, and Sir Arthur Wellesley's
military conduct; when they formed themselves
into Misionary Societies—Bible Societies—Tract
Societies—Native Education Societies—School
Book Societies—Agricultural, and Horticultural,
and Literary Societies—Companies for clearing
single Tracts—building Theatres, &c. &c. when
they came forward to assist in the preservation
of order and save expense, by forming unpaid
Magistracies—when they set up Orphan Schools
—Hospitals—Dispensaries—and similar institutions—when they were called to receive (as an

H

acknowledged Public) from Lord Hastings a *compterendue* of the greatest political and military operations ever undertaken in India—when they hailed the liberation of the Press in speeches and addresses, and, in short, did every thing which a Public, not actually holding any share in the Government or Legislation could well do, *to prove its existence.*

95. Times indeed are somewhat changed within the last few years, every thing thus savouring of free institutions is now carefully and jealously put down—the Press is destroyed ; and the Supreme Court, an Independent and Royal Court of Judicature, has *not* scrupled to rivet the fetters of publicity, and to accept at the hands of Government, which this Tribunal was instituted to check, *a scandalous immunity against free scrutiny and remark on the conduct and opinions of the Judges!!* a thing as yet unparalleled in the annals of British Justice elsewhere. The privileges of the inhabitants have been variously curtailed in the control over the public Charity-fund, which the Government have handed over to a close self-selected Vestry; and in the abolition of their ancient

right as a *grand Jury to assess their* own house-tax.

96. But in the midst of these mutations, all of which are in the same spirit favourable to power and against the community, it is somewhat consoling to observe that the noble privilege of voting *agreeable* addresses remains unimpaired, provided always that things be done with the ceremonial prescribed by jealousy to take away real freedom of speech and opinion, while preserving all the appearances to the world of perfect independence. Since the epoch when the " public " voice was solemnly declared in print, by Governor Adam, to have no existence legal or actual, this very same unreal mockery of a Public appears to have rewarded (or ridiculed) that illustrious declarent, by voting him empty compliments and a substantial picture. The same shadowy body has also performed the usual Ko-tou before the shrine of the new Ruler of their destinies;—and another section of this phantom—the non-existing Public—has even gone so far (headed indeed by a Major-General on the staff) as to congratulate Governor Adam, and *itself*, on his triumphant completion

of the work, he had long it seems meditated, of crushing the last remnant of free opinion, and crowning it by a sacrifice—not indeed of himself—but of a defenceless individual, his family, and prospects, which are all reduced to ruin by Mr. Adam's act! This temporary Governor is not ashamed to take part in this despicable comedy ; he affects to consider this addressing, but non-existing, Public, of military station, headed by their General, as an honest independent body " daring to be honest in the worst of times." He answers—*admitting their right to approve* and disapprove political acts, coquets as to his own merits, and finally allows that he *deserves* that praise they are so well qualified to bestow! True it is that all this consistent stuff has recently been exchanged between these personages; and to complete the humour of the thing, it is all carefully sent to the English news-papers by some officious person or other, just as the discussions are coming on. But injudicious friends would do well to learn, that similar addresses are utterly valueless, and below contempt, in a community where all hold actually and prospectively, at the will

of the person addressed ; and the reason is, precisely *because* they are signed publicly.   In such
a country, *anonymous* praise is worth a wilderness
of addressing major-generals, because good ground
must be assigned for the good opinion, and the
anonymous *be-praiser* cannot be suspected of interested motives.   Herein lies the marked difference
between a free and a servile community.   It is only
in the former, that *open* praise is of value ; in the
latter all such is justly suspicious.   What value
in his heart can Governor Adam set upon the
approval of those who, as he has written and
printed, are not free to *dis*approve ?

SECTION V.

Conclusion—and Connection of the Press with
Colonization.

98. The case, as originally proposed, is now
closed.   It is believed to be proved,

FIRST, that if the good of the great body of the
governed be truly desired, it is quite indispensable

they should be protected against the severity of the Government, and misconduct of European and Native servants.

SECONDLY, that as no INSTITUTIONS of any sort, independent of the Government, exist in India, the only possible substitute is, the Press, which enables men freely and *anonymously*, but under severe *legal* responsibility, to intercommunicate their thoughts, and to exercise an *indirect* control and check on the measures of Government, and the conduct of its servants.

THIRDLY, that none *ought* to have a greater interest in the operations of the Press, than, 1st, *The Indian Governments*, who cannot possibly govern their immense regions without some such auxiliary to their direct superintendance. 2dly, The *Court of Directors*, who cannot otherwise know both sides of every story, or what is really going on abroad. 3dly, The *Proprietary Body*, who desire to review the acts of *all* their servants fully, at home and abroad.

FOURTHLY, that if this expression of public opinion through the Press be limited to England, it must necessarily be without EFFICACY, or even

PERMANENT SAFETY to the common interests of the people of India and England.

FIFTHLY, that in India alone, it can be exercised with *complete* EFFECT and *perfect* SAFETY.

99. One only topic remains to be noticed, and that addresses itself chiefly to those persons in England, whether manufacturers, stockholders, Indian annuitants, ship-owners, under-writers, or others, who are connected with India, and interested in its prosperity.

100. It is vulgarly supposed, and no little pains have been taken to spread the notion, that the body of men in question have no near interest in the establishment of a more liberal system and institutions for British India. There cannot be a more entire or fatal mistake.—None can possibly have a *nearer* interest than they, in the development of the vast resources and powers of that country ; and they are cautioned to turn a deaf ear, or rather a well-prepared ear, towards such as, for their close and sordid purposes, endeavour to inculcate this selfish doctrine, and thereby, to keep India from obtaining the good wishes and power-

ful aid of friends in England, in order that they may have her all to themselves, to serve their little turn.

101. Nothing is more undeniably true in political economy than this : that a nation cannot import more than she can pay for by exports. If India be not allowed to make the most of her natural products, in silk, cotton, sugar, indigo, saltpetre, coffee, &c. how is it possible she can take the manufactures of England to any amount? —If, in these respects, India were allowed to do her utmost, there is scarcely a limit to her power of taking manufactures. What hinders her from making the most of her products ? Why does she not substitute, in her infinitely varied soil and climate, the finer cottons of the West for the inferior staples, which are indigenous to her? Why does she not indefinitely extend the growth and fabrication silk ? Why not improve the manufacture of sugar, according to the more finished processes of other countries ?

102. The reason is two-fold, 1st. European skill intelligence, and superintending industry, are excluded from employment, owing to the absurd

and pernicious prohibition of Colonization. 2d.
European capital is excluded from overflowing
and enriching that boundless field, Indian agriculture. What *might* be done by European skill
and capital, we see, by the creation, in our own
times, of the indigo culture and manufacture. It
had scarce any existence thirty years ago: now it
produces, annually, eight or nine millions of
pounds, and the finest qualities, equal to the old
indigo of Mexico. All this is *entirely* the work
of European skill and capital, it is believed to be
owing chiefly to the policy of his Majesty's Ministers, that India was so far thrown open to enterprize.—A second such effort has never been made.

103. But nothing can be done towards this
great work without COLONIZATION—not by means
of a resort of labouring men ; for such there is
no room, nor would the climate admit of their
working—but by a resort of men possessed of
capital, education, and talents to direct the labour
of others, and willing to render *militia*-service in
case of invasion or rebellion.

104. COLONIZATION can never take place until
that absurdest of bye-laws is repealed which

I

hinders Europeans from holding land in their own names,—a law that encourages and winks at mendacity and public immorality.

105. COLONIZATION can never take place until every man's property and person, of whatever class, colour, or religion, be put under the protection of *known* and equal laws, that leave no pretext for imprisonment, banishment, fine, or confiscation, but by the sentence of impartial, public, and independent tribunals. To this end the power of transportation by Government, without trial, and the system of licensing Europeans at all, must be repealed, as the very first preliminaries.

106. COLONIZATION would increase the imports of British manufactures into India, not only by adding incalculably to the amount of exchangeable exports—not only by adding immediately and remotely to the numbers of consumers, but also by diffusing a taste for luxuries and conveniences, and gradually raising the *standard* of want, and thereby of happiness. India is at present at the very bottom step of the *ladder* of civilized life. The food, raiment, shelter, requi-

site for mere support of life are all of the common-
est and scantiest kind ; in consequence of this
and of the unfortunate stimulus given to early
marriage by the pernicious customs of the Hindoos, the country swarms with redundant—but
wretched—population, and the smallest scarcity
carries with it the same tremendous effects as in
potatoed Ireland.

107. All impartial travellers admit that the
districts of India where European Indigo Planters
have settled most thickly are by far the most
flourishing and prosperous. Such are the undoubted effects of European capital and example.
All India might be *such* as these Indigo districts
are.

108. But owing partly to the prohibition against
investing European capital in land or agriculture,
it is prodigiously accumulated in the hands of the
great capitalists at the principal settlements. Unable to find a profitable, secure, and reasonable
vent, it seeks investment in the Public Funds,
which bear no proportion there to the wants of
the capitalists, and which the Company are every
day reducing still further in amount, to the great

distress of thousands, and disquiet of those who think that one of our great securities for Native attachment is the vast quantity of the Public Funds which they hold in perfect confidence.

109. Thus the Public Funds rise prodigiously, and the general rate of interest falls vastly below the level at which it *would* stand if capital were free to find its level in employment, whether agricultural or other.

110. The consequence of this unnatural rise of Funds and fall of Interest is that the Government. seize the occasion of paying off capital Debt, and reducing Interest, thereby adding immeasurably to the distresses of absentees, annuitants, and others, in England; of public charities, settlements, &c. &c. in India, all of which are invested in the stocks, because they are arbitrarily hindered from investment in landed property. But for this unjust prohibition, the acts of Government in paying off and reducing interest would be quite right: as it is, they profit by their own violence and wrong.

111. These are some of the views which it was at one time hoped the Freedom of Discussion by

the Press in India might have helped to accomplish. Certain it is, that *without a Free Press there*, none of the benefits mentioned above, as so anxiously desired for India by her real friends, could, even if procured, be preserved against the vast power and influence of a government, which may be said *substantially* to hold in its hands the legislative, judicial, and executive powers, with all patronage, and not a corporation or institution of any kind to oppose it in any thing. It was believed that the shortest and surest way to obtain these benefits, in the first instance, was to bring men's minds, by dint of discussion, to see the necessity for such improvements. Perhaps this may have been the very reason why, from its outset, the Indian Press was viewed with such unmeasured hostility and alarm. It cannot be expected that the Company or the Company's servants should take the same interest in the improvement of the resources of India, and the happiness and productive powers of the people, that others do who are virtually Colonists, from *birth* or connexions, or whose fortunes and families are staked on the welfare of that country. The revenue of India already overpays its charges—what more could the Company gain by troubling themselves with dreams of improvement? What could the Company's servants gain beyond their salaries, of which they are quite secure in the present condition of the country?

112. It is now for the Merchants and Manufacturers of this country to determine whether they choose to support the present close system, or to compel—for compel they *can*, if they *will*—a more liberal one. Of one thing, however, they may be assured,—that the Question of the Press is inseparably bound up with their interests and those of India—interests which are but one and the same, AND WHICH MUST SOONER OR LATER PREVAIL.

A PROPRIETOR OF
INDIA STOCK.

MARCHANT, PRINTER, INGRAM-COURT, FENCHURCH-STREET.

HISTORY OF THE

PUBLIC PROCEEDINGS

ON THE QUESTION OF THE

EAST INDIA MONOPOLY,

DURING THE PAST YEAR.

WITH AN OUTLINE OF

MR. BUCKINGHAM'S

EXTEMPORE DESCRIPTIONS

OF

THE ORIENTAL WORLD.

PRICE TWO SHILLINGS.

LONDON:

HURST, CHANCE, AND CO., ST. PAUL'S CHURCH YARD;

AND SOLD BY ALL BOOKSELLERS.

1830.

Bradbury and Co., Printers, Oxford Arms Passage.

NEW QUARTERLY REVIEW.

THE increased and increasing interest now awakened throughout the Country, on every topic connected with the Eastern World, whether as regards the conquest of Turkey by Russia—the independence of Egypt under its present Pasha—the Steam Communication with India, by way of the Mediterranean and Red Sea—the approach of European armies towards our Indian Possessions by land—or the abolition of the East India Company's exclusive Monopoly, which will be the subject of Parliamentary discussion in the approaching Session—has determined MR. BUCKINGHAM to commence an entirely New Series of his Periodical Journal, with the commencement of the present year, 1830, and to make it QUARTERLY, instead of MONTHLY, in order that it may admit of being conducted on the same plan as the Edinburgh, Quarterly, and Westminster Reviews, by giving careful, copious, and complete Analyses of the best Standard Works that have been already published, and of all New Books that may appear, the contents of which are in any degree connected with Turkey, Egypt, Palestine, Syria, Mesopotamia, Persia, India, China, and the other vast and populous regions of the Asiatic World, as well as occasional Original Articles on Eastern Affairs : and, more especially, a critical examination of every Publication for or against the existing Monopoly, which cramps our intercourse with that interesting quarter of the Globe.

This new Publication will be entitled *The Oriental Quarterly Review*, and, in addition to the continued labours of the Editor, it will receive the contributions of the most distinguished writers of the age. It will be of the same form, size, and price, and be conducted exactly on the same plan, as the established Reviews of the day, confining itself to those topics which are of the highest and most enduring interest, to the exclusion of all merely temporary matter, with which Monthly Journals, almost of necessity, abound.

The first Number will appear on the 20th of January, 1830, and the succeeding Numbers will be published regularly every Quarter, in April, July, and October ; and as the annual cost of this Quarterly Publication will be much less than half the original price of the Monthly Journal, being only 24s. in the year, and consequently much less than the expense of even a weekly Newspaper, it will be brought within the reach of every Merchant, Manufacturer, Ship-owner, and Trader, of the kingdom, as well as of every Family, and of every individual Philanthropist and Patriot, who may desire to assist in forwarding the great end to which it will be chiefly directed—the extending and improving our knowledge of, and intercourse with, the unnumbered millions of the East.

As no extra number will be printed beyond the copies actually ordered, it is important that the Proprietors and Managers of Public Libraries, Book Clubs, Reading and News Rooms, and every other class of Subscribers, who may desire to be furnished with the first Number of the New Review, when it appears, should give early directions to that effect, as orders for the work will be received by all the Booksellers in town and country.

The closing Number of *The Oriental Herald* was published on the 1st of December last, and contained an entire copy of the present Charter of the East India Company, as passed at the last renewal—completing a work that has extended to 23 octavo volumes, of nearly 15,000 pages, in which is contained a greater body of information respecting the countries of the East, than in any Public Journal that has ever before issued from the English Press.

[The Appendix to the First Number of The Oriental Quarterly Review will contain Official Copies of the several Resolutions passed by the Public Associations formed at all the places named in this Narrative, where they will be preserved as a permanent record, always to be found in that publication ; and by a reference to what has been already done in these, towards opposing the renewal of the East India Company's Monopoly, it is hoped that other Towns will be encouraged to follow the example. It is intended, by periodical additions to this Appendix, to include the Resolutions of all other Towns that may join in forming similar Associations, so as to have a complete History, in the pages of The Oriental Quarterly Review, of the origin, progress, and end, of this great Public Question.]

PUBLIC PROCEEDINGS

ON THE

EAST INDIA MONOPOLY.

BY J. S. BUCKINGHAM.

An entire year having now elapsed, since the measures, of which these sheets are intended to comprise the history, were first put into operation, it is thought desirable to shew what has been done, by unremitted perseverance, in even that brief period : as nothing is more encouraging to the exertions of the future, than a retrospective glance at the success which has attended the exertions of the past. On my first landing in England from India, in the Summer of 1823, after an absence of upwards of ten years, I made a hurried tour through the principal districts of England and Scotland, partly for the acquisition of general information respecting their condition, but also for the purpose of ascertaining how far any disposition existed to take an interest in the fate of India—considered as a part of the British empire, and as such having a strong claim on patriotic attention. During the whole of this tour, which occupied about four months, I found everywhere the most extraordinary want of information respecting our Eastern possessions to prevail even in the best circles. Scarcely one person in a hundred appeared to know more of India than that it was a country at a great distance, where the climate was very hot, the people very savage, and fortunes easily made by those who escaped the cholera morbus, or the liver; but, this very absence of all accurate or detailed information on the subject, was perhaps one reason why every communication that I had an opportunity of making to others respecting any part of the Asiatic world was listened to with avidity, and with such an evident delight, as to convince me, that when the proper time arrived, I could render no better service to my country, or to mankind, than by making a second tour throughout the kingdom for the purpose of explaining verbally, to as many auditors as could be collected, whatever I deemed worthy of their attention in that part of the East with which I was best acquainted. I naturally concluded, that if 20 persons would suspend conversation at a dinner table for the purpose of listening with great silence and earnestness to a description of some scene, or a narrative of some event of which I had been a witness in India, there could be no good reason why 200 might not be equally ready to listen with the same attention to similar communications elsewhere. I accordingly formed the resolution of waiting until the near approach of the Parliamentary Discussions on the East India Company's Charter should give an additional excitement to public curiosity, and then putting my plan of this personal tour into execution.

I returned to London, established THE ORIENTAL HERALD, a Monthly Journal, devoted especially to the progressive development of the state of Asia generally, and of India in particular ; continued it through five years of uninterrupted publication, from 1824 to the beginning of 1829; and availed myself besides of every opportunity that presented itself, by petitions to parliament—by appeals to the Privy Council—by proceedings in Courts of Justice—by the establishment of Political and Literary Journals—and by every means that my imagination could devise, to excite discussion and spread information respecting India through every open channel, and in every accessible spot. During this period, not less than 6000*l.* sterling, partly from my own funds—the whole of the remnant of my Indian property being devoted to that purpose, and partly from the sums contributed by others to assist the cause, were expended or sunk in furtherance of this uniform and unaltered design, of awakening the people of England to a sense of the importance of our Indian possessions, and the benefits that would accrue to both countries by a better system of intercourse between them. And if to this be added the unintermitted and laborious application of every faculty, every thought, and every moment of my time, through good report and through evil report, by day and by night, in sickness and in trouble, as well as in vigorous health and comparative tranquillity—when persecuted by enemies—sneered at by false friends—and discouraged by the anxious fears and apprehensions of real ones—I believe I may truly say, that whether as regards the application of money or of labour, no cause was ever more resolutely, or more undeviatingly, adhered to, through so many opposing circumstances, than this has been by me.

The time at length approached when I had determined to put my plan of the Tour into effect; and after making such arrangements as my temporary absence from London required, for I contemplated only occasional visits to the country at first, I made public the following announcement of my intention.

' Mr. Buckingham, having long since stated his intention of visiting personally, and in succession, all the principal towns of England, preparatory to the approaching expiration of the East India Company's Charter, intends commencing immediately with Liverpool, where he will be early in January, for the purpose of arranging with the principal Merchants of that great Commercial port the best mode of inducing the Mercantile and Manufacturing Interests of the kingdom, generally, to oppose, by all legal and constitutional means within their power, the further renewal of the East India Company's exclusive Monopoly, the discussions on which will now soon commence in Parliament. Mr. Buckingham has already announced his intention to give a Series of Lectures, during his stay in Liverpool, on the Geography, Antiquities, Productions, Population, Commerce, Resources, Government, Religion, Manners, and Customs of the Eastern World, more especially of Egypt, Palestine, Syria, Mesopotamia, Babylonia, Persia, and India; the entire profits of which he proposes to devote to the commencement of a Public Fund, for promoting such measures as may be thought best calculated to remedy those evils, which, both in England and in India, are inseparable from the arbitrary power and exclusive privileges now vested in that Chartered Monopoly.'

To satisfy, in as brief a compass as I could, the many enquiries which I knew would be made, as to my qualifications, motives, and the events that had led to my possession of the requisite knowledge for the task, I drew up also the following

BIOGRAPHICAL SKETCH.

When an individual invites the attention of the public to the facts and arguments by which he may attempt to support his views on any great public question, it is not unreasonable that those to whom his appeal is made, should ask for some proof of his claims to their attention, and demand the exhibition of his credentials before they consent to honour him with their confidence; and being myself quite as desirous of granting, as others can be of asking, such reasonable concessions, I proceed to give a Sketch of the most material grounds on which I consider my claims to general confidence to be established. It will of necessity be very brief, and merely an outline—for the history of forty years is not easy to be condensed into a few pages;—but when I add, that I shall be always ready to afford to any one who may deem it worth his inquiry, the more detailed information he may seek, by a personal interview and verbal conference, I hope I shall sufficiently acquit myself of my duty by the union of these two modes of communication.

At the very early age of nine years, I embraced, with the most enthusiastic ardour, the maritime profession ; and embarked in one of his Majesty's Packets for a foreign station. Before I completed my tenth year, I was captured, and, as a prisoner of war, passed several months in confinement at Corunna: and before I completed my eleventh year, I had been marched, with the rest of the officers and crew of the ship in which I sailed, a distance of many hundred miles bare-foot through Spain and Portugal, from 'Corunna, through St. Iago di Compostella, Vigo, Oporto, Coimbra, and Santarem to Lisbon.

Subsequent to this, I visited other countries in the same profession ; and obtained a maritime command at the early age of twenty-one. In this capacity I performed several voyages to the West Indies, the two Americas, and the Mediterranean Sea, including Gibraltar, Malta, the Greek Islands, and Smyrna in the Levant : in which, uniting as I did, the occupation of Seaman and Merchant, and conducting not merely the navigation but the commerce of the voyage, I had abundant opportunities of becoming acquainted with all the facts and circumstances bearing in any degree upon either ; of which I very sedulously availed myself: and to show the manner in which this information was used, I need only refer to the early pages of THE ORIENTAL HERALD; where, in a series of papers, entitled ' Unpublished Manuscripts of a Traveller in the East,' * will be found a very copious detail of my principal Voyages in the Mediterranean : and a Report on the Commerce of Smyrna, including a detailed history of all its peculiarities, with a minute description of its Exports, Imports, Duties, &c. &c., which may fairly challenge comparison with any similar paper, for fullness, clearness, and fidelity. †

In the year 1813, having formed the intention of resigning my command, and settling at Malta, as a general merchant, I sailed from London with that view. The attractions of Malta as a place of settlement for that purpose, consisted in its being the great central magazine or depôt, from which the continent of Europe, then under a rigorous blockade against all British manufactures, by the decrees of Napoleon Buonaparte, was supplied with every description of merchandise, both in English goods and and colonial produce ; and also in its being the great prize-port, into which all captured vessels were brought for adjucation and sale, by decrees of the Vice-Admiralty Court, of which Malta was the chief station.

Uniting as I did, in my own person, a thorough knowledge of all mercantile matters, connected either with Colonial produce or British manufactures ; being equally well acquainted with the value of ships and marine stores ; and speaking familiarly the several languages of which Malta was the seat, namely, Arabic, Greek, French and Italian ;—there was every prospect before me of a successful mercantile career, by a settlement in that island, at that particular period.

On arriving off the port of Valetta, however, it was found that the plague, which had not been known there for upwards of a century, raged with such violence as to induce the Governor to prohibit the landing of any individuals, and indeed to prevent any personal communication with the shore. The cargoes destined for this depôt were accordingly landed in magazines near the sea, and the ships proceeded to other ports ; the one in which I was embarked going on to Smyrna.

I remained there a sufficient period to be a considerable loser by the calamitous events that occurred at Malta, in consequence of the long-continued and devastating pestilence which afflicted that island ; and at length proceeded to look around that country for fresh sources of enterprise. The cordial reception given to me by the British residents there, soon obtained me the notice and attention of the Egyptian Pasha, Mohammed Ali, the present ruler of that interesting country. He was at this period just beginning to perceive the advantage of encouraging the settlement, in Egypt, of persons of skill and capital, from every quarter of the globe, for the purpose of improving the resources of his dominion ; and, extending his views also to external commerce, I had the pleasure of passing many successive evenings with him in his Divan, after all his public officers, excepting only his confidential Secretary, were dismissed, and there, with a set of Arrowsmith's charts, which I exhibited to him,

* See ' Oriental Herald,' vol. vi. p. 15. 243. 456; vol. vii. p. 46. 497 ; vol. viii. p. 471 ; vol. ix. p. 83. 268. 509 ; vol. x. p. 72. 294. 473 ; vol. xi. p. 91. 331. 545.
† See ' Oriental Herald,' vol. x. p. 72. 473.

explaining the relative positions and productions of various countries—the winds, seasons, monsoons, currents, rocks, shoals, &c., as well as the theory and practice of navigation and hydrography ;—all of which afforded him such delight, that we often sat together until near the dawn of the following morning ; and I at length succeeded in having transcribed, upon a duplicate set of Arrowsmith's charts traced by my own hand for the purpose, all the information of importance, written in the Arabic language and character.

One of the undertakings which I subsequently proposed to accomplish for him, was the re-opening of the ancient canal which formerly connected the Red Sea with the Mediterranean ; * and another was the transporting across the Desert of the Isthmus, before the canal should be opened, two beautiful American brigs then lying in the harbour of Alexandria, which he was anxious to get into the Red Sea, but feared the East India Company would prevent his sending them round the Cape of Good Hope. † But at this period, the war against the Wahabees occupied almost the exclusive attention of all parties in Egypt, and ultimately compelled the Pasha himself to repair to the seat of hostilities in Arabia ; while those to whom he confided the government of the country in his absence, were far less able than himself to appreciate the value of such works as these.

From Alexandria I proceeded to Cairo ; and from thence ascended the Nile into Nubia, beyond the Cataracts, being prevented from penetrating farther in consequence of an almost total blindness, occasioned by a long and severe ophthalmia, one of the plagues that still afflict Egypt. On my descent I halted at Keneh, and crossed the Desert to Kosseir, on the shores of the Red Sea. In the course of this journey, I encountered, nearly in the middle of the Desert, a party of the mutinous soldiery of the Egyptian army, returning in a state of revolt from Kosseir, by whom I was stripped, plundered, and left entirely naked on the barren waste, at a distance of sixty miles, at least, from any habitation or supply of food or water. The narrative of this disastrous journey would alone make a volume, if extended to all its details : I must here content myself with saying, however, that by perseverance I succeeded in reaching Kosseir, though under circumstances of the most painful and distressing nature : and that, to add to my sufferings, I was obliged to retrace all my steps, and return again to Keneh on the Nile, from the impossibility of prosecuting my route farther in that direction.†

I descended the Nile to Cairo, from thence traversed the Isthmus of Suez, explored all the surrounding country, and visited every part of Lower Egypt and the Delta, habited as an Egyptian, speaking the language, and mixing freely with the people of the country.

It was at this period that a proposition was made to me by the English merchants then resident in Egypt, to undertake, on their account, a voyage to India by way of the Red Sea : first, to survey its hydrography, till that period most inaccurately known, and thus to judge of the practicability of its coasting navigation by English ships ; and next, to ascertain how far the merchants of India—but those at Bombay more especially—might feel disposed to renew the commercial intercourse which formerly existed between India and Egypt, for the supply of all the higher parts of the Mediterranean.

I readily acceded to this proposition, and set out for Suez accordingly, profiting by the departure of a large caravan then conveying the pilgrims of Africa. collected at Cairo, to the great Temple at Mecca; and bearing also the Harem of Mohammed Ali Pasha, consisting of fifty or sixty of the most beautiful women of Asia, to his camp in the

* For a collected view of all the best information on this subject, see ' The Oriental Herald,' vol. v. p. 1.

† These are both adverted to in the Preface to the ' Travels in Palestine,' the first of my published works.

‡ The idea having been first started in ' The Athenæum ' of producing a volume, similar to the Annuals, for the benefit of the distressed foreign refugees in England, to which the leading literary men of England should be invited to contribute their assistance gratuitously, I selected, from my unpublished manuscripts, an account of this Desert Journey, written a few days after its termination, and devoted it to this purpose. I subsequently obtained the consent of that excellent man, and accomplished statesman and scholar, Sir James Mackintosh, to charge himself with the Editorship of this proposed volume, and have, therefore, great pleasure in thus drawing public attention to its object, in the benevolence of which every feeling heart must concur. (This duty afterwards devolved upon Mr. Thomas Campbell, the poet ; but the publication has since, from some unforeseen obstacle, been unhappily frustrated.)

Holy Land.* The voyage was continued, under most disastrous circumstances, to Jedda, from thence to Mocha, and ultimately to India.

The merchants of Bombay being, however, unwilling to resume the commerce with Egypt, except under securities which it was hardly probable they could obtain, I considered my mission at an end ; and, after communicating the result to the proper quarter, my attention was turned to some maritime or mercantile occupation in India itself. This was soon obtained ; for I had scarcely been a week on shore, before I was appointed to the command of a fine new frigate, just launched for the Imaum of Muscat, an independent Arab prince, who had commissioned her for a voyage to China. I was invested with the command, and was actually engaged in rigging and fitting her out, when, not less to my regret than surprise, I received a letter from the Government of Bombay, dated May 10, 1815, which is so short that it may be given entire.

' SIR, —I have received the orders of Government to call upon you to give security to proceed to England, in such ship, and at such time as may be appointed by Government, it being understood that you have no license or authority to remain in India. I have the honour to be, Sir, your most obedient servant,

J. H. STEPHENSON, Company's Solicitor.'†

To this I replied, by recapitulating all the circumstances under which I reached India: explaining, that when I left England I had no intention of coming thus far ; that I neither knew the fact of any license being necessary, to give an Englishman the *privilege* of visiting any part of the king's dominions; nor even, had I known this fact, should I have applied for it, as I considered Malta the boundary of my voyage. I therefore asked the Governor's indulgence to remain in India, under the special license which he had the power to grant, until the pleasure of the Court of Directors in England should be known ; and, in addition to this public demand, the greatest private interest was used to obtain the indulgence required. But the orders of the Directors in England were so peremptory, commanding the instant banishment of any individual, *however useful or honourable his pursuits*, who ventured to set his foot in India without a license, that the Governor dared not depart from them. This indulgence was accordingly refused : but, in an interview which I afterwards had with the Governor, Sir Evan Nepean, he himself said to me, ' My dear sir, what a pity it is that you are not an American—and I think you might very well pass for one—for then you might remain in India, and visit any part of it, without license from England, or even leave from me.' To show also that this my *first* banishment from India, and deprivation of a very honourable and lucrative command, in the service of an independent prince, which any American, French, or other foreign officer might enter without the power of the English to hinder, was not occasioned by any supposed hostility on my part to the India Company, or by any thing objectionable in my character or views, I shall subjoin the whole of the letter of the Governor of Bombay to his Chief Secretary. This letter was written in reply to the secretary's application on my behalf for permission to return to England by way of Egypt, as I had already been refused permission to go by way of Bengal, which I had wished, as the most expeditious of the two ; It is as follows :

' DEAR WARDEN, —I can have no objection to Mr. Buckingham returning to England by the way of Mocha. He came hither, I understand, by that route. But I have an objection to the allowing him to go to Bengal, or to any other part of India, being determined to discourage all attempts which may be made by persons to settle in India without the license of the Company. To the individual himself I have not the slightest degree of objection. On the contrary, he appeared to be a sensible, intelligent man : and I shall by no means be sorry to see him return with the Company's license, believing, as I do, that he would be of use to the mercantile interests, in opening the trade of the Red Sea. Your's, &c. E. NEPEAN.'

I was accordingly, without the least fault alleged against me, but even with these eulogies bestowed on my character and my views, punished with the deprivation of an honourable command, the loss of a certain fortune from this lucrative service, (which my licensed successor actually realised, to the extent of three lacs of rupees, or 30,000*l.*

---

* An account of this Journey across the Isthmus, was furnished, from my unpublished manuscripts, at the request of Mr. Pringle, the able editor of ' The Friendship's Offering,' for 1827, for the pages of that beautiful and interesting Annual, where it will be found.

† Brother of the Banker, Rowland Stephenson, whose frauds and escape have lately excited so much attention; but, unlike this brother, a most upright and honourable man.

sterling, in three years,) and subjected to transportation, as if my very touch were sufficient to contaminate a land—which we Englishmen call our own, as being won with the blood and treasure of our countrymen, and under the protection of our national flag—while foreigners alone are *free* in it, and every Englishman is virtually a slave !*

I returned to Egypt in company with Dr. Benjamin Babington,† by a second voyage through the Red Sea, in which I collected ample materials for a new hydrographical chart of all its coasts ; and communicated the result of my expedition to the British merchants at Alexandria. It was then resolved to obtain from Mohammed Ali the securities which the Indian merchants desired ; and accordingly, a Commercial Treaty was entered into, between the Pasha, the British Consul, and myself, each of whom pledged himself to certain engagements, calculated to afford reciprocal protection and profit.‡

As this was considered to clothe me with a new character, and invest me with new powers, it was agreed that I should proceed again to India, as the ambassador or envoy of Mohammed Ali, the viceroy of Egypt : being made the bearer of letters and commissions from him to the Government of India, as well as of this tripartite treaty to its merchants. I accordingly left Alexandria in the close of the year 1815, for the coast of Syria,§ landed at Bairoot, proceeded by Tyre, Sidon, Acre, and Jaffa, to Jerusalem ;—was compelled, by various circumstances, but more especially the disturbed state of the country, to traverse nearly the whole of Palestine, and the countries east of the Jordan and the Dead Sea, the Hauran, and the Decapolis ;—reached Damascus ; —passed several weeks in the agreeable and hospitable society of Lady Hester Stanhope ;—visited Baalbeck, Lebanon, Tripoly, Antioch, the Orontes, and Aleppo.‖ From thence I proceeded into Mesopotamia ; crossed the Euphrates at Bir ; visited Orfah, near Haran, the Ur of the Chaldees, the birth-place of Abraham the Patriarch, and Edessa of the Greeks ; journeyed to Diarbekr, or the Black City, in the heart of Asia Minor ; from thence to Mardin on the mountains ; and by the Great Desert of Sinjar to Moosul on the Tigris ; inspected the Ruins of Nineveh, Arbela, Ctesiphon, and Seleucia ;—made extensive researches on the Ruins of Babylon, identified the Hanging Gardens, and the Palace, and discovered a portion of the ancient Wall ; ascended to the summit of the Tower of Babel, now still erect in the Plain of Shinaar, and at length reposed in the celebrated City of Bagdad, on the banks of the Tigris.¶

After a short stay here I proceeded into Persia, crossing the chain of Mount Zagros, and going by Kermanshah to Hamadan, the ancient Ecbatana ; Ispahan, the most magnificent of all the Oriental cities ; the ruins of Persepolis ; and by Shiraz and

---

* The whole of the official correspondence relating to these transactions will be found at length, in the Appendix to the First Volume of 'The Oriental Herald,' p.3 to 5.

† See his evidence as to this voyage in ' The Oriental Herald,' vol. xi. p. 405.

‡ The original Arabic version of this treaty is in the possession of Sir Charles Forbes, Bart., M.P., and the French version of it will be found in ' The Oriental Herald,' vol. iv. p. 505.

§ It is here that my published Travels first commence, in the volume entitled ' Travels in Palestine, through the countries of Bashan and Gilead,' beginning at Alexandria, and ending at Nazareth. It is dedicated to the Marquis of Hastings, and comprises 553 quarto pages, with a Portrait and 28 engravings, exclusive of Inscriptions, Plans, and Maps. The Preface to this contains a detailed account of my track.

‖ This concludes the second volume, entitled ' Travels among the Arab Tribes, inhabiting the Countries East of Syria and Palestine.' It is dedicated to Dr. Babington, and comprises 679 quarto pages, and 28 Engravings, exclusive of Inscriptions and Map. In the Appendix to this Volume is contained all the documents and correspondence relating to the controversy with ' The Quarterly Review,' the Indian Government, Mr. Gifford, Mr. Murray, and the elder and younger Mr. Bankes.

¶ This concludes the third Volume, entitled ' Travels in Mesopotamia,' which is dedicated to the Right Honourable Lady Hester Stanhope, and comprises 578 pages, and 27 Engravings, besides the Plans and Views of the Ruins of Babylon, and the Map. It may be mentioned here, that this work having been read by Mr. James Keeling, an extensive manufacturer of porcelain at the Hanley Potteries in Staffordshire, he was so pleased with the scriptural illustrations it contained, and with the Engravings with which the Work was embellished, that he formed the design of making a beautiful Dinner Service, to be ornamented by the Views in Mesopotamia, which he brought to great perfection, and presented me with the first set sent from his manufactory. The Appendix to this volume contains the issue of the trial of Mr. Bankes ; a verbatim report of which will be found in ' The Oriental Herald,' vol. xi. p. 375.

Shapoor to Bushire. At this port I embarked in an East India Company's ship of war, bound on an expedition against the Wahabees, the Arab pirates of the Persian Gulph; visited their port at Ras-el-Khyma; went on shore with the Commodore of the squadron, and acted as his Arabian interpreter; assisted afterwards in the bombardment of the town; and finally reached Bombay at the end of 1816, having been nearly twelve months in performing this long and perilous journey.*

That such a succession of voyages and travels should be full of danger, as well as incident, may be easily imagined: but I purposely abstain from a recital of them, which would lead, indeed, to a volume of itself. It may be sufficient to say, that storms, plagues, shipwreck, battle, imprisonment, hunger, thirst, sickness, nakedness, and want, had been my frequent portion; and that there was scarcely any form under which human misery could present itself, in which I had not encountered it: or scarcely any pomp, pleasure, honour, or distinction, which mortal could enjoy, that I had not witnessed, and occassionally shared in; having in all this weary pilgrimage, invariably found the name of AN ENGLISHMAN, wherever it was safe to assume it, a passport and a claim to every favour and protection that the public authorities of *other nations* could afford, till I reached what I had hitherto regarded as a part of my own country—INDIA; where, I found this proud name the badge and symbol of every thing that was debased and enslaved—an Englishman *alone* being there subject to *banishment* and ruin, without trial, without a hearing, without even a reason assigned, merely *because* he is an Englishman; while foreigners of every other country are entitled to the protection of the laws, and cannot be touched but through the medium of a Court and a Jury,—a privilege of which all Englishmen are deprived!

The issue of my second mission to Bombay was not more successful in bringing about the wished-for trade between India and Egypt, than the former; and having by this time, through the intervention of my friend and fellow-traveller from India, Dr. Babington, who left me in Egypt, and proceeded to England, obtained the Company's license to remain in their territories, (which was sent out to me in Bombay,) I resumed the command of the Imaum of Muscat's frigate, from which I was before displaced; his Mohammedan agent having been indignant at what even *he* considered the tyranny of the Indian government, and pledged himself to reinstate me in the command, if I ever returned to India to accept it. But the three lucrative voyages to China, which I was to have performed, had in the mean time been accomplished by another, and his fortune made. The ship was now destined for the Persian Gulf, whither I sailed in her; and after visiting Muscat and Bussorah, I returned with a successful result, to Bombay.†

From hence I proceeded down the coast of Malabar, touching at Tellicherry, Calicut, Mahee, and Cochin; Colombo and Point de Galle, in Ceylon; up the coast of Coromandel, touching at Covelong, Madras, Vizagapatam, and Bimlipatam; and at length reached Calcutta in June, 1818.

Here I found that orders had reached from the Imaum of Muscat, to whom the frigate under my command belonged, directing her to proceed to the coast of Zanzibar, in Africa, to give convoy to several of his vessels there engaged in procuring slaves, as well as to convey some of these unhappy beings in my own,—a service in which, had the prospect of fortune been ten times as brilliant as it was, my abhorrence of slavery would not permit me to engage; and accordingly rather than acquire riches from such a source, I resigned the command, and with it all the prospects of competency and ease which it had hitherto promised me.

At this period I became acquainted with Mr. John Palmer, of Calcutta, who is designated, with great justice, the Prince of Merchants in the East, who holds the same rank in India as the Barings in England, and whom no man ever knew without loving as well as revering. He it was who first suggested the idea of my having talents for literary and political life, for which I ought to relinquish that of the sea; and this

---

* This terminates the fourth Volume, entitled 'Travels in Assyria, Media, and Persia,' which is dedicated to Sir Charles Forbes, Bart., M.P., comprises 545 pages, and is illustrated with an Equestrian Portrait in the costume of the East, 26 Engravings, and a Map. The Preface to this explains the circumstances under which this Volume went through the Press; and which are probably without a parallel in the whole history of literary labours.

† A short extract from the description of Muscat, composed on this voyage, will be found in Mr. Pringle's elegant Annual, the 'Friendship's Offering,' for the present year, 1829; the full account is incorporated in the 'Travels in Assyria, Media, and Persia;" and the account of Bussorah which is given at length in the same volume, will be found also in 'The Oriental Herald' for January, 1829, vol. xx. p. 36.

impression receiving considerable strength from the very flattering attention paid me by the Marquis of Hastings, the late Lord Bishop of Calcutta, and indeed all the men distinguished for their rank or learning in India, I yielded to the general solicitation, and consented to undertake the editorship of a public journal in Calcutta, to be conducted on the liberal principles which then characterised the brilliant administration of the Marquis of Hastings, and with which every feeling of my heart was in perfect accordance. The materials for this journal were purchased for 30,000 rupees, or 3,000*l.* sterling. It was issued; obtained almost instantaneous popularity; and, within three years after its first establishment, I brought it to produce a net profit of about 8,000*l.* sterling per annum. During the whole of this period, it supported, with a degree of zeal which was sometimes interpreted as adulation, the measures and policy of the existing government, which was that of Lord Hastings, who, contrary to the views of his more narrow-minded colleagues, the civil servants of the East India Company, had removed the Censorship from the Press; was disposed to elevate the condition of the Natives; to permit the settlement of English gentlemen of capital and character in the interior; and in every other manner to promote the interests both of his own country, and of that over which he ruled. The support of this noble and enlightened policy of Lord Hastings, the representative of his Majesty and the British Legislature in India,—and the fact of my having sold one-fourth of my Paper for 10,000*l.* sterling, in 100 shares of 100*l.* each, which were purchased by the principal merchants, and civil and military officers in the Company's service in India, and which, therefore, was the highest mark of honour any public writer could receive,—was the very cause of all the hatred felt against myself, and hostility to ' The Calcutta Journal,' which I conducted, by the more bigoted adherents of the Company's system, then forming his council. Accordingly, there arose perpetual efforts, on the part of the latter, to obtain my arbitrary banishment from India, for supporting the views professed and entertained by the head of the government himself; but he, like a true English nobleman, always referred them to the *law*, as the protecting power of the ruler and the subject; and declared, that while Providence continued him at the head of affairs, he would never suffer any one to deprive a British subject of that shield which was purposely created to protect him from the exercise of arbitrary power.

During the whole of Lord Hastings's government, therefore, which lasted for ten years, no arbitrary banishment of any Englishman, for opinions expressed through the press, ever took place. The law was there, as it is in England, sufficient to repress all evils arising from this source; and notwithstanding this perfect freedom, never was the empire more tranquil, never more prosperous, even according to the testimony of his enemies; for he was the first Governor-General India had ever seen, who left the country in a state of perfect repose, from the Indus to the Ganges, and from the Himalaya to Ceylon, with ten millions sterling of surplus revenue in the treasury, the people comparatively happy, the public debt in a state of liquidation, and content and prosperity marking every branch of the public service. During all this long and eventful period, in which the law had been resorted to by the enemies of his pacific administration, no single conviction for libel, or any other offence, had ever been recorded against me; though I had obtained convictions against my calumniators, (for no man ever opposed bad measures without being calumniated by those whose unjust gains were endangered,) and was even obliged to meet my opponents in the field;[*] yet, no sooner had the Marquis of Hastings quitted India—which his health obliged him to do, before his permanent successor, Lord Amherst, arrived—than his temporary *locum tenens*, Mr. John Adam,—who, being one of the oldest of the East India Company's servants, and the last that held the office of Censor of the Press, abolished by Lord Hastings, was the most deeply imbued with all its despotic principles of rule—determined to seize the first possible moment of banishing me from the country, and doing for himself what he had before often urged the Marquis of Hastings to do in vain. I had already heard, and indeed was enabled to prove, his declaration, made before Lord Hastings left India, that if he ever obtained the seat of power but for a day, his first act should be to banish me; and I exercised a proportionate degree of caution; so much so, that my enemies, whose great object it was to goad me into indiscretion, taunted me with the line from Shakspeare,

' High-reaching Buckingham grows circumspect;'

---

[*] See a detailed account of the meeting with one of the public servants of the Indian Government, here alluded to, in ' The Oriental Herald,' vol. i. p. 61.

and provided also a very easy remedy for the Government, by exclaiming, in the language of the same poet,

' Off with his head!—So much for Buckingham.'

Accordingly, the time of Mr. Adam's temporary governorship fast drawing to a close, and the impression being, that if he did not hasten to do his deed of destruction, the dagger would pass away from his grasp, the occasion was seized to do it instantly, and this was the feeble pretence on which it was attempted to be justified.

A Presbyterian Minister of the Scotch Church, Dr. Bryce, who was the head of that Church in India, had been for many years the Editor of a violent newspaper, entitled the ' Asiatic Mirror,' which had been greatly injured by the superior success of ' The Calcutta Journal,' to his very natural mortification and regret. He had subsequently connected himself with a second paper, called ' The John Bull,' set up by the functionaries of the Indian Government for the avowed purpose of defaming me : and in which a series of libels on my private character appeared, for which I obtained judgment against it, even in an Indian Court of Justice, with large damages : the Judge on the bench declaring, at the time of passing sentence, that ' the libels were so atrocious, as scarcely to be thought of without horror.'* To show upon what principles this Journal was conducted, it will be sufficient to quote a single passage of the writer of the calumnies directed against my private character, which his Letters in that Journal, under the signature of ' A Friend to Mr. Bankes,' contained. In this he openly avows, that, being unable to overturn, by reason, my arguments, (in favour of free trade, free settlement, and free publication,) and finding that my sentiments derived great weight from the excellence of my moral character, he thought it fair to *destroy* that character, in order to weaken the opinions which reposed on it ! The passage is so atrocious, that no one would believe it without its being produced. It is as follows :

' The phenomenon of a Journalist venting his sentiments without the aid of a censor, is but new in India ; and it was manifest that, in this country, such a man might prove the instrument of incalculable evil. In looking around me, I beheld the evils that might be feared actually occurring. I saw them insinuating themselves into the very strongholds of our power, and possibly paving the way for an event, which the enemies of our power have hitherto attempted in vain. Entertaining these views, the *conductor* of such a Press became, in *my eyes*, a Public Enemy ; and resting his power, *as he did*, as well on his Character as his Principles, his *reputation* became a *fair* and á *legitimate* object of *attack*, and its overthrow a subject of *honest triumph* to every lover of his country ! !'†

I will not weaken the force of so atrocious a doctrine as this, by a single word of comment.

It was almost immediately after this that Dr. Bryce was rewarded by Mr. Adam with an appointment to an office of considerable emolument, but the duties of which were the most unsuitable to a clergyman that could be imagined, and such as required very close attention, although the same individual had on a previous occasion given up the *unpaid* Secretaryship to a Bible Society on the plea of wanting time to perform its duties ! The appointment was even announced by the local Government, in an Extraordinary Gazette, as if it were a triumph or a victory ; and certainly, the unusual nature both of the fact and its mode of announcement created considerable sensation, of mirth in some, and of sorrow and alarm in others. Being rather actuated by the former than by the latter class of feelings, I was disposed to view it, and to treat it, in a playful light ; and as this was the article for which I was a *second* time banished without trial from India, (the reader will remember the first from Bombay,) and as, from our rooted notions of justice, the bare fact of any man having been banished from any country, leads all who hear it to *infer* that the individual really *deserved* his punishment, or it would not have been inflicted, it is very important that it should be given entire. It is rather long, but it will dispel the fears of many ; and show them that from the portion of my writings in India for which I was made to suffer the loss of 100,000*l.* in prospect, banishment as a felon, and the deprivation of an actual income from the labours of my own pen, of 8,000*l.* sterling a-year,—there was, at least, no probability of the empire being overturned, which is the only danger that could justify such severe and arbitrary punishment. The following is the article in question :—

---

* See this trial and sentence in ' The Oriental Herald,' vol. i. pp. 15. 348. 352.

† ' Oriental Herald,' vol. iv. p. 511.

' Appendix Extraordinary to the last Government Gazette.

' During the evening of Thursday, about the period at which the inhabitants of this good City of Palaces are accustomed to sit down to dinner, an Appendix to the Government Gazette of the morning was issued in a separate form, and coming in the shape of a Gazette Extraordinary, was eagerly seized, even at that inconvenient hour, in the hope of its containing some intelligence of great public importance. Some, in whose bosoms this hope had been most strongly excited, may, perhaps, have felt disappointment ; others, we know, drew from it a fund of amusement which lasted them all the remainder of the evening.

' The Reverend Gentleman, named below, who we perceive by the Index of that useful publication, the Annual Directory, is a Doctor of Divinity, and Moderator of the Kirk Session, and who, by the favour of the higher powers, now combines the office of parson and clerk in the same person, has no doubt been selected for the arduous duties of his new place from the purest motives, and the strictest possible attention to the public interests. Such a clerk as is here required, to inspect and reject whatever articles may appear objectionable to him, should be a competent judge of the several articles of pasteboard, sealing-wax, ink-stands, sand, lead, gum, pounce, tape, and leather ; and one would imagine that nothing short of a regular apprenticeship at Stationers'-hall would qualify a candidate for such a situation. All this information, however, the Reverend Gentleman, no doubt, possesses in a more eminent degree than any other person who could be found to do the duties of such an office ; and though at first sight such information may seem to be incompatible with a theological education, yet we know that India abounds with instances of that kind of genius which fits a man in a moment for any post to which he may be appointed.

' In Scotland, we believe, the duties of a Presbyterian Minister are divided between preaching on the Sabbath, and on the days of the week visiting the sick, comforting the weak-hearted, conferring with the bold, and encouraging the timid, in the several duties of their religion. Some shallow persons might conceive that if a Presbyterian Clergyman were to do his duty in India, he might also find abundant occupation throughout the year, in the zealous and faithful discharge of those pious duties which ought more especially to engage his devout attention. But they must be persons of very little reflection, indeed, who entertain such an idea. We have seen the Presbyterian flock of Calcutta take very good care of themselves for many months without a pastor at all : and even when the shepherd was among them, he had abundant time to edit a controversial newspaper, (long since defunct,) and to take a part in all the meetings, festivities, addresses, and flatteries, that were current at that time. He has continued to display this eminently active if not holy disposition up to the present period ; and, according to the maxim, ' to him that hath much (to do) still more shall be given, and from him that hath nothing, even the little that he hath shall be taken away,' this Reverend Doctor, who has so often evinced the universality of his genius and talents, whether within the pale of Divinity or without it, is perhaps the very best person that could be selected, all things considered, to take care of the foolscap, pasteboard, wax, sand, gum, lead, leather, and tape, of the Honourable East India Company of Merchants, and to examine and pronounce on the quality of each, so as to see that no drafts are given on their Treasury for gum that won't stick, tape short of measure, or inkstands of base metal.

' Whether the late discussions that have agitated both the wise and the foolish of this happy country from the Burrumpooter to the Indus, and from Cape Comorin to the confines of Tartary, have had an influence in hastening the consummation so *devoutly* wished, we cannot presume to determine. We do not profess to know any thing of the Occult Sciences : and being equally ignorant of all *secret* influences, whether of the planets of heaven or the satellites of earth, we must content ourselves, as faithful chroniclers of the age, with including in our records, the important document issued under the circumstances we have described.'

(Here followed a Table of the articles of Stationery required, and the quantities of each ; at the end of which was the following paragraph, as it stood in the Government Gazette, published by authority.)

' " *Conditions:*—1st. The quality of the Stationery to be equal to the musters now open for inspection at the Stationery office.—2d. The articles required for the expenditure of every month to be delivered on or before the 28th day of the month which

precedes it, and paid for by an order on the general treasury for the amount delivered. —3d. The proposals of contract to be accompanied by a written document signed by a respectable person, acknowledging himself (if the terms are accepted) to be responsible for the performance of the contractor's engagement, and engaging, in the event of deficient deliveries, to make good the value of these, together with a penalty of 50 per cent. on the amount of them.—4th. The Clerk to the Committee of Stationery to be at liberty to reject any part of the Stationery which may appear objectionable to him.   By order of the Committee of Stationery,
'"*Stationery Office, Feb.* 4, 1823.   JAMES BRYCE, Clerk Com. Sty."'

This, then, was my crime! and my punishment was more severe than the law inflicts even upon felons; for their property is not always confiscated, nor are they ever denied the right of a trial; while I, and the wife of my bosom, who had just joined me in India, after a separation of ten long years, from the period of my leaving her in England on my first voyage to Malta, were turned out of house and home, at a moment's warning; a princely fortune destroyed; an abode of happiness changed into one of mourning; and the brand of infamy, as a banished man, placed upon my forehead, for the finger of scorn to point at, and for every man to *infer*, from the mere fact itself, that I was a fire-brand, dangerous to the peace of the country, and *therefore* ejected from it by violence!

Whether my offence was of a nature to deserve this treatment, let the reader judge. But what will be his indignation when he learns that although, when we reached England,—(finding our children embarked, and almost in the act of sailing to join us in India, so sudden was the decree, that there was not even time to countermand our orders for their coming out to what they innocently deemed a shelter and a home,)— the India Company and the Board of Control had both concurred in the impropriety of the appointment I had so gently satirized, and had even ordered it to be instantly annulled; yet, when I applied, on this ground, for leave to return, I was refused, by both, this reasonable permission. The doctrine maintained at the India House, was, that their servants abroad, even if occasionally wrong, *must* be supported; and the doctrine at the Board of Control was, that as it was not a question of patronage, the India Company must be supported *also*. Of all this, then, I was the victim : and even when I asked, a few months afterwards, on hearing of proceedings against my property in India, too atrocious to be believed, and too long to be detailed, for leave merely to go to India for a few weeks to wind up my affairs, pay my debts, receive those due to me, and then quit the country for ever, these unfeeling tyrants (can any man designate the authors of such cruelty by any more appropriate term?) refused me even this : so that, to the total wreck of all I left behind, amounting to at least 40,000*l*., was added the accumulation of debts on various proceedings taken in my absence, purposely to increase my embarrassments, amounting to upwards of 10,000*l*. more; thus plunging an innocent and amiable family into almost irretrievable misery, for, at most, the indiscretion of a father, who ventured to call in question the propriety of that which the highest authorities of the country no sooner heard of, than they denounced and overturned!!

My return to India, where all my friends and hopes of fortune lay, being thus rendered impossible, I determined to use the information which Providence had thrown in my way, to benefit, as far as my humble powers would admit, my fellow-countrymen here, as well as my fellow-men and fellow-subjects in the East. I have accordingly employed the last five years of my life in conducting THE ORIENTAL HERALD, which has been almost exclusively devoted to Eastern affairs :—in establishing THE SPHYNX, a European Political Journal, to which I applied a legacy of 5,000 rupees, sent me from India by an individual whom I had never either seen or heard from before, but who left it in his will as a tribute of respect to my public character and principles, and as a mark of gratitude for the benefit which he believed my writings to have produced in India;* —and in following up the successful career of this, by THE ATHENÆUM, a Journal devoted chiefly to Literature, Science, and the Arts. In addition to these, which have all been crowned with marked approbation and success, I have also published four quarto volumes of Travels in the East, each of which has been received with favour by

---

* See the details of this in the first Number of 'The Sphynx,' for July, 1827; and in The Oriental Herald,' vol. xiv. p. 391. 394.

the literary world; and have succeeded in bringing to a satisfactory issue, my legal proceedings against Mr. Henry Bankes, the late Member for Corfe Castle, and Mr. W. J. Bankes, the late Member for Cambridge; and setting myself right, I hope, with all the reading and reflecting part of the world.

The time is now come, therefore, when I have resolved on following up my writings by the personal Tour which I had always purposed, and which, indeed, I stated my intention of undertaking some years ago, in order to communicate to others that local knowledge of which my peculiar duties and pursuits have given me possession: and to rouse the public attention to the benefits which must result to this country, as well as to every part of the Eastern World, by extending the commercial intercourse between them. I enter on this task under the most favourable auspices, and, as far as zeal and determined perseverance can effect, I hope, by the blessing of God, to bring it to as auspicious a close. If there are those who think that in so doing I am actuated by vindictive feelings towards the East India Company, I cannot wonder at their receiving such an impression; for, if ever man had *cause* for vengeance against them, that man is myself. But I confess (let those doubt who may) that I would not willingly hurt a hair of the head of any man living, not even of my greatest enemy: and as for the East India Company, it is composed of 4,000 or 5,000 individuals, including old men, old women, and young children, and has within it as much of merit and innocence as any other body of superannuated stockholders,—for the great mass of them are nothing more:—while some of the warmest and steadiest friends I ever had the happiness to possess, are members of that body, or holders of its stock; but who, though members, deprecate, as severely as I can do, the conduct which I have faithfully described.

It is not against any man or any men that my labours are directed, but against the *system*, which is unproductive of good even to those who uphold it, and fraught with all manner of evil to those who are not of that number. To this system I was as determined an enemy on the first day of my setting foot in India as I am now: and this I never concealed. I could not have been influenced by vindictive motives *before* I received any injury from the India Company, yet the views I maintain now, were those which I maintained then; no change whatever has taken place in my sentiments on those subjects, except that the longer I have lived, the more I have seen, and the more extensive and more accurate my information has become during the last ten years that I have been engaged almost exclusively in increasing my stock of knowledge from every accessible source, the more firmly have I been convinced of the truth of my position, that Free Trade to India, China, and the Oriental World in general, would be productive of incalculable benefit to all the countries engaged in it, and of danger or injury to none.

I have now, then—though I fear most imperfectly—endeavoured to show, that when I address my countrymen on the subject of shipping and commerce, I have some claim to their attention, as a seaman and a merchant; that when I describe to them the antiquities and productions of other seas and countries, I speak of tracts that I have traversed, and objects that I have seen; and that, even on questions of policy and government, as relates to the Eastern World at least, I am not altogether unworthy of being heard, after supporting the liberal policy, and enjoying, as I had the happiness to enjoy, the good opinion of the greatest and best Governor-General India ever saw; after conducting, for five years, with the greatest success, a public Journa. in India, supported and patronised by the most celebrated of the civil and military servants of the Government itself; and editing, for the same period, a public Journal in England, The Oriental Herald, which is still eagerly sought after in every part of that country, and well known and esteemed among the statesmen and legislators of this.

If these credentials are deemed satisfactory, I shall rejoice at having been prompted to produce them; and I ask only the fair and candid interpretation of whatever apparent confidence they may seem to evince. For myself, I feel that I *have* a claim to be heard; and *having* that feeling, it is but consistent with the acknowledged frankness of my earliest profession, which still influences my nature, that I should freely *say* so, whatever imputations of weakness, or of undue confidence may follow such a declaration. My sense of public duty is as clear as it is strong: its dictates I shall therefore continue firmly to follow; but the issue is with a Higher Power—whose blessing I implore.

4, Brunswick Place,   J. S. BUCKINGHAM.
Regent's Park, London.

LIVERPOOL.

AFTER this announcement, I proceeded to Liverpool, where I met, as I expected, a very cordial reception, from all classes of the wealthy and intelligent inhabitants : and there, for the first time, I determined to make the experiment of giving Extempore Descriptions of the Eastern World. They were announced as Lectures on the Countries of the East, to be given in the Music Hall of the City, and from the first were most respectably attended. Some apprehensions were felt by my friends, that this being my first attempt at a public and extempore delineation of scenes and events so varied as it was my intention to make them, I might experience some embarrassment in the execution : but I felt such inward consciousness of strength and confidence, that I was never more self-possessed than when I first opened my lips before the large assembly that attended me. The result was even more successful than I had ventured to hope : all parties seemed pleased ; and in addition to the uniform and enthusiastic approbation of the audiences, the eulogies of the press on both sides of politics, and the union of parties not usually co-operating in any public undertaking, produced by my last lecture at Liverpool, was thus spoken of by the leading papers of that City :—

' In company with a very numerous and respectable auditory, we participated in the unequivocal satisfaction of witnessing, on Monday night last, the delivery of Mr. Buckingham's first lecture, introductory of that subject to which in our last publication we directed the attentive consideration of the public. Mr. Buckingham's second lecture took place last night ; and on both occasions his talents and experience were successfully exercised. The manner of this gentleman confers additional interest on the subject-matter of his discourse, and he himself is a striking instance of the union of qualities most to be desired—the *simplex munditiis*. His style is peculiarly suited to the delivery of lectures, intended to be rendered familiar and accessible. It may be described as conversational oratory. It is complete delineation. We wander with the traveller, and scarce need a chart to guide us on our way ; we roam with him by the banks of Nilus, we descend into the Catacombs, or calculate the height of a pyramid ; and, as the Orientalist (so to call him) unfolds the stores of his enlarged conception, we take possession of his treasures, and imagination bodies forth, with the fidelity of a diagram, scenes which, so far as we are concerned, may almost be termed visionary.'— *Gore's Liverpool Advertizer, Jan.* 8.

' Mr. Buckingham's lectures, it gives us pleasure to observe, have been attended by audiences of which, both for numbers and respectability, he may justly be proud, and the applause wrung from them by the pleasing popular style of his delivery, must have proved to him an abundant source of gratification. Mr. Buckingham deserves the thanks of the community for his labours ; for they are directed to effect one of the greatest and most beneficial reforms, to advance the prosperity of his own country, and to confer inestimable blessings on countless millions of his fellow creatures. The exertions of Mr. Buckingham have already produced good results in this town : men of all parties and sects have united in this one object ; and a requisition is now in course of signature to our worthy chief magistrate, requesting him to call a public meeting for the consideration of this most important question.'—*Liverpool Chronicle, Jan.* 10.

' We have seen with very great satisfaction the cordial reception which Mr. Buckingham, the public-spirited advocate of free trade to the East, has met with during the last week, from all classes of the inhabitants of this town, and especially from the most active and enlightened of our merchants. His lectures on Wednesday and Friday were attended by even larger audiences than that on Monday, and on Friday evening the body of our Music Hall was filled almost to overflowing. We have never, on any occasion, seen larger or more respectable audiences at lectures in this town ; and the spirit manifested was one of the most cordial pleasure at the enlightened views and generous sentiments of Mr. Buckingham, mingled with astonishment at the infatuated policy of the East India Company. He said that he hoped again to have the honour of appearing before them on this subject—an announcement which the audience received with three loud and distinct rounds of applause. Mr. Buckingham expressed his deep and lively sense of the extreme kindness which he had experienced in Liverpool, and concluded his lecture amidst enthusiastic expressions of approbation from the audience. The Mayor here came forward, and said, that he could not permit the meeting to separate, without attempting to express the obligations under which Mr. Buckingham had laid the inhabitants of Liverpool, by his exertions to give them informations, and to rouse them to activity on the subject of the India and China Trade. He therefore begged leave to move,

' " That the cordial thanks of this meeting be presented to Mr. Buckingham, for his exertions in exposing the injurious effects consequent on a continuance of the monopoly of the East India Company : and that this meeting cannot permit Mr. Buckingham to leave Liverpool without expressing their best wishes for his success in the towns which he is about to visit.' " (*Loud cheers.*)—*Liverpool Times, Jan.* 13.

After being made a sharer of the cordial and splendid hospitalities of the principal families of Liverpool, and passing there a week of great happiness, I returned to London.

MANCHESTER.

EARLY in February, I set out again for Manchester, the vast wealth, productive powers, and extensive population of which, gave it an equal interest in the commercial part of the question with Liverpool itself. There also I met with the same cordial reception—the same public interest—and the same private hospitalities. In short, if there was any difference, I think the people of Manchester took a still deeper interest in the literary attractions of the subject, and quite as deep an interest in the commercial branch of it. The audiences at Liverpool had never exceeded 400, while at Manchester they exceeded 600, and even at a small village, Duckinfield, to which I went on a spare evening, by the invitation of three gentlemen residing there, an audience of about 200 was collected at a day's notice, without any further announcement than a mere written sheet of paper, sent in circulation from the house to receive names; and these remained for nearly four hours, listening with unbroken attention to what so rivetted their minds, that at the close, the universal regret was, that it could not be prolonged or continued. The following are the terms in which the Lectures delivered at Manchester were spoken of in the papers of the day :—

' Mr. Buckingham has brought forward the inhabitants of Liverpool, as one man, to oppose the continuance of the East India Monopoly, and we have every reason to believe that he has produced an equally powerful sensation here. His lectures have been attended by most of the leading and influential men of the town and neighbourhood ; and, large as the room is in which they were delivered, it was every day crowded.—Of the manners, population, commerce, and other particulars, he gave a most interesting account. The second part of his lecture, which comprehended Palestine, seemed to excite the greatest interest. His description of the holy city, of the Mount of Olives, of the lakes of Genesareth, of the fertile fields of Bashan, of the valley of Jehosaphat, of the land of Uz, and many other places mentioned in Scripture, and in which, in every particular, his experience bore out the Scriptural account, even in the very minutest and apparently immaterial circumstances, was listened to with breathless attention. The lecture lasted for three hours ; and we believe there was not one person present but would have been happy to have listened for a much greater length of time to the interesting details.'—*Manchester Times, Feb.* 7.

' We must for the present, content ourselves with an expression of what we are sure is the universal sense of those who have had the gratification of attending Mr. Buckingham's course, the deep obligation under which all the commercial interests of the kingdom will lie to that gentleman, for his zealous and most useful efforts to direct public attention to East India affairs. Throughout his lectures, Mr. Buckingham, by his clearness of arrangement, his felicity of illustration, his varied information, by the remarkable turn for observation of which he has given evidence, by his absolute *plethora* of matter (for he never hesitates or loses the thread of his discourse for an instant;) and, though these are in some, but not all, respects, of less consequence, by his very agreeable manners, his distinct articulation and pleasing delivery, has secured a very high place in the regard of his auditors, who have, we have little doubt, derived much more information from him, on the topics of which he treated, than they could have have derived by the dedication of the same time to the same object in any other manner. From the interesting nature of the facts detailed in these lectures, as well as from the lively and agreeable manner in which they were communicated, the whole course was in the highest degree interesting, and gave unmixed pleasure and satisfaction to the most numerous, the most respectable, and the most attentive audiences that ever attended a course of lectures in this town.

' We had not heard Mr. Buckingham's first lecture to its conclusion before we were satisfied, that, great as was the pleasure he was giving to his audience here, valuable as was the instruction he was communicating to them, highly useful as his ample store of commercial and political knowledge relative to the East would be deemed in whatever town he might present himself, there was yet another audience—one in the metropolis—before whom it was far more important that he should be enabled to appear and to speak. The time is rapidly approaching when the discussion of East India affairs must be commenced in Parliament : the Company are sure to have their advocates in that assembly urged by almost every inducement that can animate the exertions, and shape the conduct of man, to support their cause ; it is of the highest consequence that the public also should have their's. Forty years ago, the paid tools of even some of the Native Sovereigns in India found their way into the House of Commons. Shall the door which was opened to them be closed against an energetic, talented, and high-principled advocate of free trade ? That Mr. Buckingham should hold a seat in the House of Commons during the discussions on the East India Company's Charter, appears to us an object of extreme importance. Who is better fitted by his ready and impressive elocution, but still more by his extensive knowledge of the commercial capabilities of the East, and by the personal experience he has had as to the character and wants of the Natives, to plead effectually on behalf of free-trade and colonization ? But still more, who is at once so well qualified, and so well disposed, to cross-examine the Company's witnesses, to detect and expose false testimony, or to extract, even from his opponents, unequivocal evidence in favour of his case ? These are considerations which we would impress on the commercial public wherever our journal is read. They are, it is true, very inadequately represented in Parliament ; but they can, if they please, easily secure a seat for Mr. Buckingham. If they do not, we think they will not do justice to that gentleman ; but we think also, what in a national point of view is far more important, that they will not do justice to themselves.'— *Manchester Guardian, Feb. 7.*

BIRMINGHAM.

AFTER returning again to London, for the remainder of the month, I left town for Birmingham early in March, and there also my reception was such as would have been felt perhaps to be more favourable than it could possibly seem, after the enthusiasm of Liverpool and Manchester. The Lectures were there delivered in the Theatre of the Philosophical Society, and were attended by the principal inhabitants of the town : but 300 auditors was the greatest number the space would accommodate, and it was entirely filled. The report of the termination of the Course in the Birmingham Gazette, contained the following notice of the manner in which it was received :—

'Mr. Buckingham delivered his supplementary lecture on the state of the Trade to the East, at therooms of the Philosophical Society, on Monday last. Occupying upwards of three hours and a half in the delivery, it becomes impossible to do more than enumerate some of the prominent heads under which his most able and elaborate inquiry was pursued.—At the termination of the lecture, the President of the Philosophical Society, the Rev. John Corrie, rose and addressed the audience to the following effect :

' "I understand that at Liverpool and Manchester, where, as you have heard from him, Mr. Buckingham has been giving lectures, the audience at both places, at the conclusion of the lectures, expressed their approbation by a vote of thanks. Permit me to

ask, if it would agreeable to you that we should follow their example? The very lively
interest these lectures have excited—the numerous and increasing audiences by which
they have been attended—and especially the feelings you have so repeatedly and
warmly manifested this morning, seem to leave no room for doubt or hesitation. I
venture, therefore, without further introduction, to propose that ' the respectful and
cordial thanks of this assembly be presented to Mr. Buckingham, in testimony of our
admiration of the very able and deeply interesting course of lectures which he has
now concluded.' Circumstances compel me to be very brief in this address; but I
trust you will permit me to gratify my own feelings, by stating that Mr. Buckingham is
by far the most accomplished lecturer it has ever been my lot to hear. (*The concurrence
of the audience in this opinion was testified by loud, repeated, and long continued applause.*)
In regard to the lecture of this morning, which has fixed and delighted our attention for
nearly four hours—which has combined all the resources of eloquence—facts—arguments—vivid description of the effects of different systems of civil and commercial
policy—irony—wit—invective—in regard to this most brilliant and powerful discourse,
I will only make one observation, and I am persuaded I shall give no offence to Mr.
Buckingham, nor, I trust, to any of this audience, if I remind them of a circumstance
which, some forty years ago, occurred in the House of Commons. It was at the conclusion of that memorable speech with which Mr. Sheridan introduced one of the charges
against Warren Hastings, and which, by the great authorities of the day, was said to
have equalled or surpassed all that had ever been heard or read of ancient or modern
eloquence—at the conclusion of that speech, which had enraptured, enchanted, overpowered the House, it was thought necessary to adjourn immediately, and come to no
decision on the subject-matter of the speech in their excited and agitated state of feeling.
Permit me to recommend a similar caution on the present occasion, and to express my
hope, that, while you treasure in your memories a part, at least, of that endless variety
of novel and curious information which has been so profusely spread before you—while
you retain, as you cannot fail to retain, a vivid impression of the nature and bearing of
that evidence which Mr. Buckingham has with such extraordinary ability stated and
expressed—you would pause before you form any decided conclusion on that most important, I repeat it, *most important* topic, which was the great object of the lecture :
whatever opinions you may ultimately entertain—whatever proceedings you may ultimately adopt, at least have the satisfaction of feeling confident they have not been the
result of momentary excitement, but of cool, deliberate, and mature reflection."

' The proposal was seconded by Joseph Walker, Esq. High Bailiff, or Chief Magistrate, of Birmingham, and the vote was passed amidst the most animated applause of
the company.'—*Birmingham Gazette, March 6.*

BRISTOL.

From hence I proceeded direct to Bristol, where some difficulties were at
first apprehended, in uniting the West Indians with those who wished a Free
Trade to the East. By the aid of some kind friends, and the force of the cause
itself, these apprehensions however gradually wore away; and although
Bristol was at this period in a state of great excitement from the divided
opinions of its society on the Catholic Relief Bill, then in its progress through
Parliament, a small audience was collected, at first not exceeding 60
persons, which progressively increased, however, to nearly 600 : exceeding
Liverpool, almost equalling Manchester, and leading to a union of all parties
and sects in one common object, in a way that had hardly ever been experienced for many years. The following from the Bristol papers will sufficiently
evince the feeling that prevailed.

' Mr. Buckingham gave his supplementary lecture this morning to one of the most
respectable audiences we ever saw assembled in the room. And, perhaps, never was
an audience so entertained, or so delighted, not only by the vast information they received, but by the pleasing way in which it was conveyed.

' It would be vain in the confined limits of a weekly journal, to attempt to give any
analysis of a lecture occupying upwards of four hours in its delivery ; suffice it to say,
the lecture exposed, in a very masterly manner, the monstrous abuses of the overgrown
monopoly of Leadenhall Street, and pointed out the very great advantages which would

accrue to this country by the extension of her commercial intercourse with India, and by the opening of the trade to China. The lecturer having impressed on the minds of his hearers in a most emphatic manner, the absolute necessity of union and co-operation in the great cause he advocated, sat down amidst much applause.

' At the conclusion of Mr. Buckingham's last lecture, the applause was intense, and the cheering continued for several minutes. When it had subsided, the Mayor, John Cave, Esq., rose, and addressed Mr. Buckingham to the following effect:

' " Sir, as the Chief Magistrate of the City of Bristol, I cannot suffer this numerous and respectable assembly to depart, without expressing, on my own behalf, as well as on theirs, our deep sense of the important service which you have rendered to us, and to our common country, by the able manner in which you have developed the evils of a system which you call upon us to assist in amending. I am sure, Sir, that I speak the unanimous sense of this assembly, when I say that the City of Bristol will give you their most cordial support, and will gladly unite with Liverpool, Manchester, Birmingham, and other great towns of the kingdom, in immediate steps to obtain a removal of the existing restrictions on our Commerce with the East. (*Cheers.*) For the entertainment and instruction conveyed to us in your animated and accurate descriptions of the several countries through which you have so delightfully led us, you are entitled to our warmest thanks, (*cheers,*) and for the still greater object of your present Lecture, which is to show the existing evils of our rule in the East, and point out the means of benefitting both this country and its empire in that quarter of the world, you are entitled not merely to our thanks but our cordial co-operation ; and that co-operation we will zealously and cheerfully accord. (*Cheers.*) I am persuaded, Sir, that such a cause, in the hands of such an advocate, must ultimately triumph ; and I am confident that the City of Bristol will be always ready to hail your re-appearance within its walls with pleasure.

' " In the name, Sir, of the citizens of Bristol, I tender you their cordial thanks and best wishes for your continued success in your public-spirited and patriotic career." '— *Bristol Journal, March* 27.

LEEDS.

From Bristol I went direct to Leeds, and there also my reception was most flattering. The principal manufacturers of this town having frequently supplied the Americans with goods for China, which could not be conveyed there in English vessels, except by the India Company, the subject had before engaged their attention, and a very strong feeling was manifested by all classes, as soon as my arrival, and the intended delivery of the Lectures were announced. What the issue was, may be gathered from the following testimonies given by the papers of the town itself.

' On Monday last Mr. Buckingham commenced his course of lectures on the countries of the East, in the Music Hall, in this town. All the lectures descriptive of those countries have now been delivered, and whether we judge of them from our own feelings, from the testimony of those with whom we have conversed, from the increasing numbers who have every day attended them, or from the strong and unequivocal expressions of pleasure and admiration with which they have been received, we have no hesitation in saying that they have been the most interesting and eloquent course of lectures that have ever been delivered in this town, or that we have ever had the pleasure of hearing, either here or in any other place. They have possessed every charm which eloquence and wit can communicate to the narration of the most interesting events, and the description of the most interesting scenes ; and have not been more admirable for those qualities, than for the benevolence of heart and liberality of sentiment which they have every where displayed.'—*Leeds Mercury, April* 4.

' At the close of the last lecture, Benjamin Gott, Esq., one of the principal merchants of Leeds, rose and addressed the assembly as follows :

' " Having been a witness of the intense interest manifested towards Mr. Buckingham by the largest and most respectable audiences that have ever been assembled at any delivery of lectures in this town ; and seeing how these audiences have gone on increasing daily, until this Music Hall is filled, as I now behold it, to overflowing, I am sure I shall but speak the sentiments of every one present when I propose that the cordial thanks of this assembly be presented to Mr. Buckingham, for the high gratification he has afforded to us all, by his eloquent, animated, and accurate descriptions of the most interesting features of the Eastern World : and that in addition to our thanks we tender him our best wishes for his health, and continued success in the valuable services he is rendering to his country and to mankind."

' This motion was seconded by William Aldham, Esq., merchant of Leeds, and was carried by acclamation, amidst the most enthusiastic applause.'—*Leeds Patriot, April* 9.

LONDON.

THE course at Leeds was closed on the Saturday, April the 4th at about eight o'clock, the concluding Lecture having lasted four hours : when, notwithstanding the continued labours of the week, the lectures being delivered every day consecutively, I stepped from the Lecture Room into the Mail, drove home, without stopping on the road, and after a journey of nearly 200 miles, was at the City of London Tavern, on Monday the 6th, to commence a course there at noon, for the Merchants of London. It required some firmness, however, to bear the change ; for instead of the crowded Halls of Liverpool, Manchester, Birmingham, Bristol, Leeds, and the enthusiastic plaudits of their brilliant and elegant assemblies, here was a frigid, as well as a small audience of nineteen individuals, and though upwards of 100*l.* had been expended in advertising in all the London papers, in printing large and small bills, sending invitations by messengers, and every other device that could be thought of, the audience never exceeded fifty, during all the week that it continued ! Nevertheless, the few who did attend, were at the end as loud and enthusiastic in their approbation as in the largest assemblies; and the following expression was given of the general feeling, by J. T. Rutt, Esq. of Clapton, who addressed the assembly as follows :

' GENTLEMEN,—Before Mr. Buckingham leaves the situation which he has occupied so much to the instruction and highly rational entertainment of those who have listened to him, you will, I hope, allow me to propose to this respectable meeting, that we unite in an expression of our thanks and satisfaction. I will not venture to detain you another moment, but beg leave to submit to your acceptance the following Resolution : " That this meeting cannot separate without respectfully presenting to Mr. Buckingham, their grateful acknowledgements for the valuable information, so agreeably communicated in his lectures on the important and interesting objects of inquiry connected with the Eastern World, and for the patriotic zeal with which he has explained and recommended a system of wise and equitable national policy, under the extending operation of which, an intercourse with that too long-neglected portion of the globe would eminently conduce to the advancement of the moral, political, and commercial interests of the British Empire."

' The Resolution was seconded by J. Wilks, Esq., of Finsbury-square, in the following terms : " The proposition made by my venerable and intelligent friend is to me an ' agreeable surprise.' It is a surprise, because completely unexpected ; and agreeable, because the respectful tribute it affords has been so amply deserved. For many years a proprietor of East India Stock, I have no hostility to the welfare of that Company, and, unconnected with commercial affairs, I am quite uninfluenced by the desire of gain ; cheerfully, therefore, do I second a proposition which all who have attended this course of lectures will gladly support. I speak because it would be ungrateful to be silent ; and because it is pleasant partly to repay the obligations conferred. Without adopting all the opinions Mr. Buckingham has avowed, and deprecating any alteration whereby the political power and patronage of India should become more absolutely vested in the Crown,—who has not been gratified to accompany Mr. Buckingham through the Eastern regions to which he has been our guide ? Who has not been charmed by those accurate and vivid descriptions which no books can supply ? Who, after treading with him in imagination the margin of the Ganges, the Jordan, and the Nile, will not eagerly tender to him their acknowledgments of praise ? But he has yet

more won my esteem by the intrepidity with which he has entered on his new career—
by the liberal principles he illustrates as well as propounds—by his exposures of the
evils of that commercial monopoly which India and Britain alike deplore—and by the
solicitude he displays, that commerce, wealth, knowledge, freedom, religion, and happiness, should far more widely prevail.   Therefore, mainly, I repeat, do I second this
proposition; and as a patriot, a philanthropist, and a Christian, must wish him success."'

Though somewhat discouraged by the slight attendance at the City of London
Tavern, yet considering the influence of the East India Company in this,
their strong hold; and considering also how much the merchants of London
generally are impressed with an idea that the abolition of the monopoly, though
beneficial to the country at large, would take away a large portion of what is
now the exclusive privilege of their single port, I was not so much surprised.
What did, however, I confess, somewhat astonish me, notwithstanding my
experience of the London press, was the fact, that scarcely any assistance was
rendered to the cause by that powerful instrument here, but that on the contrary, not a line, by way even of announcing the time and place of delivery,
could be inserted in the principal papers of the day *without payment;* while no
report or mention of the lectures was in any case gratuitously undertaken, as
is usual in similar cases.   I need not attempt to divine the *cause* of this: it is
sufficient for me to record the fact, and to express the confident assurance, that
when the tide of popular opinion is strongly set in *favour* of the views I advocate, the London Press will then be as loud in their advocacy of them, as
they were now silent; their almost uniform practice being, not to *direct* public
opinion into right channels, which, with their vast power it would be so easy,
by some sacrifice of popularity and profit, to do; but to find out in what
directions that public opinion runs, and then to *follow* it as the easiest and
most popular career.   I am aware of the consequences of avowing this; but I
conscientiously believe it to be true; and therefore I have no scruple in declaring it, and bearing the evil that may follow.

Supposing it possible, however, that the apathy or hostility evinced in the
City might not extend to other parts of the Metropolis, I remained in town
for the purpose of repeating the effort again; and between April and June, I
delivered no less than seven distinct courses, of seven Lectures each, in seven
different places;—the first was in the City of London Tavern, Bishopsgate
Street; the second in Freemason's Hall, Great Queen Street; the third at
Almack's Ball Room, St. James's Square; the fourth at the City Concert
Rooms, Finsbury Circus; the fifth at the Crown and Anchor in the Strand;
the sixth at the King's Concert Room of the Italian Opera House; and the
seventh at the British Coffee House, Charing Cross.   Every hour of the day
and evening was tried in succession, from one o'clock till eight: and every
day in the week had its chance; but, though no expence was spared to excite
public attention, scarcely any one audience at either of the places named
exceeded 100 persons, and very frequently they were under 25; on one
occasion only 15, and on another only 7 attended!   The result was, that
upon the whole of the London Courses, a sum of about 350*l.* was *lost*, in actual
expences incurred and paid beyond the receipts; without accounting the time,
labour, anxiety, and disappointment, which twice that amount of *gain* would
very inadequately repay.*

* Among the most constant attendants on these Lectures delivered in London, was Sir Sydney Smith (who has seen, perhaps, more of the Eastern World than any other officer in the
British Navy), with the ladies of his family.   At the close of them, he sought an introduction
to me, when, after expressing the high satisfaction he had received from their delivery, he presented me a rare and curious volume, written in Spanish, on the legal rights of the Christians
to their sanctuaries in the Holy Land, with the following inscription on the title-page, written
in his own hand:
"To Mr. Buckingham, in acknowledgement of his benevolent views, and perspicuity and
energy in their developement, from Admiral Sir Sydney Smith, after his Lecture on Palestine,
April 16th, 1829."

Another circumstance which added greatly to my mortification was this:—
that in consequence of the exclusive attention which I had given to this undertaking since January last, and the consequent abandonment of my publications to the management of other hands, they had so declined in sale, and all
my business concerns had become so deranged, that I was placed in this unfortunate dilemma ; being compelled to choose whether I would relinquish the
plan I had marked out for rousing the Country on the state of our Eastern possessions by those personal exertions, and by returning to my publications restore
them again to the state in which they were when I first left them to the management of other hands; or whether I would abandon them altogether as matters
of property, and by one effort make the requisite sacrifice, and continue steadily
to prosecute to the end what I had at so much hazard begun. It was a hard
struggle between the private claims of my family, and the duty which I conceived I had taken on myself to discharge to the public ; but the latter conquered. I gave up all hope of the benefits which these publications had already
realized, and which might, by my return to their management, and relinquishment of my tour, have been permanently secured : and winding up my affairs, by
a transfer of some portion of the property, and a sale of the remainder, I retired
from it with a loss of more than 2,500*l.*, bestowed on two of the publications alone,
the SPHYNX and ATHENÆUM—and a loss of at least 1,500*l.* more, on the leases,
stock and materials, engaged in their establishment. I mention these particulars,
not for the purpose of attaching more importance to them than they really deserve, but chiefly as an answer to the ever-ready accusation, and often-repeated
calumny, that self interest and individual benefit are the sole motives by which
I have been actuated in the course I have undertaken ; while to those who say
that, in addition to these motives, my opposition to the India Company has been
created solely by my having received injury at their hands, I need only reply,
that I opposed the system of Despotism and Monopoly in India, long before I
had ever received such injury ; that I was, in short, removed from that country,
because of my opposition to the system by which it is ruled ; which is a very
different thing from opposing that system, because of my removal. *My opinions*
respecting the East and its rulers, have never changed, and if the Government
of that Country, because of my conscientious opposition to their system there,
thought proper to remove me from *that* scene of action, and to plant me here in
England, which is *their* act and not mine, I should be wanting in every right
feeling as an Englishman, if I did not avail myself of that change, to speak
freely and openly to my countrymen here, that which I was scarcely permitted
to breathe in stifled whispers there. My motives are known only to God and
to myself, and I am satisfied with their purity. The facts and arguments I
may advance, are fair and legitimate objects of critical examination, and to
that I am always willing to submit; but if those who advocate Despotism and
Monopoly claim for themselves unexceptionable motives and conscious integrity, I can conceive no good reason why those who advocate Freedom and
fair and open Trade should not be equally entitled to credit for the sincerity
of their motives and the integrity of their intentions also.

In consequence of the Lectures delivered in the several Provincial Towns
before named, and almost immediately succeeding them, Public Meetings were
held in each, and Resolutions entered into for following up what had been
already so auspiciously begun, by more active measures to promote the opening
of India and China to free intercourse and trade. One of these measures was
the appointment of Deputies from the several Towns alluded to, to repair to
London, and there, in conjunction with Mr. Woolryche Whitmore, the Member
for Bridgenorth, who had given notice of his intention to move for a Committee
of Enquiry into the state of the Trade between Great Britain, India, and China,
and with whom I had been in frequent correspondence and conference on this

subject, and with Mr. John Crawford, formerly in the service of the East India Company, and since constituted or deputed by the Merchants of Calcutta, as their Agent in England, to confer with Ministers on the steps necessary to be taken, for effecting their object. When the Deputies arrived in town, consisting of about twenty-five of the most eminent merchants and official authorities of Liverpool, Manchester, Birmingham, Leeds, Bristol, and Glasgow, I had a meeting with them at their Hotel in St. James's, and after some deliberation as to the propriety of associating me in their proceedings, it was thought prudent that the Deputation to wait upon the Ministers, should consist only of the Gentlemen appointed by their respective Towns ; Mr. Whitmore, as the Member of Parliament who had given notice of a motion on the question ; and Mr. Crawfurd, who came as the Agent of the Merchants of Bengal. This arrangement, excluding me from all participation in the *public* proceedings of the Deputation, was alleged to be made in deference to the scruples of *some* of the Members of it, who were not unwilling to have the full benefit of all the aid that I could render to their cause, in a separate or individual capacity; who were willing to admit that the public meetings which had led to their appointment and journey to town, owed their very existence, this year at least, (with the one exception only, that of Glasgow, and even this followed closely in the train of Liverpool and Manchester), to the Lectures I had delivered in each, and to the excitement of the public mind, and through its best organ, the public press, by the discussion of the facts and arguments advanced in them ; but who were yet unwilling to permit such an instrument to share with them any part of the *public* credit, or *public* importance attached to their mission, because he did not happen to be deputed by any particular persons, or particular town ! The reasoning of this, to say the least of it, was *singular ;* but the excuse for any apparent defect in the logic of the determination is, that it was a matter of *feeling* and not of *judgement.* This feeling was an unwillingness to admit that a large town could be moved by an individual, and that individual a stranger ; a sort of jealousy, lest the municipal reputation for public spirit and alacrity should be tarnished by the fact that they were quickened in their exertions, and accelerated in their movements, by one who came from without, and who formed no part of their municipal body. Such a notion is purely English, and has no parallel in any other country with which I am acquainted. An Arab, or a Turk, for instance, barbarians as we deem them, will not only adopt any good measure that a stranger may recommend, but be ready to give such stranger the full credit and full honour due to him for his suggestion. In England, however, though civilization is much farther advanced than in Arabia or Turkey, the notion of being indebted to a foreigner, or of being led by a stranger, is repulsive; and accordingly the number of followers in any particular path is not dependant on the excellence of the object to which it leads, or the fitness of the means by which it may be attained, so much as on the name, rank, station, and even fashion, of the *person* who points it out. It is thus that in England *principles* are of much less weight with the multitude than *names ;* and I believe it is the only country on the globe where men professedly of wealth, education, and high character, will condescend to avail themselves of the information, skill, labour, and even self-devotion of others, as long as these shall be calculated to promote the object they have in view: and yet, when the question of reward and reputation comes to be considered, will disdain all participation with the very instrument that has chiefly effected the accomplishment of their wishes, and cast him off as of no *further* use, when their end is attained. This has been the case with almost all the individual advocates of great public measures in England, and it might, perhaps, be added, in the Colonies and Dependancies of England also, where the offspring has imbibed at least *that* defect of the mother country, to its full extent ; and therefore, not expecting to find myself an exception to the general rule, I was not to be discouraged from persevering in the course I had laid down, from higher motives, I hope, than the mere love of popular applause, by the truly *national* spirit evinced in this determination. I accordingly continued my private interviews with the Deputies, and laboured as zealously within their circle and without it, as if I had been their leader, or public associate.

This disclaimer of participation was first indirectly attempted in the speech of Mr. Samuel Hope, the Banker, at Liverpool, in the following paragraph :—

' He begged leave to correct a very general error with respect to that meeting. An opinion prevailed that the efforts they were now making were immediately owing to the exertions of Mr. Buckingham, during the course of lectures which he recently delivered in this town. The gentlemen who attended those lectures must feel themselves under deep obligations to Mr. Buckingham, for the talent and amenity of temper with which they were delivered. (*Loud applause.*) He certainly succeeded in diffusing a mass of most valuable information, in a manner which did the highest credit to himself; (*applause;*) but, though it was not generally known, there existed, long antecedent to that period, a conviction that some measures should be adopted with a view to the great object they were now met to consider. They owed a large debt of gratitude to his Worship, the Mayor, for the manner in which he came forward at the conclusion of those lectures, (*great applause,*) and, without sheltering himself under the restrictive dignity of his office, too generally supposed to be inseparable from those walls, (*great applause,*) in his character of an English merchant, returned thanks to Mr. Buckingham for the information thus afforded to him and his fellow-townsmen. (*Redoubled applause.*) '—*Liverpool Mercury, Jan.* 30.

To this, the following reply, from the pen of another Liverpool merchant, Mr. William Rathbone, was given in the papers of the day :—

' *To Samuel Hope, Esq.*

' Sir,— I am very unwilling to fritter away strength in discussing with whom measures originate, when all our strength will be required to carry the measures themselves. Yet I cannot permit an assertion of yours, in your speech on the India question, to be left upon record without attempting its refutation.   In that speech you contend that Mr. Buckingham's Lectures were not the *immediate* cause of the public meeting here. I venture, Sir, to differ with you in opinion, and to think that we owe the suggestion of having a public meeting at this time entirely to Mr. Buckingham. Had Mr. Buckingham not found the pile, he might have applied the torch in vain, there would have been no fire. Nor is it any disparagement of the zeal of the Liverpool merchants, that the additional facts he communicated to the crowded audiences he drew to his instructive lectures, and of which even *they* were ignorant, should have called their attention more immediately to the subject. The Liverpool merchants have already given proof of their continued attention to the subject from the year 1792 to the present time, and will, I trust, give still further proof how much they are in earnest to promote their own interest and that of the country. In the mean time, I feel no hesitation (and I believe it to be a very general impression) in admitting my obligations to Mr. Buckingham for the increased interest he has given to the subject, for the important facts he has communicated verbally and through "The Oriental Herald," and for the assistance he has afforded in leading the merchants to think of a public meeting at this time, thereby producing an effect which will, I hope, end in serving every man, however humble his station, in the kingdom, and will call down blessings on our heads from millions of our brethren in the East.   I remain, Sir, your's respectfully,   W. R.'

The interview which the Deputies from the country had with the First Lord of the Treasury and the President of the Board of Trade, led to the promise that every attention should be paid to their representations, and a conventional pledge, that if they would consent to waive all pressure of the subject on the attention of Parliament, for the present session, a Committee should emanate from their (the ministerial) side of the house, early in the next : and in the interval, such documents as were calculated to elucidate the subject in the way of evidence, should be laid on the tables of both houses, for the information of their members.

On this understanding, the motion of Mr. Whitmore, for a Committee of Enquiry, was brought forward on the 14th of May, and after a Debate of some length, (which was reported in full, with copious notes on the statements of the several speakers, in the ORIENTAL HERALD of June), * the pledge given by the President of the Board of Trade, to the Deputies, in their interview, was publicly repeated in parliament, on which Mr. Whitmore withdrew his motion, and thus, for the session at least, all public proceedings on the question, in either House, were suspended.

After the rising of parliament, when the Deputies repaired to their several homes, and when London began to be, in the fashionable phrase, ' empty,' I prepared for a second Tour through the country, in prosecution of the plan marked out, and partly executed in the beginning of the year; being now determined to take the circle of Scotland and the North of England first, and then return southward in the winter. This was not to be accomplished, however, without some sacrifices, and considerable difficulty. The constituted Agent of the Merchants of Bengal, though retired from the East India Company's Service with a provision and a fortune—both justly and honourably earned by services of corresponding value—had not merely his expences paid, but a salary of 1500*l.* a year allowed him for his labours. The Deputies from the several towns, though all wealthy merchants, had their charges also paid from a fund raised by subscription in the respective towns from which they came ; and to them, therefore, the movements and measures in which they were engaged, were comparatively easy. For myself, however, I was very differently situated. Being the ' representative' only of the opinions entertained and advocated by myself for the last ten years of my life ; and having, instead of being rewarded with wealth, been visited with all the sufferings and losses already adverted to, as a punishment for the crime of persisting in maintaining them ; having, also, since my return to England, been subjected to various other embarrassments arising out of my present pursuits ; looked coldly on by the London Press, and by the Country Deputies, from a similar feeling of jealousy and exclusiveness, which appears to have been the acting cause in both, my abandonment of the publications before described, and the losses incurred by the seven courses of Lectures in town, occasioned my difficulties so to increase, that I was twice arrested, during their progress, and once at the door of the Lecture Room itself, at the instigation, as I have reason to believe, of parties wishing to increase rather than lessen my difficulties, from hostility to my public views. This compelled me to receive back from the Liverpool Committee the sum I had originally given them as the foundation of the public fund for carrying on the measures contemplated, and which, even from the first, there had been a great reluctance on the part of those who wished to keep aloof from " connection with any individual" to receive. This repayment, did not, however, take place, until *after* the determination of the Committee to exclude me from all participation in their *public* proceedings : and on that ground alone did I feel justified in receiving back a contribution, which, having been in the first instance voluntarily tendered, and apparently as cordially received, could not with satisfaction to either party, remain on its originally intended footing, after the one had shewn such reluctance to be *publicly* associated with the other, in pursuing the object privately desired by both. This, however, was quite insufficient of

---

* This method of attaching notes to the speeches made in debates at the India House, in Parliament, and at public meetings on Indian Affairs, has been uniformly observed in the Oriental Herald, correcting errors and putting down fallacies as they occur, and constitutes one of the most valuable features of that Work. If this could be done with the speeches in Parliament as they appear in the papers of the day, it would be of the highest value to the public cause.

itself to relieve me from the difficulties by which I was on all sides pressed, and among which may be numbered the defalcation and disappearance of a confidential agent or publisher, (during an illness—quinzied sore throat—contracted by the cold drafts of the stage at the King's Theatre, while delivering the Lectures there, which kept me speechless for many days, and from which my recovery was for some time despaired of), with a deficiency of nearly 1000*l.* in acceptances and monies due.   Subsequent to, and in consequence of this defalcation, about half the sum, 500*l.* was obtained from this person's securities, in their acceptances to that amount—but spread over five years of time! so that for all available purposes the whole amount was lost; and a part of the deficiencies being for money due by the agent to the Stamp Office for duties on the publications issued by him, and which had been rendered to me in account as actually paid ; the Stamp Solicitor having his option to seize upon myself or the publisher, issued his writ of execution, and would only be satisfied with the payment of the amount, (about 200*l.*) in cash.   In this dilemma, and with other accounts of charges for printing, advertising, and rooms, connected with the London Lectures, still due, and pressing for immediate payment; having learnt from the Agent of the Merchants of Bengal, that in addition to his salary of 1500*l.* a year, he had had a sum of 1200*l.* placed at his disposal for general purposes in aid of the cause, I applied to him for a temporary loan, or assistance from that fund, towards the expences actually incurred in the endeavours to excite public attention, and to enlist public feeling in favour of the Free Trade to India and China, in London ; but it was declined.   I made a similar application to various parties in the country who had taken a lead in this matter, and who, from their wealth and station might have rendered all the aid required, without feeling the slightest inconvenience. To almost all these applications, I received for answer, an abundance of commendation, great encouragement to proceed—as far as words could give encouragement—and regret that no public fund was yet provided, from which the assistance required could be furnished : but the only instances in which any thing more than complimentary expressions, and good wishes were offered towards the execution of my object, were in the case of two gentlemen of Liverpool, two of Leeds, and one of Birmingham, in all, 5 individuals, (out of at least 500 that were addressed on the subject), whose joint contributions amounted to 250*l.*.   With this, and the appropriation of the additional means that my own resources afforded me, I was enabled to make such provisional arrangements as to admit of my leaving London, free from the danger of further arrest, to prosecute my Tour in the country, for which purpose, however, I was enabled to reserve only 10*l.* with which I left home for Scotland, trusting to the issue of my visit there, for means to proceed further in the cause.   I mention these details for two reasons: First, to shew that I have never been employed by any Association, or Public Body in England, to execute any purpose of theirs ; nor received the least assistance from the Agent of the Merchants of Bengal, or any other parties deputed from India, to forward any designs of theirs ; as has been continually asserted by the opponents of Free Trade ; and that even the slight assistance rendered by private individuals who were favourable to the object, was confined to five in number only, and bore but a very small proportion in amount to that which I had actually lost and expended from my own funds alone, during the six months that had elapsed since I entered on the task. And secondly, to shew that, so far from private gain or personal advantage being the only motive which impelled me to the undertaking, as asserted by others, there was no evil of a pecuniary nature that I was not willing to encounter rather than abandon my pursuit, and no personal inconvenience that could induce me to turn aside from the course I had laid down, in which I was determined, as long as life, strength, and means were spared to me, to persevere.

EDINBURGH.

I ARRIVED in Edinburgh on the 10th of July, and announced the delivery of my first Lecture at the Hopetoun Rooms in Queen-street. It was attended by 170 persons, of the highest respectability, who expressed their approbation in so marked a manner, as to give a sure earnest of increasing interest in the subject. On the succeeding evenings, the audience so increased in numbers, that the Rooms were insufficient to contain them; and we accordingly removed, first to the Assembly Room in George's Street, and afterwards to the Great Room at the Waterloo Hotel, where, at the concluding Lecture, the audience was nearly 500 in number, and the demonstrations of feeling more marked, than had been witnessed in the capital of Scotland for a considerable period of time. This was the more remarkable, as it happened at a period of the year when the Colleges and Courts were vacant; when the principal families had gone to their seats, or the watering places; and when, in the usual phrase, the town was at the dullest point of the year. The few following extracts from the papers of the day will, however, sufficiently indicate the feeling that prevailed :—

' Few men in our day have made a greater figure in the world than Mr. Buckingham. In one way or other his name has been almost continually before the public. The arbitrary and tyrannical act of oppression which drove him from India, and ruined his rising fortunes in that country, first engaged the attention, and we may truly add, enlisted in his behalf the sympathies of the people of England. Persecution of every kind invariably defeats its own object. When the strong, merely because they are strong, in the very wantonness of conscious power, employ their strength against the weak, and convert the authority with which they have been clothed for the benefit of a great community into an instrument of undisguised oppression against an individual, the generous feelings of our nature are immediately awakened in behalf of the victim of injustice, and the public at once take him under their protection. Hence the very means which were taken to crush Mr. Buckingham, and to ruin for ever his prospects in life, at once marked him out as a person of consideration, and excited universal indignation against the petty tyrants who had attempted his destruction. His first introduction to our notice, therefore, was by means of a passport, signed and counter-signed, if we may so express ourselves, by his Indian persecutors. And since that time we have been rendered familiar with his name in a great variety of aspects; as an enterprising and intelligent traveller, who had indefatigably explored and ably described some of the most interesting countries on the face of the earth; as a sturdy claimant for justice and reparation, thundering at the gates of the India House, and disturbing the slumbers of the merchant princes of Leadenhall-Street; as the triumphant defender of his literary reputation against the ungenerous and unmanly attack which had been made upon it by Mr. Bankes; as the parent of a whole generation of periodicals, political and literary; and, lastly, as the preacher of a general crusade against the East India Company's monopoly. We confess, therefore, that we felt no ordinary degree of curiosity to see and hear a person who had made so much noise in the world, and connected his name with so many great interests, remarkable occurences, and distinguished individuals; and that with expectations considerably excited, we repaired on Monday night to the Hopetoun Rooms, where it was announced that Mr. Buckingham would deliver the first of a short course of Lectures on the Eastern World. Nor were these expectations in any degree disappointed.

' Of the subject of the Lecture we shall speak presently. With regard to the Lecturer himself we must say that he appears to us admirably qualified for the task he has undertaken. Full of the subject, on which he evidently possesses the most abundant information, he spoke from the printed heads of his lecture, which are exceedingly brief, with the greatest ease and fluency, and in a style of elocution equally simple, graceful, and unpretending, displayed a talent for communicating knowledge in a clear, vivid, interesting, and popular manner, far surpassing any thing of the kind we have lately witnessed. The best proof of this we can mention is the fact, that for nearly three hours he kept the attention of a numerous and most respectable audience so rivetted by his graphic descriptions and illustrative anecdotes, told frequently with an archness and effect peculiarly *frappant* and felicitous, that, forgetting to take any note of time, his auditors, at the conclusion, seemed actuated only by a feeling of regret that the lecture had so soon been brought to a close. As a *conteur*, indeed, Mr. Buckingham might almost rival some of his friends in the Desert, of whom he cherishes so many pleasing recollections ; nor is it possible to conceive any thing more engaging than the style in which he brings before his audience the scenes, the manners, the characters of the gorgeous East ; not in frigid description, but in full presentment, as it were, touching our own imaginations by the happy power he possesses, and enabling us almost to *see* what, in fact, he only after all *describes*. But never for one moment did he lose sight of his main object, namely, to demonstrate the expediency or rather the necessity of breaking up the Company's monopoly, and opening a free trade with the East. To this almost all his numerous illustrations were skilfully made to converge ; and many of the facts and circumstances which he adduced in support of the measure he recommends, were unquestionably calculated to make a deep impression upon the minds of his hearers. Beyond all question, Mr. Buckingham is the most formidable enemy with whom the sovereign monopolists of Leadenhall-Street have yet had to contend. Commercial or political reasonings and speculations, when read in the closet, make but a faint impression ; and many will not even read them at all. But when truths of the very highest importance to the interests of the nation, are clothed in so fascinating a garb, and surrounded with so many accessary attractions, their force is immediate and irresistible. They sink deep into the mind, and become at once, as it were, part and parcel of itself ; while, in this way, the ignorant are informed, at the same time that the instructed and intelligent have their opinions confirmed, and the desire to reduce them into practice stimulated and awakened. Hence, we anticipate the very greatest benefits to arise from the progress that Mr. Buckingham is now making through the kingdom, teaching and preaching anti-monopolist doctrines, in a style and manner so captivating and attractive. By this, in conjunction with other means that have been employed, the mind of the country will be thoroughly awakened ; and, in due time, public opinion will acquire a consistency and force sufficient to surmount every obstacle, and to overcome all opposition, founded on old errors, and anti-national interests.'—*Caledonian Mercury, July* 16.

'On Monday night, this celebrated traveller commenced his Lectures in the Hopetoun Rooms, on the manners, antiquities, and policy of the Eastern countries. The company was numerous and genteel ; and for the two hours during which his discourse continued, he was listened to, as he deserved to be, with the most profound attention. He has since delivered two other lectures which have not been less favourably received. Mr. Buckingham, we believe, is the only traveller who ever resorted to this method of communicating the result of his observations verbally to the public, in place of publishing them in a printed volume; and every one must at once see how greatly these *viva voce* communications must excel in vivacity and interest any written composition, whatever be its merits, especially when the person who makes this experiment is so eminently qualified to give it effect as Mr. Buckingham appears to be. As a lecturer his merits are very great. His elocution is easy ; his manner quite natural and agreeable ; and he seems to carry on his discourse without the aid of any written notes. He has indeed all the ease, readiness, and alacrity of a finished speaker, and so simple and familiar is his style, that in place of a public audience we might suppose him to be addressing an account of his adventures to a circle of his private friends. He has none of that ease, however, which degenerates into carelessness ; and he never approaches to any thing like tameness. On the contrary, though he is obliged, in consequence of his limited stay in this city, to protract his lecture for two, and sometimes nearly three hours, he never flags for a moment, but seems to gather new vigour, as he enters more deeply into his subject ; and goes on, to the last, fluent, animated, and impressive. Yet he does not evince any anxiety to shine ; his sole object seems to be, to convey instruction to his audience ; to tell them what they did not know before, and to tell it in the easiest and briefest manner. His style is accordingly simple. He does not go out of his way for flowery descriptions or embellishments of any sort, but seems to rely entirely for his success on the sterling value of the information he communicates, and which is only a portion of that larger store which he has collected in the course of his travels. His acquaintance with those eastern countries which form the subject of his discourses, seems to be most perfect; we were particularly struck with the mastery which he displayed over every part of his subject; with the fulness, the freshness, the vivacity of his sketches; the force of his illustrations; the prodigality of his details; and the skill with which he disposed and arranged to the best advantage, his extensive information. There are many travellers ingenious and well informed, who have perfectly accurate and just notions of all that they have either seen or heard, but who yet fail to give any distinct or vivid impressions of interesting objects; who set the mind afloat, as it were, among vague and general ideas, and there leave it. Mr. Buckingham is quite the reverse of this. Whatever be the matter on which he is discoursing, whether it be any point of local usage or manners, any interesting relic of antiquity, or any question of antiquarian research, he is sure to make it clear before he has done with it, and to bring it home to the standard of our ordinary ideas, by some ready and familiar illustration. He does not seem to be much given to ingenious or doubtful speculations; yet he misses no opportunity of illustrating the manners and policy of the Eastern countries; and, without being a theorist, he is frequently very successful in tracing particular facts to the general state of manners, in striking out an unexpected light, where the mere antiquarian would grope in darkness, and in thus bringing out the *rationale* of many ancient customs, by reasonings that display at once his research and his judgment.'—*Edinburgh Evening Courant, July* 16.

'Having been thus particular in regard to the adventures of Mr. Buckingham, we shall now speak of his appearance in our city. In his lectures on Arabia and Palestine, the two at which we were present, he stated very little that is not familiar to every intelligent reader; but at the same time, what he did state was so happily expressed and so agreeably illustrated by personal anecdotes, that we believe every body in the room was heartily sorry when he brought them to a close. We were in particular greatly struck with his picture of Damascus, than which nothing oral could be more graphic and enchanting; *and it recurred to us repeatedly, that were such a man to devote himself entirely to delineating the face of the earth by word of mouth, he would do more to advance geographical knowledge than all the professors in Britain.* It is Mr. Buckingham's object to draw attention to the Eastern world, and of course he paints the orient as strewn with paradises; but still, with the full persuasion that his pictures are in danger of being overcharged, we are not prepared to say that we detected any palpable exaggerations—or at least any that a lecturer might not legitimately employ. The knowledge that he had seen the towers and temples—traversed the deserts—bathed in the waters—slept in the groves—eat of the fruits—and conversed with the people he described, added greatly to the effect of his details. Though he never lets slip a favourable opportunity of giving his old oppressors a kick, he does not employ any vituperative language against them, or in anywise intrude his own grievances into the subject. On the whole, we regard him as a very formidable enemy to the Company. He has undertaken to render it unpopular; and with the undeniable facts that he can adduce, and the tide of public opinion setting strongly in his favour—for there is not one man in a hundred but is hostile to the further extension of the charter—he will do much to accomplish it.'—*Edinburgh Observer, July* 17.

'Mr. Buckingham's lectures which commenced on Monday last, and have continued every evening during the week, appear to be exciting much interest, and giving great satisfaction, in this city. We are, for our own part, heartily disposed to approve of the favourable impression which he has made. We have heard him with no common degree of pleasure; and consider ourselves called upon to declare, that we were never before in possession of such vivid and accurate notions of all that is remarkable in the countries he undertakes to describe, as those with which we have been supplied by him. Egypt, Arabia, Palestine, Mesopotamia, and Persia, have been successively delineated, with all their wonders, both of art and nature, in a manner which makes us now feel comparatively at home upon these subjects. Numerous circumstances concur in recommending Mr. Buckingham's lectures to the public, viewing them merely in a literary and popular point of view, and altogether apart from the grand national question, with which, however, they are all more or less connected. In the first place, Mr. Buckingham has himself been in the countries of which he treats, and has seen with his own eyes every thing he describes. If he speaks of the Pyramids, he has stood on their top; if of the Nile, he has bathed in its waters; if of Mecca, he has made the pilgrimage to the holy shrine; if of Palmyra, he has been among its ruins. In the second place, information conveyed orally has a great advantage over that which comes to us through the medium of books. It is amazing how much the looks and gestures of the speaker contribute to give distinctness and graphic force to the picture he attempts to sketch. A book is the best substitute we can have for its author, but it is only a substitute. Mr. Buckingham is both the book and the author in one, and the effect produced is therefore doubled. In the third place, Mr. Buckingham's manner is exceedingly prepossessing and agreeable. One sees at once that he is a gentleman, and entitled to respect as well as to attention. He is a man past middle life, but hale and active, and with a modest but energetic and business-like mode of delivery, which effectually prevents the minds of his audience from wandering. In addition to all this, he is excellently skilled in the art of pleasing a popular assembly by intermixing with his graver and more important matter, a number of light and amusing stories.'—*Edinburgh Literary Journal, July* 18.

' MR. BUCKINGHAM.—Yesterday this celebrated traveller concluded his course of Lectures on the Eastern World, to the great regret, we venture to say, of every person who had the good taste to attend him. As we anticipated, his audience gradually increased as he drew nearer and nearer to the grand topic to which all his details, whether descriptive or argumentative, converged ; and on Saturday and yesterday the great room in the Waterloo Tavern was crowded with several hundreds of the most intelligent and respectable of our citizens, all intent to catch the winding-up of his prelections. The ladies supported him staunchly all along ; and, judging by their looks at least, we may safely assert that his advent has created quite a sensation, and completely annihilated in many a fair bosom the popularity of the gigantic monopoly which he strives to subvert. Our own favourable opinion of Mr. Buckingham, not merely as a lecturer, but as a man of most extensive intelligence, has steadily progressed ever since we first heard him speak ; and we are now confirmed in the opinion, that there are few men in the British islands equally qualified, and certainly none better, to expose the erroneous principles on which our vast territories in the East are governed ; and the imperious necessity of the people at home making a firm stand against the extension of a charter which militates so monstrously against the improvement of eighty-five millions of the human race. It cannot be, we know, that Mr. Buckingham is without a bias in the contest. No man could have battled so long and so obstinately with a very powerful enemy, without having his perception quickened by a spicing of vindictiveness towards his adversaries ; but we must say, that so far as our judgment goes, he has to boast of a very large share of philanthropy, and that it is not easy to listen to his arguments without feeling respect for the man, and aversion towards the system of moral and commercial bondage which he labours to overturn.'— *Edinburgh Observer, July* 21.

' Mr. Buckingham's supplementary lecture on the East India Company's Monopoly, and the advantages which would result from throwing open the trade to India and China, was delivered in the Waterloo Great Room, on Monday last, to a numerous and highly respectable audience. It occupied nearly four hours in the delivery ; but from the interesting nature of the subject, the multiplicity of the details introduced, and the engaging qualities of the lecturer himself, whose talent for communicating knowledge in a clear, animated, and attractive form is really of a very high order indeed, the attention of the auditory was kept up, with unabated intensity to the last ; and if we may judge from our own feeling and observation, the discourse might have been almost indefinitely prolonged without producing any sensation of lassitude or of exhaustion.'—*Caledonian Mercury, July* 23.

' On Monday, the subject of Mr. Buckingham's lecture was the constitution, policy, and government of the East India Company, and the condition of the population of Hindoostan, and it was delivered to a more crowded audience than any that has yet attended him. He continued expatiating on this important subject with such varied powers of eloquence, argument, and wit, that for the space of nearly four hours he enchained the attention of his hearers. Every new appearance which Mr. Buckingham makes, confirms and increases the first impressions of his great and original talents. On Monday he surpassed all his former exertions. He was animated apparently by the presence of so large an audience ; and he rose at times to the highest tone of impassioned eloquence ; while he enlivened the dry details of argument in a manner so extremely amusing and original, that we never before saw entertainment and instruction so happily combined. He was occasionally quite dramatic in his statements, and the delight of his audience, testified by frequent plaudits, seemed to react upon him, and to inspire him with new energy. He improved in fluency and ardour, and presented every topic upon which he touched in a new and more striking aspect, by the force and vivacity of his delineations.'—*Edinburgh Evening Courant, July* 23.

' Mr. Buckingham.—Last night this gentleman gave the first of three supplementary lectures on the Eastern World, to an audience consisting of upwards of 500 ladies and gentlemen, among whom we noticed a great many individuals of the highest intelligence and respectability. Mr. Buckingham, while he touched on all the countries which he had described in his previous lectures, was careful to avoid repetition, his object in extending his course being rather to supply facts omitted, than to rivet those which he had before communicated. In this attempt he was exceedingly happy —this lecture being fully more diversified, and richer in anecdote, than any of its predecessors. Mr. Buckingham's stores of information regarding the East appear to be quite inexhaustible ; and he opens them with a facility exclusively his own, and which makes us regret every time we hear him, the impossibility of doing justice, in a report, to a tythe of the topics which he illuminates.'—*Edinburgh Observer, July* 24.

In addition to these unsought eulogies from the public press of Scotland, emanating from nine different papers of all shades in politics, the private hospitalities and friendly attentions with which I was everywhere greeted, by the warm-hearted inhabitants of this beautiful and interesting city, were such as led me to feel myself no longer among strangers, and to bring away with me recollections of pleasure and attachment that I believe I shall carry with me to my grave. It was not to be expected, however, that such a stream of popularity as this would be permitted to flow on entirely without interruption. Accordingly, during the course of this period, an attack was opened on me, by a writer in one of the newspapers, (the Editor of which, however, had expended his highest eulogy on my character and proceedings), calling himself ' A Friend to Dr. Bryce.' and reviving all the thousand-times-refuted accusations respecting the cases of Bankes, Burckhardt, Bryce, Adam, and others. It was replied to through the same channel, and at last led to the disclosure of the name of the writer, who proved to be Dr. Bryce's professional Agent, and was therefore labouring in his vocation, and had possibly began to think of the blessings of a ' suit at law,' and all its comfortable emoluments. In this, however, he was defeated, as the mere disclosure of his name, in Edinburgh, *where* he was well known, was deemed sufficient to deprive his lucubrations of even the little value which, had they continued anonymous, they might still perhaps have retained.

ABERDEEN.

From Edinburgh I proceeded to Aberdeen, where the kindness of friends had already prepared the way for me, and where I accordingly met with a most cordial reception. The magnificent Public Rooms of that flourishing town were readily accorded for the delivery of the short course of Lectures which I intended giving there ; and of the effect produced by these, the following extracts from the Aberdeen Papers may, perhaps, be deemed sufficient evidence :—

' On Monday and yesterday evenings we attended the Lectures of this gentleman in the Banqueting Hall of the Public Rooms, Union-street; both of which, and especially the last, was attended by a numerous and highly respectable audience, including many of the principal families of the town and surrounding country. In consequence of a desire expressed by several of the leading members of the community, Mr. Buckingham gave a Preliminary Lecture, in which he introduced a selection of the most remarkable things contained in his longer Course.

' It would be difficult to say which of these portions gave the most unmixed satisfaction to the audience—they appeared to be delighted with all; and although the first Lecture lasted from seven o'clock till nearly ten, every one seemed reluctant to depart when it was brought to a close. We have never, on any occasion, witnessed more unequivocal satisfaction and delight.

'The second Lecture, which was given last evening, was still more fully attended than the first; and the regret was continually felt and expressed that Mr. Buckingham's stay was confined to two evenings only. We were glad to see, however, that his allusion to an intended repetition of his visit in the next year was received in such a manner as to manifest the most cordial support of all who heard it; and we doubt not but his full course would be attended here with very ample numbers.

'The Lecture on the East India Company's Monopoly, being the essence of the whole, was listened to with profound attention; and we doubt whether there was a single individual who before had any idea of its being so full of mischief to the country, or who did not leave the room with a fixed resolution to do every thing within his power to prevent the renewal of the charter of exclusive privileges, which is productive of such unmixed evil.'—*Aberdeen Journal, July 29.*

'Mr. Buckingham, who lectured in the County Rooms on Monday and Tuesday last, was attended on both occasions by numerous and respectable audiences. The appearance of this gentleman confirms all that has been said of his previous talents. He has eloquence, fluency, argument, and wit; and such powers of striking illustration that he arrests the attention of his audience, and gives at the same time such comprehensive and clear views of his subject, as impress the truth irresistibly on the mind. The subjects treated of by Mr. Buckingham are of the deepest importance, with a view to the great question, so soon to be discussed, of the renewal or non-renewal of the East India Company's charter; and he has very clearly proved, that this political anomaly of a trading company ruling our vast dominions in the capacity of a sovereign, is of the most pernicious nature, and has been attended with the worst consequences. The government of the East India Company has always been directed to one plain, simple, and selfish end, namely, the preservation in their own incapable hands of their vast possessions, at whatever expence. To this end every thing has been sacrificed, the happiness alike of the millions whom they govern, and the interests of Great Britain. The commercial sovereigns of Leadenhall-street have behaved to their subjects in every respect like the false mother, who would rather divide the child in two than part with it. They have resisted the most obvious improvements—opposed the wisest laws—and countenanced the basest idolatries and the most bloody superstitions, from a slavish fear of some nameless perils, arising from what was to benefit their subjects; and the only object they have been at all solicitous about has been to extort money from them, and to remit it home. It is clear that the colonization and settlement of Europeans in India, is essential to the improvement of the country; it is in this manner only that European improvement, both in arts, in morals, and in religion, can be diffused over this vast continent. Yet, this is rigidly prohibited by the East India Company, in whose dominions alone it is that the name of an Englishman is the badge of slavery.'—*Aberdeen Chronicle, August 1.*

DUNDEE.

DUNDEE was the next place of my visit, and there also the subject had already excited attention. The public authorities of the town evinced their approbation of the undertaking by a visit to me on my arrival; and the effect is thus spoken of in the Journals of Dundee:—

'MR. BUCKINGHAM.—This celebrated Orientalist commenced his first lecture, yesterday evening in the Thistle Hall, Union-street; and was enthusiastically greeted on his entrance by a numerous and respectable audience. We cannot, at this late hour, even venture upon an outline of his lecture: suffice it to say, that the facts he produced were so intensely interesting, and his manner of delivering them so vivid, familiar, and free from any thing like affectation, that not one of his auditors exhibited the least impatience, or left the room till the conclusion—so completely were they riveted by his eloquence for upwards of three hours. To show their respect for the character and talents of Mr. Buckingham, and their zeal for the great cause which he is advocating, several of our principal merchants waited upon him at the hotel, and conducted him to the Lecture-hall. This, we trust, is a symptom that our merchants are alive to the importance of a free trade to the East.'—*Dundee Advertiser, July 30.*

' Mr. Buckingham's Lectures took place here on the evenings of Wednesday and Thursday last, in the Thistle Operative Hall, Union-street, and were heard throughout with the deepest attention, and we may add, with conviction, by all present. Mr. Buckingham has distinguished powers as a lecturer. His readiness, his fluency, his eloquence, his complete mastery over the subject in all its details, his lively and apposite illustrations, as well as the point and sarcasm of his observations, all concurred to impress on his hearers the most profound admiration of his talents, and to secure attention, which is the first great step to conviction.—There cannot be a doubt, we think, that Mr. Buckingham made out a most triumphant case against the East India Company; proving that their whole attention was directed, not to the happiness of the people, or the prosperity of the country, but to the more selfish end of preserving those dominions for a possession to themselves. Accordingly Europeans are prevented from colonizing the country and settling in it, and by that means, of introducing among the Natives the industry, the arts, the manufactures, and, though last, not least, the intelligence and morality of Europe. If European merchants were allowed to settle freely in the interior, and to establish houses of agency, British goods would be dispersed throughout every corner of that immense continent, which would be a vast and profitable market, that would excite a demand in all parts of the country, and would give employment to our superfluous capital, and to our idle and necessitous workmen. This, and the opening of the China market, would certainly give a spring to industry, and would be of immense benefit over all the country. And why, it may be asked, should the British merchant be shut out of the China market, to which the Americans freely trade ? Is there any policy in this ? Is there any common sense in it ? We are not only excluded however, by this Company—by those princely grocers of Leadenhall-street—from a most beneficial branch of trade, which is engrossed by foreigners, but we *pay* for being excluded. We absolutely pay a heavy tax of three millions per annum to support our own exclusion from this excellent market for our goods ! We should really think that this grievance must be redressed when the Company's charter expires.

' From a notice by Lord William Bentinck, inserted in a former column, it will be observed, that the East India Company are beginning to think a little about the improvement of their dominions. The speedy expiry of their charter is a decisive argument; and they wish, before the question comes to be discussed, to have it to say that they have not altogether neglected the good of their subjects. That this is not the motive for this tardy act of justice there is little reason to doubt; otherwise, why would such an obvious duty have been so long delayed. This measure is clearly extorted from the fears of the Company, rather than from any overbundant anxiety for the happiness of their subjects.

' Mr. Buckingham was waited upon at his hotel by the Dean of Guild, the Deputy Chairman of the Chamber of Commerce, Baillie Brown, and several other respectable merchants, by whom he was accompanied to the new Hall in Union-street, and introduced to his audience, consisting of about 150 of the most respectable people in the place. On Thursday evening there might be 300 present.'—*Dundee Courier, Aug 4.*

GLASGOW.

From Dundee I passed through Perth, where not more than twenty or thirty persons could be collected to form the first audience; and a further stay there being deemed a loss of time, I proceeded to Glasgow, where I arrived on the 2d of August.

I had before this enjoyed the pleasure of an acquaintance with some of the leading merchants of this large and opulent city, and was now glad to renew my intercourse with them, in the mutual pursuit of an object so eminently beneficial to themselves. On communicating, however, with the East India Association already formed here, the Deputies from which had been in London in May, I found the same spirit of separation and exclusiveness to prevail as in London. The leaders in this Association were gentlemen who seemed to think it quite possible to carry the measure of opening the Trade to India and China, and entirely to destroy the exclusive Commercial Monopoly, and yet leave the *Government* of India in the hands of the East India Company. They were for Free Trade only, but not for Colonization; as if it were possible for the benefits of the one to be fully reaped without the admission of the other; and they were for taking away the trading character of the India Company only, and leaving them all the revenues, patronage, and political power they possess; as if it had not been shewn, beyond all possibility of doubt, that the latter could not be supported by them at all, without the profits derived from their Monopoly on Tea; and that on this issue they must all stand or fall together. In consequence of this imagined 'moderation,' as the parties were pleased to call it, an idea seemed seriously to be entertained by some of them, that it was quite possible to obtain the abolition of the East India Monopoly, and yet do nothing that should in the least degree offend the East India Directors! and this temporizing policy was that which the majority of the Glasgow Association adopted. There were some exceptions, however, to this rule; and accordingly although the Body took especial pains to keep itself aloof from all supposed connection with the labours I had undertaken, to effect the end they professedly desired—namely, the opening of the Eastern Trade; yet the excepted individuals exerted themselves with great zeal and earnestness to compensate for this luke-warmness, and gave their most cordial support and countenance to the measure in operation.

The First Lecture was delivered in the Assembly Room of Glasgow, on the 3d of August. It was attended by about eighty persons, who expressed their satisfaction in an enthusiastic manner. The succeeding ones were attended by increasing audiences every day, and the closing Lecture on the Monopoly and Government of India, produced a more striking impression than in almost any previous instance. The effect may be judged of from the following extracts from the Glasgow papers.

'The efforts of Mr. Buckingham, since his arrival in this country, to enlighten the public mind on the religion, literature, commerce, &c., of Oriental countries, and to expose the evils and injustice of monopoly in connection with some of these, afford at the same time a singular and striking proof of its impolicy and absurdity. Who have a British public to thank for the mass of valuable information that has thus been communicated, and for the admirable exposé that has been made of maladministration in the affairs of India? It is to the East India Company themselves, it is to the very intolerance and illiberality of their government that we are indebted for this. For it was the Company and their government who banished this gentleman from India, nay, who sent him in glorious exile back to his native country. What a master stroke of policy was this? Was there not another spot on the face of this wide terraqueous globe, to which this sworn foe to monopoly and oppression might have been banished? Was there no solitary, no barren rock of the ocean, from which his uplifted hand could not have beseeched release, and from which his lonely voice could never have been heard? Why was not the El Dorado of emigration-mania selected as she appropriate residence of the man who had provoked Demetrius, incensed the craftsmen, and attempted to turn the Eastern world upside down? But no, even though he had, with bare and bended knee, intreated the choice of any of these alternatives, the boon would not have been conceded—a decree, irrevocable as the laws of the Medes and Persians, has willed it, and home to Britain he must infallibly go. Thus has the champion of anti-monopoly been admitted within the walls of the citadel, and like a wise and skilful tactician, he is closely following up the advantage.'—*Glasgow Chronicle, July 22.*

'MR. BUCKINGHAM.—This distinguished Oriental traveller commenced his Lectures here on Monday last, in the Assembly Rooms, Ingram-street, to a very respectable and highly intelligent audience. His subject on Monday was Egypt, and yesterday Arabia; and we feel assured that we express the sentiments of every one who heard him when we say, that he crowds more information and entertainment into a short space, than any Lecturer who ever before addressed a Glasgow audience. His utterance is rapid, yet very distinct,—although occasionally, at the close of the periods, he permits his voice to fall so low as to escape the hearing of those who sat at any great distance; his elocution at the same time is good, his ideas acute and striking, his gestures animated, and his manner and appearance very gentlemanly and prepossessing. He is thoroughly master of every detail connected with his subjects, and he thus, with as much ease as familiarity, pours out upon the minds of his hearers a flood of knowledge, at once varied, extensive, original, and interesting. Perhaps his most distinguishing characteristic is his graphic power, by which he conjures up before the imagination, in as much vivid distinctness as if if were actually present, every image (and they are most multitudinous) of which he attempts the delineation. At the progress of so eloquent and able an advocate of freedom in commerce and legislation as this, the East India Monopolists have had good reason to become apprehensive.'—*Glasgow Free Press, Aug. 5.*

' Mr. Buckingham.—We are truly rejoiced to see the extraordinary manner in which the audiences attending the Lectures of this gentleman have increased since Wednesday. His popularity is now unbounded, and were he to repeat his whole Course three times over, he would each successive time have an enlarged attendance. This, we are glad to perceive, has induced him to give us an evening Course before his departure. By that means hundreds of our fellow-citizens will be enabled to embrace the opportunity of hearing him, who cannot leave their places of business at the present early hour. Yesterday Mr. Buckingham, in a splendid Lecture, gave us his *description* of India : to day he is to grapple with the *Monopoly ;* when we earnestly call upon every one who takes an interest in the question to attend, and witness this modern Hercules of the commercial world strangle our modern Nemean Lion.

' As a proof of the rapid manner in which the question respecting Free Trade with India is forcing itself on the attention of all classes of the community, since the commencement of Mr. Buckingham's tour through the country, for the purpose of awakening the public mind to a due sense of its importance, we may here mention that the College of Glasgow has proposed, for a Prize Essay, the following subject :—' The probable effects, both in England and in India, of removing all the existing restrictions on the commerce between the two countries.'—*Glasgow Free Press, Aug. 8.*

' The close of Mr. Buckingham's Lecture on Saturday was marked by the loudest and most enthusiastic applause, which continued to be reverberated and prolonged from every part of the Hall. Before it had subsided, Mr. Spiers of Culcreuch, a leading Member of the East India Association of Glasgow, rose, and addressed the assembly to the following effect :

' " Ladies and Gentlemen.—After the brilliant display of eloquence with which you have heard the subject of India and its administration treated to-day, and after the enthusiastic manner in which you have evinced your admiration of the talented individual to whom we are indebted for this exposition, I am sure that I shall only be expressing the unanimous feeling of every one who hears me, when I beg to propose that we tender to Mr. Buckingham our united and cordial thanks, for the vivid and convincing manner in which he has condensed and arranged the vast mass of information submitted to us to day ; and the triumphant case which he has established against the East India Company ; so as to satisfy the most scrupulous, that we ought to unite with the other great towns of the kingdom to prevent the renewal of their exclusive privileges, from which so little of good, even to themselves, and so much evil to others, have already sprung."

' The vote of thanks to Mr. Buckingham was seconded by Mr. Douglas of Barloch, and carried by loud and long-continued acclamation.

' Mr. Buckingham acknowledged his deep sense of the honour conferred on him, in very feeling and appropriate terms, and the meeting then separated, the Speech, or Lecture, having lasted nearly four hours ; and being kept up with increasing intensity of interest, both in the speaker and the hearers, to the very last.'—*Glasgow Herald, Aug. 10.*

In ' The Glasgow Chronicle' of August 12, immediately after the close of the Lectures, appeared the following letter, addressed to the Editor:

' Sir,—At the conclusion of a very powerful address of Mr. Buckingham, on the

D

India Monopoly, by which, on last Saturday, he exceeded every expectation of his most sanguine admirers, and engaged for four hours the untired and eager attention of a most respectable and numerous auditory, nothing was more gratifying than the universal expression of ardent approbation which followed the motion of Mr. Spiers of Culcreuch, of thanks to Mr. Buckingham for his conduct, and for the extensive and valuable information which he had compressed into so small a compass, and conveyed in a manner so particularly interesting. The repetition of the lectures in an evening course, is most judicious, and will, no doubt, be attended by the large proportion of the reflecting part of the community, whose interests are so deeply engaged in this question, but who could not spare so many business hours of the forenoon.

‘ On Saturday, a very general feeling was expressed in the respectable mercantile and manufacturing circle assembled at the Lecture—that if the commercial metropolis of Scotland had, like Liverpool, any power to elect a Parliamentary Representative, those who had witnessed Mr. B.'s capacity for abridging the largest subjects, and simplifying the most complex details of commercial affairs, or state policy—his distinctness in argumentative discussions—his correct easy style—and graceful and animated delivery and action—his equal facility of transition from the grave to the gay—from playful irony or pleasantry to the pathetic and deeply impassioned—the general result of a profound impression of the importance and truth of his doctrines—would bestow, by acclamation, a seat in Parliament on one so well qualified by peculiar knowledge and capacity for meeting with effect the Parliamentary manœuvres, which the great Leviathan of Indian Monopoly will assuredly spare neither cost nor exertion to put in motion, to exclude the British nation from a free-trade intercourse and settlement in the Eastern world.

‘ The best method of securing an advantageous arena on which this able champion of the public cause may meet its wily and potent adversaries, is to raise a national subscription from every class in proportion to their stake and their means—the very interest of which, vested in the funds, would defray every needful expense, and the principal, under the charge of local committees, be returned to the subscribers to this Grand—National—Free—India Trade Savings' Bank.

‘ That there are public spirited merchants and manufacturers in this city, and in the West of Scotland, who would be zealous and proud to lend a little of their time in organizing such a scheme, and in superintending the conduct of the efforts for obtaining free admission to the soil and trade of India, under the protecting influence of British law—it would be an insult to the extensive knowledge, enterprise, talent, and spirit of the public to doubt.

‘ If a general expression of opinion to this effect were first collected by subscriptions, obtained by a few active individuals to a short paper, the principle would at once lay hold of the public attention, and a sense of its advantages diffuse it over the whole kingdom. This expression of opinion would undoubtedly induce one of the many patriotic noblemen whose families have for centuries devoted their Boroughs to the patronage of men who have disclosed talents for upholding any branch of British liberty, or public right, which was peculiarly endangered—of Fox, Burke, Sheridan, Mackintosh, Brougham—to introduce to the senate the oppressed advocate of the Liberty of the Press, of British law, of free ingress and egress to all British subjects to a colony conquered by our own blood, and retained in dependence by our own efforts ; more especially when the shutting of some foreign markets, and the glutting of all, have produced such a depression in every branch of our national industry, and when the question is, whether we shall for another quarter of a century be excluded from one half of the world for the mere pleasure, not profit, of a Company, whose monopoly ‘ not enriches them, while it makes us poor indeed.’

‘ The feeling on this subject is not at present so strong and general that it only requires direction and motion from a very few merchants and manufactures of good sense and activity.   I am, Sir, yours, &c.
‘ A Glasgow Merchant.’*

---

* In the Glasgow Chronicle of the following week, this notice appeared in reference to the Letter given above :

‘ The Sheffield Iris ’ thinks that the suggestion of our Correspondent ‘ A Merchant, in favour of a subscription for procuring a seat for Mr. Buckingham in Parliament, is well worthy

During the period of my stay at Glasgow, there were two occasions of which I was glad to avail myself, to add to the feeling of interest already excited on the subject of India, and its affairs. The first of these was the laying the foundation stone of a new bridge across the Clyde, at which a Masonic procession took place, in the presence of 150,000 spectators, which was closed by a public entertainment in the evening; the second was the opening of the Royal Exchange at Glasgow, a splendid building, where upwards of 600 persons sat down to a sumptuous feast. On both of these occasions, my name having been associated with the progress of Free Trade, especially with India and China, I took occasion to increase the feeling of interest in the cause, by addresses which will be found at the end of this narrative. The last Lecture given in Glasgow was on the 20th of August, in a larger room than the former, the Trades' Hall, which was closed by the following proposition, as reported in the papers of the day :—

' Mr. Buckingham having been earnestly pressed to give a developement of his views on the question, '' What is to be done with India ?'' for this purpose, a supplementary lecture was delivered yesterday afternoon (Thursday, August 20) in the Trades' Hall, Glasgow, to an audience more numerous and fashionable, if possible, than on any former occasion. For the gratification of the ladies, the lecture was preceded by an account of a very perilous journey, undertaken by Mr. Buckingham in the Arabian desert, also by some interesting details of the life, habits, and manners of Lady Hester Stanhope.

' At the conclusion of a Lecture, which lasted upwards of two hours, and was listened to with intense interest and great applause, Mr. Buckingham took leave of his audience in very feeling terms.

' After the applause consequent on this ardent expression of the Lecturer's feelings, had subsided,

' LAWRENCE HILL, Esq. rose, and expressed his regret that some one in the assembly, better qualified than himself, had not made some proposal or suggestion, to evince that Mr. Buckingham's Lectures had not been lost upon them, and that they had given rise to some beneficial result. However, the conviction he felt of the importance of the subject on which Mr. Buckingham had just addressed them, compelled him not to allow the meeting to separate without offering them some resolution. With this view, he would propose,

' '' That after the repeated and convincing proofs which Mr. Buckingham has given to the world, and of which we ourselves have been this day witnesses, of his rarely united qualifications, to advocate the great cause of a more extended intercourse with India and China, by his abundant information, his unwearied zeal, his great eloquence, and his capacity to bring all these into operation in the most crowded and intellectual assemblies, it is the opinion of this meeting, that a subscription should be immediately opened, and a committee appointed for the purpose of taking such measures as may be most expedient, and likely to make Mr. Buckingham's talents and information available to the country, and as may be most conducive to the desirable object of a free trade with the Eastern world, and beneficial to the other important interests involved in that great question.''

' JOHN WILSON, Esq. of Thornly, in seconding the resolution, said, he considered it as a tribute and a testimony due to Mr. Buckingham, for his zeal and talents in a

the attention of all whose interests are involved in the speedy settlement of the great question now in agitation; the more so, as neither cost nor exertion will be spared by those who have too long enjoyed the exclusive right of trading to the Eastern world. As Glasgow, although containing a population of 200,000, has only the privilege of returning one-fourth (other three boroughs, Dumbarton, Renfrew, and Rutherglen, sharing the honour,) of a member to the ' Collective Wisdom ' of the state, it recommends the public-spirited and enlightened merchants of that city to take the lead in promoting the measure suggested by their fellow-citizen, of seeking to obtain for Mr. Buckingham a seat in the House of Commons. It only requires (says 'The Sheffield Iris ') that a beginning be made, and there can be no doubt of the willingness of the inhabitants of Manchester, Birmingham, Leeds, and Sheffield, to lend their aid, in forwarding a cause which so much concerns their future prosperity.

great cause, and for his delightful method of conveying information with a view to the promotion of that cause, to the understanding and the heart.

' The resolution was unanimously carried, amid the acclamation of the meeting.

' Mr. Buckingham, evidently much affected at this unexpected demonstration of regard, briefly returned thanks. Whatever might be thought of his talents or capacity, he hoped no one would call in question his ardent zeal in the cause; and which, if it were ever his lot to address another assembly, he hoped would not be found to have become relaxed in the slightest degree. Supposing it to be possible that he should be compelled to choose between offering up his life as the only sacrifice by which this cause could triumph, or of living in ease and affluence, but yet compelled to witness the continuation of the system, he declared, that though bound to society by the strongest of all possible ties, and having a family, every individual member of which was as dear to him as himself, yet he knew he had still sufficient of the Roman in him to prefer the former course. And he took heaven and earth to witness the sincerity of this vow, that so long as he possessed life, health, and adequate strength and means to maintain this crusade against the despotism and monopoly of the East India Company, nothing should prevail on him to turn aside from so holy a path. All he asked or hoped for was the sympathy and support of his countrymen; and if he had but this, their triumph would be certain and complete.'—*Glasgow Chronicle.*

CARLISLE.

From Glasgow I proceeded to Carlise, where the Assizes happened to be then holding, a circumstance which occasioned many of the Country Gentlemen to be present, and of whose attendance I was glad to avail myself. The Lectures there were confined to the subject of the East India Monopoly only, as the time of my engagements at other places prevented my staying longer; but they were attended with all the good that could be wished, and ended in the passing of Resolutions, for the formation of an East India Association, which received the support of the principal inhabitants of the town. The following was the report given in the papers of the town, of the termination of this course :—

' At the close of Mr. Buckingham's last Lecture on the East India and China Monopoly, delivered at Carlisle, on the 26th of August, to a highly respectable audience, including a great number of the county gentlemen, who had been attending on the assizes, it was moved by John Dixon, Esq., seconded by William Halton, Esq., and carried by acclamation:

' " That the cordial thanks of this meeting be tendered to Mr. Buckingham, for the able and agreeable manner in which he has opened to us the vast fund of his information respecting the trade with India and China; and that we offer him our best wishes for his health and continued success in the great cause which he is so effectually advocating." '—*Carlisle Journal.*

DUMFRIES.

Dumfries was the next place that I visited; but there, partly from the extreme severity of the weather, the country being then deluged with rain, and partly, perhaps, from the existence of an old East India Interest in that quarter of Scotland, the Lectures were but thinly attended, and led to no immediate results. In this corner of the island, where I had not expected to meet a single creature that I had ever seen before, I was agreeably surprised, when on a visit to the venerable widow of the Poet Burns, to meet with an individual whom I had seen before at Ispahan, the capital of Persia, where we had passed some days together, and with another gentleman whom I had before conveyed as a passenger in my ship in India, from Bombay to the Coast of Malabar.

GREENOCK.

I proceeded from hence to Greenock, and if I were called on to name any one place where the interest in the subject of my visit was more lively and vivid than in another, I should certainly name this. Nothing could exceed the zeal, and even fervour of the inhabitants, including all classes :—the following extracts from the Greenock paper will explain the rest:—

' Mr. Buckingham.—This gentleman concluded his course of Lectures on the India and China Monopoly, and the discussion of the important question, ' *What will be done with India?*' on Wednesday evening. He was attended throughout by the most respectable inhabitants of Greenock, Port-Glasgow, and the neighbouring watering places, who testified their high sense of his important labours, by loud and repeated cheerings. It gives us pleasure to announce to our readers, that he has complied with the earnest wish of several ladies and gentlemen, to deliver his lecture on Palestine and its holy places, this evening, in the Assembly Rooms, at seven o'clock. The Journals speak in the most unqualified manner of the deep interest which is excited by his description of the Holy Land, and the impression which it leaves on the minds of his audience ; and if he enter upon this lofty and arduous subject with his usual simplicity, distinctness, and energy, it cannot fail to be listened to with breathless attention, embracing, as it does, a description of Tyre, Sidon, Jerusalem, and the Mount of Olives, the tomb of our Saviour, and the various worshippers who resort to it; the Land of Uz, and the valley of Jehosaphat; the seas, lakes, rivers, and plains; and the manners, religion, population, and government of the people. These, with many illustrations of Scripture—particularly of passages difficult to comprehend, but which in the hands of so acute and attentive an observer as Mr. Buckingham, and so intimately acquainted with the customs and language of the Eastern World as he is, cannot fail to be equally interesting to the Divine, and the Christian World in general.

' As an orator, Mr. Buckingham is entitled to rank amongst the first in the first rank of extempore speakers. He is never at a loss for language, distinct and appropriate, in which to clothe his ideas, which flow upon him in quick and fervid succession, each one loftier and mightier than that which preceded it. His voice is clear and agreeable, and capable of every variety of modulation and tone,—he is cool or impassioned, serious or jocular, pathetic or indignant, encouraging or commanding, as the nature of the subject he is discussing requires ; his feelings are always in accordance with it,— like his language, illustration, and instructive anecdotes, they are always under his command. The same may be said of his gesticulation ; it is chaste and varied, and adapted to the nature of his discourse. It seems to come upon him unsought for—he could not repress it if he wished to do so. Indeed, we venture to say, that, in the eagerness to reach the understanding and conviction of his hearers, he is scarcely aware that he uses an arm, yet he is never caught in an ungraceful attitude. The East India Company never had an opponent so powerful, and completely fitted to expose the evils of the exclusive privileges which they have so long enjoyed. Our enterprising merchants we are sure will follow up the proceedings which they have already adopted, and unite with the other great commercial towns in the kingdom, in lending their aid to remove the disabilities under which they have so long laboured.

' We are glad to understand that, in consideration of the vast fund of information which Mr. Buckingham has conveyed to them on this most important subject, and in testimony of their admiration of his character and talents, several of the principal merchants of Greenock are to give Mr. Buckingham a dinner in the Tontine Hotel, and afterwards accompany him to the Lecture Room.'—*Greenock Advertiser, Sept.* 4.

' Dinner to Mr. Buckingham.—The strong and general interest excited by the delivery of Mr. Buckingham's lectures in this town, so increased with each succeeding day, that a number of the principal inhabitants came to a resolution to manifest their approbation of this gentleman's labours, and their concurrence in his views, by entertaining him with a dinner at the Tontine Hotel, on Friday evening last, just before his setting out for Edinburgh. Baillie Leitch, Chief Magistrate, in the chair; James Watt, Esq., croupier.

' In the course of the evening, various toasts were proposed, in harmony with the spirit of the meeting, which was addressed by the Chief Magistrate, by Mr. Buckingham, Mr. Wallace of Kelly, Mr. Watt, Mr. Thom, Mr. Fairrie, and others. In these, the principal topics were, the evils under which the whole country is now labouring, in consequence of its productive powers being so great, while the existing markets for consumption are all supplied; and the indispensable necessity, therefore, of claiming from the Legislature a free admission to all the markets of the globe to which our power extends.

' When the health of Mr. Wallace was given, allusion was made to his being a large West India proprietor, who had the intelligence, experience, and the liberality to admit that the interests of the class to which he belonged, ought no more to be maintained by a monopoly than the interests of the East India Company, but that fair com-petition and equal protection should be granted to all branches of property or trade. Mr. Wallace, in a very feeling and happy manner, expressed his entire concurrence in this view of the subject, and showed, by references to his past opinions and actions, as well as by the conduct of the people of Greenock itself, that even if it had been other-wise, and that partial evil might be expected, which he did not, however, apprehend, both his conscience and the example set him by the public-spirited merchants of this port, would concur in inducing him not to think of setting up his own individual interests as an obstacle to the accomplishment of a great public good.

' This speech was followed by a second, from Mr. Buckingham, in which, having already expatiated on the interests of the East India Trade, he undertook to show, and that by fact and argument in detail, that if the question merely turned upon the ad-mission of East India sugar only, as a free article from the East, the interest of the sugar-growers in the West might be supposed likely to suffer; but taking all the other articles of Indian produce into account, and more especially the opening of China, and the highly improved state of all the countries which might, if the existing monopoly were abolished, engage in a commerce with the East, it was certain that a much larger quantity of all kinds of colonial produce would be required than is now supplied, and that, therefore, the West Indies might still hold their ground, and even participate in the general benefits which the opening of the East would give to all classes of pro-ducers. This subject was pursued at much greater length than our brief outline would embrace, and its reception was such as to show that it was cordially and reciprocally entertained.

' Mr. Fairrie stated, in which he was followed and confirmed by the Chief Magistrate and Mr. Watt, that at the last expiration of the Charter, the merchants of Greenock were the first in the field to oppose its renewal. They had derived considerable infor-mation and some impetus towards the cause from Mr. T. Attwood, the public-spirited and intelligent banker, of Birmingham; and as early as the year 1811, they sent up a deputation, which was soon after joined by one from Hull, though the country generally did not engage in the struggle until long after. In May last, also, there was a public meeting held at Greenock, and another of the county of Renfrewshire (the only county meeting yet held in the kingdom on this occasion), at both of which strong resolutions were passed, committees formed, and every preparatory step taken to enter into more active operations when the time for action arrives; so that the spirit has continued here as vigorous as at first, and will now be in no danger of abatement.

' The entertainment was altogether one of the most agreeable description, equally honourable to the givers and the receiver: and notwithstanding that most of the indi-viduals had, on the preceding evening, been engaged in the festivities of opening the Royal Exchange at Glasgow, there was as much freshness, vivacity, and even enthu-siasm, as if the longest interval had intervened between.—*Greenock Advertiser.*

' Mr. Buckingham's Lecture on Palestine.—This lecture was attended on Fri-day evening by the most numerous and fashionable audience we have ever seen within the walls of the Assembly Room. The Orator spoke for more than three hours. The breathless silence with which he was listened to, interrupted occasionally by immense cheering, evinced the intense interest that prevailed. The audience were completely under his sway—they could no more resist the impression he wished to make, or fail to catch a portion of his spirit, than he himself could resist the impulse of deep feeling with which he was borne away. It was indeed a highly interesting and imposing discourse—one continued and unconstrained torrent of eloquence, ' deep, fervid, limitless, and strong.' We will not lessen the effect which it produced by at-tempting even an outline of it. It is much to be regretted that he did not favour us with his lectures on Egypt, Arabia, and Mesopotamia; they would have been as much appreciated in Greenock as any other town which Mr. Buckingham has visited.

Indeed, if he had had time to do so, previous to his departure from Scotland, we feel assured that it would repay him for his labour.

'In our last we stated that he was the most powerful opponent the East India Company ever had. He seems to have been destined for the task, and we are much mistaken if he do not sap the foundation of this odious monopoly, and eventually overturn it altogether. There is a union of every quality in him for the work. Oratory, natural and unassuming—energy, determination, and an inexhaustible fund of information—a heart sympathising with the woes of suffering humanity—a philanthrophy which embraces in one wide grasp the myriads of our fellow creatures who are still immersed in the darkness of superstition. The mercantile world cannot but follow and support him, the Christian world cannot but aid him with their prayers, for the successful issue of his crusade ; for a wider field never was opened for Christian benevolence than will be opened at the expiration, we trust, of the present charter.'—*Greenock Advertiser*, *Sept.* 8.

From Greenock I returned through Glasgow to Edinburgh, and there gave a concluding Lecture on the question 'What is to be done with India ?' which was attended by an audience of about 500 persons, and a large number went away, from inability to obtain seats. It was most enthusiastically received, and ended by a vote of thanks being moved by Mr. Baillie Spittal, and seconded by Mr. J. Macfarlane, thus closing my labours in Scotland for the year. I had visited Paisley and Leith ; but the one of these was so near to Glasgow, and the other to Edinburgh, that the majority of the inhabitants who felt an interest in the question had attended the Lectures at the larger places ; but it might be safely said, on the whole, that not less than 20,000 different individuals had been *hearers* of these Lectures in Scotland, while, from the continued agitation of the subject in the newspapers of the country, there could scarcely have been an individual capable of reading, to whom the question had not become one of almost unavoidable interest.

SCARBOROUGH.

I left Edinburgh for Scarborough, in the Steam Packet, hoping to find there an assemblage of Members of Parliament, and wealthy families, for which it is a favourite summer retreat. The experiment was, however, so unfavourable, from the intervention of the Doncaster Race week, which had drawn off nearly all the company, that not more than 30 persons attended. At the suggestion of some of these few, who expressed great pleasure at what they had heard, the conclusion of the Course was postponed for ten days, and in the mean time, I proceeded to Whitby.

WHITBY.

My arrival at this place was just at the period of Mr. Sadler, the Member for Newark, having visited it, and dined with the principal shipowners, on which occasion he delivered a speech, replete with denunciations of Mr. Huskisson, the free trade policy, and all its abettors. This was preceded by a letter, written by an intelligent magistrate of that town, who had been himself a shipowner, in praise of Mr. Huskisson's system, and published in the *Liverpool Times*. The circumstances arising out of this may be best understood by the following extract from the *York Courant* of the date referred to :—

'In our last, we stated, that the celebrated Orientalist, Mr. Buckingham, was about to deliver a series of Lectures at Whitby, in the course of which he would undertake to show the fallacy of Mr. Sadler's views respecting the shipping interest. These lectures have, we are assured, had an effect upon the minds of his enlightened and respectable auditories, which is calculated to *unsettle* their faith in Mr. Sadler's politics, notwithstanding the vividness of that gentleman's oratory. A contemporary has thus noticed Mr. Buckingham's Lectures :—

'Mr. Buckingham's arrival at Whitby was just after the dinner given to Mr. Sadler, and while the town was almost exclusively occupied with the denunciations with which the latter gentleman had assailed the principles and practice of the free-traders and political economists. The moment was therefore thought peculiarly unfavourable for the successful reception of Mr. Buckingham's views, as to the advantages of that free trade which Mr. Sadler had just taken so much pains to misrepresent, as well as to decry. We mentioned in our last, that a highly respectable magistrate of Whitby, Mr. Richard Moorsom, had issued a small pamphlet, containing an address to his fellow townsmen, and embodying his views as to the shipping interest and the general misconception which attributed its depression to Mr. Huskisson's measures; which pamphlet, opposed as it was in every respect to Mr. Sadler's notions, was rather un-courteously treated both by this gentleman himself, and by those of his party, to whom it was sent for previous perusal. Mr. Buckingham having been long since known to Mr. Moorsom, by correspondence, arising out of the similarity of their commercial views, became, with that portion of his family who accompanied him in this part of his tour, Mr. Moorsom's guest. This was another circumstance which it was thought might operate unfavourably at the present moment, for the popular reception of Mr. Buckingham's views; and, altogether, the prospect was considered to be unusually discouraging. Notwithstanding this, however, Mr. Buckingham issued, in addition to the usual announcement of his Lectures, an especial invitation to the ship-owners and merchants of Whitby, to whom he pledged his readiness to prove, to their entire satis-faction, that they all suffered great injury from the continued exclusion of their ships and capital from ports under the control of the East India Company, where foreigners resort freely, though British vessels and British subjects are shut out; and that it is not *by* free trade, but by the existing obstacles which are still interposed to *prevent* that free trade being extended to all parts of the world, that the depression of the shipping interest has been produced.

' And what has been the result ? Why, that the Lectures of Mr. Buckingham, held in the very room in which the dinner was given to Mr. Sadler, have been attended by nearly twice the number of auditors which that gentleman had, though such powerful interest, and such especial pains were taken to collect them in the one case, with the attraction of a sumptuous dinner, and excellent wines super-added ; while in the other, no step beyond the ordinary announcement by advertisement, was taken, and the fare to be supplied was wholly intellectual. Mr. Buckingham's audiences increased in number each succeeding evening, and on the third, the last to which our information extends, not only was the room entirely filled, but a number of persons, for want of room below, occupied the music-gallery. Among the auditors have been seen the principal merchants, ship-owners, and gentry of the town and surrounding country. Our worthy member, Colonel Wilson, (who, strange to say, happens to be Mr. Buck-ingham's next door neighbour in London), was observed to be among the audience. Mr. Edward Chapman, the chairman of the dinner given to Mr. Sadler, has been throughout a constant and punctual attendant, as indeed have most of the persons who participated in that festivity. It is to be regretted, that the honourable member for Newark, Mr. Sadler, did not himself remain either to gather new laurels by his exposition of Mr. Buckingham's errors, if errors they be, or to yield the palm to his truths, if, upon examination, they should be found to deserve that character ; for either one or the other at least they must be. That he was duly apprised of Mr. Buckingham's inten-tions, and even urgently pressed to attend them, we happen to know from good autho-rity ; but the tranquillity of Redcar appeared to have greater attractions for the honour-able gentleman, than a further sojourn in Whitby—flattering as had been his reception among the inhabitants of that place. To be sure, there might have been some dis-advantageous comparisons and contrasts, between a speech upon the shipping interests, by Mr. Sadler, who despises all theorists, and will admit of no evidence but that of practical men ; but who at the same time, can really know nothing whatever of ships or seamen, except as a theorist—having been all his life bred and occu-pied as a trader in linens, in an inland town, and never having either performed voyages by sea, or lived amongst those who had :—we say, that a speech on the ship-ping interests from such a man, might perhaps have been rather disadvantageouly con-trasted with a speech on the shipping interests by Mr. Buckingham, who went to sea at nine years of age, who commanded a ship before he was twenty-one, and who has visited almost every part of the globe, by sea and land, as a navigator, a merchant, and

Mr. Sadler at Whitby. 41

a traveller. The shrewd ship-owners of Whitby, most of whom have themselves been
sailors—could not fail to distinguish the wide difference between a man speaking of
that which was perfectly new, and scarcely intelligible to himself—and a man explaining
to others that with which he had been familiar from his cradle, and which had formed,
indeed, the principal object, and as it were the natural and professional pursuit of his
life. Yet this is just the distinction between Mr. Sadler and Mr. Buckingham, as
speakers or writers on the shipping interest; and we really cannot help thinking, that
if the ship-owners of Whitby or Hull, of Whitehaven or Newcastle—of Greenock,
Liverpool, or Bristol—think it essential to their interest to have a representative in
Parliament, or an advocate at public dinners—a seamen and a navigator is a more
appropriate person than a farmer or a linen-draper: and he who unites to theory the
most extensive experience and practice—a better man than one who is destitute both
of the one and the other.

Mr. Sadler may be a very fit and appropriate person to represent the Duke of Newcastle, in the House of Commons, his Grace himself being confined to the narrow
limits of the House of Lords; and he may very adequately discharge all the important
duties imposed upon him by his Grace's tenants and retainers in the borough of
Newark-upon-Trent: but we repeat again, that on any question connected with shipping and commerce, Mr. Buckingham's practical knowledge and multifarious experience must render him a much more appropriate representative of the shipping and
mercantile interests of this great maritime and commercial community. As to the
other qualification, the power of communicating vividly, clearly, and agreeably his
own thoughts and feelings to others, it is admitted on all hands, by the universally
concurrent testimony of writers on both sides of politics, and by auditors of all
parties, that Mr. Buckingham is pre-eminently successful in its display: and the most
striking manner in which we can show this, by comparison, is by saying, that while
Mr. Sadler, after all the comfort and excitement produced by an excellent dinner,
found it difficult to preserve the sustained attention of his hearers for an hour and
three quarters—himself and the whole party halting twice on their way to refresh themselves with a glass of wine (that *detestable* foreign production, which by the mischievous
free-trader has been made to supplant the home production of pure water springing from
our native wells, but which there is no sin in drinking, though the political economists
who encourage its importation ought to be exiled for commending)—Mr. Buckingham,
without any such aids, and without a single pause or interruption for even a moment of
time, so completely rivetted the attention of an audience of double the number, at the
same place, and in the same room, that during a period of more than three hours, the
silence might be described as almost breathless, and its conclusion was, in each instance,
terminated by a burst of applause, which sufficiently indicated the feeling universally
expressed from all quarters of the room, that the auditors could have remained for
three hours longer, without the least sense of weariness or fatigue, so deeply had their
feelings and their judgment been interested in the facts, arguments, and illustrations, by
which Mr. Buckingham supports the very opposite position of Mr. Sadler's policy, and
shows that in proportion as nations have encumbered their intercourse with each other,
by restrictions, they have declined from their high and palmy state, and become power-
less and wretched; while in proportion as they have made that intercourse free and
unrestrained, they have become wealthy, powerful, and happy.

'We are further enabled to add, that in addition to the interest excited in the shipping
and mercantile circles of Whitby itself, we learn that a number of wealthy and intelligent individuals, who happened to be there as visiters from Scarborough and the neighbouring country, were also deeply impressed by Mr. Buckingham's Lectures, as to the
importance of opening to British enterprize the present monopolized markets and ports
of the East. Among those visiters were Messrs. Strutt, of the extensive Manufacturing
Establishment, near Derby, who were accompanied by Mr. Gisborne, a gentleman
recently from India, and Mr. William Evans, the late Member for Leicester, whose
philanthropic and liberal views on all questions of policy and trade are well known.
From each of these gentlemen, who attended Mr. Buckingham's Lectures during their
stay in Whitby, he received invitations to visit their part of the country, with assurances
of a cordial reception, and every aid in the promotion of his public views. Mr. Buckingham returns from Whitby to Scarborough, at the latter end of the present week, in
compliance with a very general wish communicated to him by the visiters still at that
place, to give the concluding portion of his course; and from thence, we believe, proceeds

towards Newcastle, visiting Stockton and Darlington in the way, and returning from Newcastle through Durham to York. The communications from Whitby speak of the continually increasing interest excited on the East India Question ; and state, that already the formation of an East India Association, in Whitby, is preparing to co-operate with the other sea-ports and towns of the kingdom, in their efforts to prevent a renewal of the East India Company's India and China monopoly.'—*York Herald.*

At the close of the last Lecture at Whitby, Resolutions were moved, seconded, and carried, without a single dissentient voice, for the formation of an East India Association, to oppose the existing Monopoly, and open India and China to British enterprise, so that the triumph of the friends of liberal principles was complete.

From Whitby I proceeded to Stockton and Darlington, in Durham, and thence to Newcastle, Sunderland, and Shields.

STOCKTON.

At this place my first audience consisted of 15 persons only, and 13 of these were of one family ; they gradually increased, however, every evening, and at last amounted to 260, which, with reference to the size and population of the town, was larger than an audience of 50,000 in London, where more than 100 persons had never yet been collected to attend a discourse on the same subject ! The spirit evinced, too, was one of cordial co-operation in the measures proposed, for effecting a change in the existing system of intercourse between this country and India.

DARLINGTON.

At Darlington, where a large portion of the principal inhabitants are of the Society of Friends, the commencement was more auspicious, the number of the first audience being 70, and going on increasing gradually to 280. The principal difficulty here, indeed, was to obtain a room large enough to accommodate the auditors; and some obstructions were experienced in that particular, not very commendable to the individual (for it was from one person only that the objection came) who so injudiciously, but happily ineffectually, endeavoured to discourage, or, at least, to inconvenience, those who gave the cause their presence and support. The result in both these small towns was such as to justify the belief that there is scarcely even a village in the kingdom in which there is not now sufficient of intelligence to perceive the evils, of virtue to feel indignant at the vices, and of public spirit to oppose the further progress of the mischiefs, arising out of the present system of governing India, provided they could be made acquainted with the facts by means of such personal visits among them as this.

NEWCASTLE.

At Newcastle, the great Metropolis of the North, still greater success awaited my labours. The Lectures were there commenced in the small Assembly Room, and were attended at the first by about 100 hearers. These, however, increased nightly, with such rapidity, that we were obliged to go from the apartment first selected, to the large Assembly Room, which has no superior for size and proportions out of London; and on the last night, even that was found but barely sufficient to accommodate comfortably an audience of nearly 600 persons. The impression made by the whole Course was evidently of the most favourable description ; and the last, that on the Monopoly of the East India Company, was deemed so important, that, at the request of a great number of the leading individuals of the town, it was repeated in the Theatre of Newcastle, which, on that occasion, contained an audience of more than 700 individuals, and among these, were included some of the principal families of the surrounding country, as well as all the leading inhabitants of the town.

SUNDERLAND AND SHIELDS.

AT Shields and Sunderland the effect was quite as powerful, in proportion to their population, as at Newcastle; and at each, a change of room became necessary to accommodate the constantly increasing number of the attendants. At each place, too, the private hospitalities of which I was made a welcome participator, were such as to shew, that great private, or individual interest, was felt in the instrument of the cause, as well as great public zeal experienced in desiring to promote its success. At all the five places last named, being within a short distance of each other, public meetings were held after the Lectures were closed ; public thanks voted to me for my labours in each ; public resolutions passed, and public Associations formed, for prosecuting with vigour, such measures as might be deemed best calculated to secure the object in view.

RETURN TO LONDON.

AFTER having been thus instrumental in exciting this spirit through so wide a range of country, from London in the South, to Aberdeen in the North, and from Bristol, Liverpool, and Carlisle, in the West, to Newcastle, Sunderland, and Shields, in the East, with many of the great cities and towns lying between these wide extremes ;—after having been absent from my home for nearly six months in continuity ;—and during the whole of that period (with one single interruption arising from a second attack of quinsey at Glasgow) having given at least one Lecture *every day*, (Sundays alone excepted); sometimes two, and on one occasion three, at three different places ; occupying never less than two hours, frequently three, and on some occasions four, and even five in the delivery ;—having never suffered even journeying to prevent this daily labour, frequently travelling 70 or 80 miles in the morning, and addressing a crowded assembly on the evening of the same day ;—and in addition to this, profiting by every occasion that presented itself, whether at a Masonic procession, a festive entertainment, or a social private party ; at a missionary meeting, in a theatre, or at a public ball—wherever and whenever the opportunity offered, to make it a medium through which to enlist the sympathies, and at which to obtain the pledges of individuals, in behalf of the cause ;—after all this, I returned to town, and rejoined my own domestic circle, in the month of December 1829.

In reflecting on the great pleasure that I received from the private hospitalities and friendly attentions lavished upon me during this Tour, I feel it difficult to express in adequate terms my sense of so much unmerited honour, and quite as difficult to say in what quarter of the island I found myself most completely at home. A hundred names at least occur to me, as those of bosom friends, a thousand as those of most agreeable and cordial acquaintances, (indeed their very number prevents enumeration of them in detail); and independently of all the public good which I hope and believe will be achieved by the labours of the past year, I would not exchange the private and individual happiness which I derive from the pleasurable recollections it affords, for that of any single year of my existence.

ADDRESSES.

As a close to this Narrative, I subjoin the several addresses, which, in the course of my last journey I had occasion to make, including that delivered at the Meeting of the Bible Society at Whitby,—the Reply to Mr. Sadler's Speech on the Shipping Interests, made at a public dinner at the same place,—the Address to the Masonic Body, on laying the foundation stone of a Bridge across the Clyde,—the Speech at the Opening of the Royal Exchange at Glasgow,—and the Letter to the Ladies of Northumberland after the Ball at

Newcastle,—each of which will tend to confirm the assertion previously made, that on every occasion that presented itself, I was ready to turn it to the best account, as a medium for enlisting the sympathies of the British public of every rank, class, or sect, in favour of the great cause of Indian Improvement.

REPORT OF THE SPEECH

Delivered at the Eleventh Anniversary of the Whitby Auxiliary Bible Society, on Friday, the 18th Sept., 1829.

In rising to second the motion which has been so ably and eloquently introduced to your notice by the accomplished speaker who has just concluded his address, I may venture to say that I participate as largely as any individual member of this crowded assembly in the general satisfaction which the object and conduct of this meeting are so well calculated to afford. I might, perhaps, under ordinary circumstances, have contented myself with merely expressing this satisfaction, and permitting the motion to pass at once to the vote ; but, having been so pointedly alluded to by the several speakers who have preceded me, and invited by name to give some details respecting the countries I have traversed in the East, I should be wanting in respect to those who have so honoured me, and in justice to the cause itself, were I to remain entirely silent on this occasion. I fear, however, that what I have to offer will be infinitely less agreeable than what has been already presented to you , for, hitherto you have been chiefly flattered with the pleasing representations of the great good which your united efforts have actually achieved : while it must be my less grateful province to point out to you how much yet remains to be accomplished, and thereby, if possible, to stimulate you to new sacrifices and to renewed exertions. The greater number of those whom I have now the pleasure to address must, of course, be aware that the immediate object of my visit to Whitby is of a specific and peculiar nature ; it being my wish to call the attention of its inhabitants, as ship-owners and merchants more particularly, to the importance of improving our political and commercial relations with the East : but, though this is the main purpose of my visit here, yet so important do I hold the object which has brought you together in the same place, that I pledge myself to forget, for a moment, the predominant feeling of my own mind, and to confine myself, in what I shall now say, to the strict limits of our present purpose, by shewing you the condition of the Eastern World generally, with reference to its religious wants and the best means of supplying them, and the state of India more especially, with reference to its degrading superstitions, and the wide field which that country offers for the exercise of your benevolence and zeal.

Before I enter upon this topic, however, allow me, in support of the views maintained by those who have already addressed you, to supply a very striking example, which seems to have escaped them, from our own history, of the wonderful and beneficial change produced by the circulation of the Scriptures in countries where they before existed, but only as a sealed book : because, from what *has* been, may very fairly be inferred what may *again* be the result of such a step. The period to which I allude is that of our great, and as it is often most appropriately called, glorious Reformation. The principal feature of that great work was to break down the spiritual dominion then exercised by the Pope, and to place the Scriptures in the hands of all classes, in a language intelligible to all, with perfect freedom, not merely of perusal, but of interpretation or acceptation of its contents. And what was the issue ? Why, that men becoming possessed of what was hitherto sealed up from their inspection, exercised their diligence in examining, and their judgment in interpreting it for themselves ; so that the dominion of the priesthood was destroyed, and religion became what it ought every where to be, a free and unfettered communion between the soul and its Creator. Take, thus, the picture of England, Holland, Germany, and other northern countries then under Papal sway, and lay it beside a picture of the same countries since they have been emancipated from the priestly yoke, and see the amazing difference : in the one case, bigotry and ignorance were the greatest characteristics of the age ; in the other, liberality and intelligence have happily succeeded : and to this no single event has, perhaps, more powerfully contributed than that which placed the Scriptures in every man's hands, with full liberty to judge for himself of all that they contained. In short, in comparing, even at the present moment, the several countries of the earth that are nominally under what are called Christian Governments, you will find that where the Bible is still withheld from the inspection of the people at large, and where even the few who are permitted to read it are obliged to shape their faith according to the dictates of their spiritual teachers, as is especially the case in Spain and Portugal, bigotry and ignorance still prevail ; while in those countries in which the Scriptures are most freely circulated, and where religious liberty is most extensively enjoyed, as is the case in England and America, there the very opposite picture is presented, and there freedom, intelligence, morality, and happiness, are the fruits which it produces. But let me pass to the condition of that portion of the globe which I have been more especially called upon to describe.

The first of the eastern countries which it was my lot to visit, as a traveller, was Egypt ; and it was, of course, impossible for me to tread the banks of the Nile, from among the bulrushes of which Moses was taken up by the daughter of Pharaoh,—to traverse the land of Goshen, or cross the Red Sea to the Desert of Wandering,—to behold the stupendous monuments, in the erection of which, it is at least probable, that the enslaved and captive Israelites were employed—and not to feel an additional interest in every thing connected with its scriptural history, or to be indifferent to the state and condition of the people among whom those Scriptures were still held in esteem. The government of that country, as you are aware, is in the hands of Mohammedans, by whom Christianity is rejected, and its professors subjected to disabilities and oppressions. Accordingly, the circulation of the Scriptures is extremely limited in Egypt. Nevertheless, inasmuch as there are still a number of professing Christians, of the several sects denominated as Greeks, Armenians, Copts, Nestorians, Maronites, &c., having religious establishments and places of worship in Egypt, the introduction of the Scriptures among them might not be a work of difficulty, and from them it might the more readily pass into the hands of those who would be otherwise inaccessible ; while in consequence of the degraded and corrupt state of the Christians themselves, it may be said that the Scriptures, if presented in a language in which they could be familiarly read, would be likely to effect as great a change among them as among those who profess not their faith ; for scarcely any thing can be conceived more remote from the simple purity of Christianity, than the rites, ceremonies, and dogmas designated by that name in the East.

The countries that I next visited, and which may be well associated together on this occasion as one, namely, Palestine and Mesopotamia, possessed a still stronger Scriptural interest than even Egypt ; for, while gazing on the walls and towers of Jerusalem,—crossing the brook Kedron by the Pool of Siloam,—treading the Mount of Olives, and entering Bethany and Bethpage, Bethelehem and Nazareth,—who could be indifferent to the Sacred Volume that recorded all the events of which these spots were the scenes and witnesses ?—If I bathed myself in the waters of the Jordan, or lingered on the shores of the Dead Sea,—if I hung with delight on the glorious prospects from Lebanon, or reposed among the bowers of Damascus,—in short, whatever path my footsteps traced, whether it led me through the ruins of Tyre and Sidon, or the fields and vallies of remoter solitudes, every rock and every eminence, every brook and every rivulet, had its own especial history, and roused up a thousand Scriptural associations. Yet here, too, as in Egypt, the government is in the hands of Mohammedans ; and though there are not wanting professing Christians in considerable number and variety, both as residents and as pilgrims, yet the Scriptures are so little known and understood among them, and so little vigilance is exercised by those whose duty it is to be always active in the cause, that they correspond exactly with the description given by the prophet, when he speaks of the "shepherds that sleep" while the fold is in danger, and the "watchmen who slumber" while the citadel is invaded.

In Mesopotamia, the darkness is even greater still. At Ur of the Chaldees, the birth-place of Abraham, and over all the country beyond the great river Euphrates, Christianity is less and less to be found, even in name, and still more remote from its original purity in character ; so much so, that there is one sect who consider themselves to be in some degree Christians, as they profess to follow a gospel of St. John ; but their claim to that appellation may be judged from the fact of their actually paying divine honours to Satan, and quoting a passage of this gospel in their defence. The awful ruins of Nineveh and Babylon stand upon the banks of their respective streams, the Tigris and Euphrates, in all the silent gloom of utter desolation ; and traversing their vast remains with the Scriptural descriptions of their grandeur fresh in my recollection, it was impossible not to feel all the sadness which characterized the captive Israelites of old, when, instead of singing the songs of Zion as in happier days—they hung their harps upon the willows, and sat themselves down by the waters of Babylons and wept.

In passing from thence into Persia, there was not much improvement, although there a ray of hope had begun to illumine the general darkness. In every part of that country, the European character is so highly respected, that almost any measure coming from Europeans, and Englishmen especially, would be sure to meet with less resistance than in any other part of the Mohammedan world. While Persia is, there-fore, quite as destitute as all the other countries of Asia, in a moral and religious sense, it appears to me that it offers a less obstructed channel for the introduction of a great hange in this particular respect, than any other of the surrounding states. I may add to this general assertion a fact which came under my own personal observation, and which tends to shew what might be done in Persia by judicious men and judicious measures. The Rev. Henry Martyn, whose name must be familiar to most of you, and whose character stands high wherever his name is known, was in Persia, just previous to the period of my passing through that country ; and at Shiraz, I met with several Mollahs, or teachers of the Mohammedan faith, from whom I learnt that Mr. Martyn's life and conversation had produced the most surprising effect in softening the usual hostility between Mohammedans and Christians ; that the most learned Muftis had conversed freely with him, on points of faith and doctrine, and that they had come to the conclusion, that there were not such insuperable barriers between them as they had at first conceived. Such a step as this is most important, because from the moment those who are in error can be brought to listen patiently to the truth, hopes may be entertained of its final triumph ; for, as Milton has beautifully observed, "though all the winds of doctrine were let loose upon the earth, so truth be among them, we need not fear. Let her and falsehood grapple : who ever knew her put to the worst, in a free and open encounter ?"

From Persia I proceeded to India, and there I remained as a resident for several years. It might be expected that in a country so long under our dominion as that has been, the same backwardness with respect to the spread of truth and sound religion would not have been observed ; but I regret to say that while in India the reign of superstition is more widely spread, and more terrible in its degrading effects, than in any of the countries I have yet mentioned ; the obstacles thrown in the way of those who are impatient to substitute a better order of things, are quite as great as in either of them. Let me mention only one or two of the revolting practices which their super-stition engendered, and still upholds, and you will then see what a vast field a hundred millions of beings, so immersed in darkness, must afford for British benevolence and Christian reformation.

The most popularly known of these Indian rites, is that of the burning of Hindoo widows on the funeral piles of their husbands. To such a frightful extent is this carried, that, in the course of ten years, according to a parliamentary report made on this sub-ject, nearly seven thousand Indian widows were burnt alive ! Even if the practice were undoubtedly enjoined by their sacred books, and were always performed volun-tarily, there is something in it so revolting to humanity, that it ought not to be per-mitted ; but it rests upon very doubtful authority even in their own writings, one of the most learned of their Brahmins having written several works to show, that the practice is at least but optional, and of comparatively recent date ; and in by far the greater number of cases, it is not voluntary, the parties being drugged with opiates, deluded by priests, and terrified by threats, into compliance. In addition to this they are frequently bound down with cords and ligatures to the funeral pile, so that their escape would be impossible, however much they might desire it ; and in those few in-stances in which the parties have been left unbound, and have leaped off the pile as soon as the flames began to envelop their slender frames, they have been most inhu-manly seized by the fanatic by-standers, and flung back again into the flames, with their scorched and mangled limbs dropping off from their bodies, thus expiring amidst the most horrid and protracted tortures that the human imagination can conceive !

And all this under the sanction, by the authority, and with the countenance and protection, of a Government calling itself Christian!—that of the East India Company.

What appears to me to add greatly to the horror of this diabolical sacrifice, is the consideration that it puts out of existence those who are the most worthy to live; as, whatever there may be of voluntary submission to this rite on the part of those who are its victims, must spring from one of these motives : either first, the devotional motive, or a willingness to offer up life, and all that can endear it, rather than forfeit the hope of future happiness, or incur the displeasure of the Supreme Being,—which though their faith be grounded in error, they may most sincerely believe, and act upon in the way they think most conducive to that end ; or secondly, the domestic motive, an extreme attachment to the object of their affections, and an unwillingness to survive him who was not merely their husband and protector, but their best and only friend ; or, thirdly, the social motive, or an abhorrence of living in a society without a full participation in its honours and enjoyments, and an unwillingness to have their lives prolonged, if they could only live as outcasts, repudiated by their relatives und families, and despised even by strangers as well as friends. These appear to me to be the only conceivable motives of such a submission to suffering on the part of the unfortunate, but still amiable and interesting, widows of the East. And yet, surely, these are motives which do them honour, and which prove what excellent materials must exist in a society capable of producing such instances of self-devotion, for the construction of a better and happier community. For who is there among us that does not honour, with the highest distinction, the female penitent and devotee, who, rather than do that which should forfeit her the hope of heaven, would sacrifice her life, and all that she held at her disposal ? Who is there among us that does not equally honour with our sympathy and our admiration, the young and affectionate widow, whose sorrow at the death of her husband and lord so surpasses all ordinary bounds, as to evince itself in paroxysms of grief that drive the unhappy victim sometimes to the verge of insanity, and leave her in such a state as will permit her to see nothing but perpetual gloom in the prospect of the future, so that if the sublime faith of Christianity had not taught her that self-destruction was a crime against the awful majesty of the Creator, she would be as much disposed as the Indian widow to sink at once into the grave that seems about to close upon the remains of all that the earth held dear in her estimation? Who, I may also ask, can there be among us, that does not equally honour the female, be she virgin, wife, or widow, whose strongest feeling, next to devotion, is her love of an unsullied reputation, who could not bear the thought of sustaining existence otherwise than honourably, and who would rather die a thousand deaths, than live to have the finger of scorn pointed at her as one who had outlived her untainted name? And shall all these be deemed *virtues* in Britain, and *vices* in Hindoostan? It is impossible. The motive is in both cases equally honourable ; and the mis-direction of that motive in the case of the Indian widows, appears to me only to strengthen their claims on our sympathy and commiseration, as where so good a soil exists, the seed cannot be sown in vain.

The other abominable rite of which I shall now speak (for I confine myself to the two prominent ones, although there are a hundred that might be detailed), is the pilgrimage to Juggernaut. This is the name of an idol which is worshipped at a place called Pooree, on the sea-coast of Orissa, between Madras and Bengal, and to whose shrine pilgrimages are made from different parts of India. The lives annually sacrificed to this monstrous idol surpass all credibility ; but it may be sufficient to say, that the approach to the temple is indicated, for fifty miles on all sides round, by the mangled and decaying carcases of those who have perished as his victims. Will it be believed that the East India Company, not content with remaining merely indifferent spectators of all these atrocities, which, of itself, would, I think, be sufficient to warrant their condemnation—absolutely make these horrid and revolting rites a source of pecuniary profit to themselves? Nay, more ; not only do they receive all the revenues arising from fees and tribute paid to the idol, themselves defraying the costs of his maintenance, providing him with meat and drink and clothing, and keeping up a brothel, or establishment of courtezans and prostitutes, for the service of the priests ! paying, therefore, the wages of sin and death, and placing the surplus among the unholy and polluted gains which swell their common treasury ; but they go farther still, and, in order to augment these gains, they have organized a body of pilgrim-hunters, under the name of Pundas and Purharees, whose especial business it is to go abroad all over the country, and traverse it in every direction, in search of pilgrims, for the purpose of bringing them in companies to Juggernaut. Lest the ordinary motive of superstition should be insufficient to induce these wretched emissaries to perform their tasks with proper zeal, the East India Company have superadded the motive of what, in this instance, may be truly called "base lucre;" for these pilgrim-hunters are actually paid, at a fixed rate per head, for every fresh victim they can bring! They accordingly extend their excursions for hundreds of miles from the bloody and revolting scene; and wherever they find a man who has a sufficient sum of money in his possession, the hard earnings, perhaps, of years of industry and frugality, they seize on him as their victim, persuade him to leave his wife and family, and go on a pilgrimage to Juggernaut. He quits his home, with the promise, perhaps of a speedy return; but, alas! the hour for his recrossing the threshold of his cottage never arrives. He is led, by these delusive guides, to the idol and his car. In the expense of his journey, in fees to the India Company, and in the premium, or head-money, paid to his decoyers, every farthing will be exhausted. He enters the temple, joins in the horrid din of its filthy and brutal uproar, comes out of it naked and pennyless, and, before three days are passed over his head, perishes for want, in the very precincts of the temple, where thousands are annually expended in the grossest sensualities! and the whole plain, for fifty miles round in every direction, is literally whitened with the bones of the victims thus offered up as sacrifices to this most monstrous of all superstitions, or, should I not rather say, to its chief supporters and abettors—the bigotry and fanaticism of the Brahmins, and the heartlessness and avariciousness of the East India Company?

These things are so extraordinary, as well as so revolting, that I should have almost hesitated to put my own reputation for veracity in jeopardy, by even alluding to them at all, were I not speaking under the sanction of the highest and most unquestionable authorities. In a very copious and excellent Report of a Speech made at the East India House, only a year or two ago, by a Proprietor of East India Stock, Mr. Poynder; in a very valuable little volume, entitled "India's Cries to British Humanity," written by Mr. Peggs, an inhabitant of Coventry, who resided some time in India: in a still more recent work, entitled "Reflections on the Present State of British India," published by Hurst and Chance, of London, in the present year, 1829; and in the various Parliamentary Papers that have been, from time to time, produced on this subject, all these facts are stated in detail, on the authority of men in the service of the East India Company itself, and in such a way as to render its accuracy and authenticity beyond all doubt.

And shall the Christians and philanthropists of Britain remain silent and inactive under such a a state of things as this? It would be so deep a reproach to them to suppose it, that I will not, even for a moment, entertain the bare supposition. That the existing government of India, with all its repeated professions of a readiness to assist in the spread of Christianity in the East, have no such wish really at heart, I could adduce a thousand proofs; but their supporting and profiting by such a superstition as this that I have just described, will, no doubt, be deemed sufficient. Let me add to this the fact, that the largest establishment of Missionaries now in India, those at Serampore, were obliged to plant themselves in this foreign settlement, (for it belongs to the Danes,) rather than in Calcutta, or any other spot under the dominion of the English; because, in the foreign settlement they were allowed perfect toleration, and the enjoyment of a free press; whereas, in the English settlement they could only be tolerated from day to day, with the liability to be transported at a moment's warning, without trial or hearing of any kind whatever, and for any reason or no reason, as the Government need not condescend to give any to those whom they banish; besides being subject to a rigid censorship or control over the press, which gives to the India Company's servants the same monopoly of religion as their masters enjoy of political power and trade; which, therefore, enables them to compel every writer to shape his opinions and expressions according to the Government standard of orthodoxy, (not allowing even Mohammed to be called a false prophet, though any Mohammedan in India may preach in any mosque of the country that Christ and his apostles were impostors): and which, if Christians should be sufficiently imbued with their Divine Master's spirit, to love truth better than falsehood, and to speak plainly and honestly, whether those in authority liked such qualities or not, gives to those invested with rule in that country, power to suppress any publication they dislike ; first interrupting the public good it may be doing, and then inflicting ruin by the destruction of all the property of those who may be instrumental in doing it. The last law passed on that subject in India, the work of Mr. John Adam, during his brief and temporary rule of a few weeks only, but never yet repealed, gives the Government the power to prohibit, not merely the printing and publishing, but also the selling, distributing, or even lending for perusal, any book or paper whatever, whether printed in England or elsewhere, to which the Governor-General, in any fit of caprice or ill-humour, may happen to take a dislike !

This, Sirs, is the actual state of things in India at the present moment : and the monstrous and absurd pretence upon which it is attempted to be defended is, that if knowledge be spread among the natives of India, they will be alarmed at our intended interference with their superstitions, and this will lead them to rebel and expel us from the country. In such an assembly as this, I need hardly waste a moment in combatting so monstrous and untenable a position. We all know that increased knowledge produces increasing benefits ; and as to the danger to be apprehended from any reasonable, persuasive, and legislative measures, to interfere with the superstitions of the natives, I need only refer you to the publications I have already named, to show you that in every case in which this has yet been done (and they are numerous) the change has been effected without a murmur ; and that, according to the testimony and opinions of the best informed among the civil and military servants of the East India Company, whose evidence has been given on the subject, the two revolting practices that I have already described to you, the burning of human beings alive, and the sacrifice of victims at the shrine of Juggernaut, might be as easily abolished by a mere decree embodying the wish of the Government, as was the destruction of female infants in Guzerat, and the throwing children into the Ganges at Saugor.

But I will not detain you longer than to express my hope that the earnest attention with which you have listened to these details, may be an indication of that zeal with which you will follow up such measures as seem best to you for amending the existing state of things. In the circulation of the Scriptures where the people most need them, you are actuated by a desire to increase the temporal, and secure the eternal happiness of those to whom it is presented. In my humble, but not altogether different sphere, I am anxious to attain the same great ends, by other though not opposite means. In seeking to arouse the dormant spirit of this great and wealthy nation to a due sense of the importance of destroying the present, and substituting a better system of commercial and political government for India, I have really no personal motives whatever. I am neither a merchant, a ship-owner, nor a manufacturer ; and as to pecuniary benefit, I know of none that I could derive from the adoption of my views respecting India to-morrow. But, as a philanthropist merely, without reference to any particular system of speculative belief, it is impossible not to feel an interest in the fate of a hundred millions of human beings, be they in what quarter of the globe they may. As a patriot, that interest becomes greatly increased by the consideration that these hundred millions are under British dominion. And, as a Christian, the interest rises still higher, by contrasting the advanced condition of those countries in which Christianity is most pure, with those in which it is still encumbered and disfigured with the grossest corruptions ; and, therefore, I desire strongly to see the simple yet sublime precepts of the Gospel supplanting the degrading and demoralizing superstitions of Idolatry, in every portion of the habitable globe. I believe good political institutions and free commercial intercourse to be among the best pioneers in the cause of morality and true religion. Where the former are established, justice will hold her seat, and tranquillity and contentment be found ; where the latter is permitted, knowledge will flow in from a thousand different directions, and through a thousand different channels, until its united streams so overspread the land, that those things only which are just, and true, and holy, can retain their place in general estimation ; and, believing that both your labours and mine will each, in their respective spheres, conduce, under the blessing of God, to this great end, I rejoice at the occasion which has now presented itself for our acting together in so holy a cause.

The close of this Speech was followed with loud and long-continued cheers from all parts of the assembly.—*York Herald.*

E

REPLY TO MR. SADLER,

Introduced at the Close of the Lecture on the East India Monopoly, delivered at Whitby, on the 28th of September, 1829.

The intimate connexion between this portion of my exposure of the evils of the East India Company's Monopoly, and the Shipping Interest of Great Britain, leads me, by a very natural transition, to advert to the Speech recently delivered in this Hall, and to many of the auditors who now fill it, when Mr. Sadler attempted to denounce, in general terms, the whole system of Free Trade, and to claim for his supporters, in the monstrous proposition of reverting back again to the Monopolies of the restrictive system, the Ship-builders and Ship-owners of Whitby, This appeared to me so inconceivably absurd, that I thought there must have been some misrepresentation of his views, or some misconception of their purport; and it was not until I saw the copious report of his speech, put forth with all the apparent accuracy of an official or authorised version, that I could give full credit to the idea of the Shipping Interest being appealed to, in favour of monopolies and restrictions.

It is remarkable that, but a few weeks before, the Ship-builders, Ship-owners, and Merchants of Greenock,—a port certainly no less eminent than Whitby, whether as respects its population or its tonnage, whether as regards the number and size of its ships, or the variety and importance of the voyages in which they are employed—gave a similar entertainment to myself, at which the chief magistrate presided, on the very opposite view to that which seems to have actuated those who invited Mr. Sadler to Whitby :—namely, in testimony of their conviction that the Free Trade to India, into which they were the first to enter, had been productive of the very highest advantage to the Shipping Interest : and that, instead of reverting back to the monopolies and restrictions, as Mr. Sadler recommends, the greatest benefit that could be conferred on the Ship-builders, Ship-owners, and Merchants of every port in the Kingdom, would be to destroy the giant Monopoly of the East India Company, which still excludes British ships and British seamen from the most valuable part of the globe—China and the Eastern Seas—where the Americans have, for years past, been reaping an abundant harvest ; the Ship-owners of Boston and Salem growing rich at our expense, and the seamen at New York and Marblehead mocking us with derision, and rejoicing in our folly.

Let me add, however, that the people of Greenock were unanimous in their views, or, at least, that no dissentient voice was heard ; whereas, at Whitby, so far from unanimity prevailing, it is well known that Mr. Moorsom's excellent pamphlet, which exhibited in their true light the causes that had operated to lessen the employment for English ships, and which pointed out the only cure for the evil, namely, the still further extension of the principles of Free Trade—represented the sentiments of many other of the principal residents in Whitby ; and of the dread entertained of its power, among those who wished it had never appeared, some idea may be formed from the fact, that two of the copies, sent by the printer, at the author's request, to Mr. Sadler's host, were returned to him as rejected, and the copy sent to the same individual for Mr. Sadler himself, intercepted, so as to deprive him of the opportunity of becoming acquainted with its contents.

I advert to this fact, however, principally to shew, that when the honourable member for Newark pretended, in allusion to this pamphlet, not to have seen it until he entered the room, and on that to ground an apology for his hasty and imperfect analysis of its contents, it was not for want of opportunity, as it was gratuitously and extensively circulated throughout the town, and was in the hands of all those who had uncourteously and, let me add, illiberally, rejected it.

If he had remained among you but a few days,—and as his retreat is at Redcar, but a few miles distant, that might, no doubt, have been easily accomplished,—I should, certainly, have taken some pains to increase his information on the Shipping Question, of which he appears to know so little : and, hostile as he declares himself to be to any innovation on that portion of the wisdom of our ancestors which established the Monopoly of the East India Company, I should have claimed his alliance, as one of its most determined opponents, on a ground on which, I think, he must have been compelled either to recant all his former lamentations, or to co-operate with me. He condemns the system of Mr. Huskisson, because it brings the foreigner up to a level with the Englishman. What then will he say of the system of the India Company, which altogether excludes the unlicensed Englishman from the interior of India, where the unlicensed foreigner may roam at pleasure ; and shuts out from China and its rich markets all English ships and seamen except their own ; while foreigners, of every nation, are free to enter them without hindrance or molestation, and while Americans, more especially, are acquiring vast wealth in channels of maritime commerce, from which all British ships and seamen are pertinaciously excluded ? (*Cheers.*)

Now Mr. Huskisson's system of reciprocity, be its effects what they may, is forced upon us by the legislators of foreign countries, who, as long as they are sovereigns in their own respective territories, will make such laws as suit themselves, and who accordingly say to us—" If you impose restrictions upon such of our vessels as enter your ports, we will impose equal restrictions upon such of our vessels as enter our harbours. If you will employ any of your shipping in foreign trade, it can only be by consent of us foreigners : and we decree, whether it be agreeable to you or not, that, unless you admit us to an unrestricted intercourse between our own ports and yours, we will close up our harbours to your navigation, and destroy your foreign trade entirely." What answer can we make to this ?—We are not at war with all the world, and thereby enabled to command the maritime carrying trade of all nations. We are, happily, at peace, and every coast that borders on the sea, sends forth its fleets and squadrons. If in the mere coasting trade of the British Isles, and the intercourse between Great Britain and her own possessions, sufficient employment could be found for all the tonnage now possessed by us, we might then reject with impunity all overtures or propositions of foreigners. But it is notorious, that not half of our shipping could be advantageously employed in these channels only. The Baltic and the Cattegat—the Mediterranean and the Euxine—the Gulfs of Lyons and of Mexico—the Orinoco and La Plata,—are all insufficient to exhaust our mercantile marine ; and yet to none of these can we trade without the consent of the several nations that occupy their borders, which consent they have the right as well as the power to fetter with such restrictions as they please. It is utterly impossible, therefore, however much we might desire it, for us to force those foreign nations to receive our ships into their ports without the imposition of heavy burthens, unless we will agree to receive their vessels into our own, upon equal terms:—so that unless the Ship-owners of England will consent to limit themselves to the trade along their own coasts, and with their own possessions,—and be ready to burn all the ships which may be found over and above the number necessary for this purpose (which would be about half the tonnage of the kingdom) there is no alternative but that of Free Trade, and equal duties, in all foreign commerce at least.

In the reciprocity system of Mr. Huskisson, therefore, we are acting under a necessity imposed on us by the inconvenient, perhaps, but, certainly, the very natural and defensible conduct of foreigners who *lift themselves* up to our level, whether we approve of it or not. But in the monopoly system of the East India Company, no such foreign influence exists.—It is an evil wholly inflicted on us by our own Legislature, for foreigners have nothing to enforce in the matter : and is the greater, inasmuch as even the few for whom it is professedly granted, derive no permanent advantage from it ; while every Ship-owner, nay every individual in the country, not belonging to the East India Company, is deeply injured ; and from the wreck and ruin of their interests, the unfettered foreigner goes on accumulating every year fresh stores of wealth, and establishing himself in new channels of enterprize and profit, from which it will soon be impossible to dislodge him.

Does Mr. Sadler know all this, and yet contend for no alteration in the East India Company's Monopoly ? If he knows it not, then is he unfitted, by his want of knowledge, for a representative of the Shipping Interests of England : if he does know it, and in the same breath contends that the Free Trade, which brings the foreigner up to our own level, ought to be condemned, while the Monopoly which puts the same foreigner far above that level, and makes *him* the freeman, and the Englishman the slave, should be upheld—then is Mr. Sadler doubly traitorous to the cause he attempts to defend ;—the single treachery being a pretended knowledge of that of which we are ignorant,—but the more than double treachery consisting in a perverse concealment or misapplication of knowledge actually possessed, to the injury of the very cause it is calculated most to serve.

Let me, however, for a moment refer to a few of the passages of Mr. Sadler's address; not as he affected to treat Mr. Moorsom's, professing not to have even seen it till the moment of its being commented on; but after having deliberately read and examined every portion, of which I shall speak. It will of course be quite beside my purpose to advert to those parts of this oration, which, though delivered in Whitby, related to any thing but the subject which Mr. Sadler was expected to dilate upon. I shall confine myself to that portion which more especially affects your peculiar interests; and which, it would appear, from the report of Mr. Sadler's speech, that the honourable gentleman had nearly forgotten. There are some, indeed, who think that his reputation would have suffered nothing by the omission; since, full as is the whole with fallacies, the small portion devoted to the Shipping Question is thickly strewed with error in almost every line. It would, perhaps, have been something like the play of Hamlet, with the part of the Prince of Denmark omitted by particular desire: but it would have saved the author from the imputation now inevitable, that of pretending to treat familiarly a subject of which he knew not even the rudiments, with a degree of presumption almost without a parallel in the annals of political declamation. He attempts, it is true, to deprecate criticism, by affecting merely to advert to the Shipping Question as a thing that has just occurred to him *en passant*, and sets out by observing that he knew nothing whatever of the manner in which the documents representing the tonnage of the country at different periods was made up; whether they included Steam-vessels or not. But, one naturally asks, why, in this state of avowed ignorance, attempt to build up a system, with utter contempt for the most important part of it, a knowledge of the facts on which it ought to be founded? He says, indeed, "without any appeal to documents whatever, I am *fully certain* that to allow full scope to the reciprocity system in regard to Shipping, cannot but be fatal to prosperity."—But Mr. Sadler's *certainty*, however full it may be to his own mind, is a very inadequate substitute for facts and proofs.—If his convictions were built on these, it would have been easy to have communicated them, and they might have carried conviction to others also. If his certainty was not so founded, then it is as utterly worthless as any other conviction clinging still to error. Still, however, though he knows nothing whatever of the way in which any of the documents respecting the Shipping Interest are made up, and cannot, therefore, discriminate between those that represent the tonnage as increasing, or those that shew it to be on the decline:—he rejects the former, and adopts the latter, merely because he wishes to make some shew of cause for lamentation and weeping. In the amount of the tonnage belonging to Whitby, there is no doubt a decline; as there is in the amount of the tonnage belonging to the Navy—some of the largest and finest ships of which are to be seen dismantled in the harbours of Plymouth and Portsmouth, Deptford and Sheerness: and from the self same cause. One of the great branches of employment for the ships of Whitby was the transport-service. Fleets of 300 and 400 sail of ships, conveying or waiting upon armed expeditions in all parts of the world, was no unusual sight during the war: and the fortunes derived by the Ship-owners of Whitby, among others, from ships employed in the transport service, at high prices, with cheap equipments, and little occupation for wear and tear, must have been, no doubt, very agreeable to those who accumulated them. But to lament that the ships and men thus employed had fallen off in number and amount, and to infer from this the symptoms of national decay, is just about as wise a proceeding as to lament the falling off in the number of line of battle-ships and frigates that were formerly employed; the melancholy decline which has taken place in the number of men once filling the ranks of our gallant army; and the still more deplorable defalcation in the consumption of gunpowder and cannon balls. Alas! that innovation should ever have disturbed these halcyon dreams! that either our fleets or our constitution, both of which Mr. Sadler tells us was founded by our great Alfred, should ever have been broken in upon! and that we cannot again return to those golden days, when it was denounced as an unwarrantable luxury for a church dignitary to have clean straw placed in his drawing room every day, while nobles and princes were content to change it once a week; or when Scotch herrings and English brawn were deemed sufficient for the costliest table, and ale was the only liquor that sparkled on the board,

It seems, however, that though the old English archers, and those who made their weapons, were lawfully displaced by the musqueteers and cannoniers who succeeded them, and the mixture of charcoal and saltpetre superseded the consumption of the ashen arrow or the beechen bow; though steam-ships have as legally superseded, in many instances, those which could not be made to sail in the winds' eye; and fuel and water have succeeded to canvas, rope, and wood; though all this has taken place without any complaint of the injustice of such supercession, the ship-owners of Whitby, whose transports are unemployed, are, by a mere relaxation of the navigation act, as much robbed and plundered as if their ships were sunk, burnt, and destroyed. Hear Mr. Sadler's own words, "that act (the navigation act) formed an essential part of the naval constitution of England, so to speak; it was on the faith of that sacred engagement—for sacred it had become in the sight of successive generations of Englishmen—that you, gentlemen, (the ship-owners of Whitby) embarked your property, which is now, much of it, (the unemployed portion of their ships) sacrificed and lost, by as *direct an act of spoliation*, as if the same power had seized a portion of your estates, which you hold only under the same sanction, that of the law!" Can any thing be more grossly ignorant, or more disingenuous than this? If the laws of England were like those of the Medes and Persians, any change made in them for the first time might excite an outcry; but in a country where old acts are repealed, and new ones enacted, almost every day during the sitting of Parliament—to hear a member of that Parliament designate a deliberate revision of any law, after infinite investigation and debate, as " a direct act of spoliation and plunder," leaves one in doubt whether most to admire the ignorance or the arrogance of the speaker.

But what could be expected from one whose previous habits and pursuits can have given him no *practical* knowledge of any thing relating to Shipping; and who despises all knowledge derived from theory; who is utterly unacquainted with the documents relating to the subject, and even of the manner of their being compiled; and who does not seem even to know (though he says he has always *understood* it, from common report, to be so) that Whitby is a noted ship-building station? He had visited it once before; yet, though this arose from a wish to view so interesting a spot, he remained only for a *few hours*, and yet pretended in that short time to become intimately acquainted with its splendid prosperity in every branch. He comes a second time, and at a long interval, not because he again wished to add to his deficient knowledge from the stores of others, or to communicate any thing of his own to them, but because he is *invited* to lament over the fallen fortunes of Whitby, and the decline of the Shipping Interest; and, then he accordingly observes nothing around him but proofs of misery and decay!

Gentlemen, is this really so? Is there any town or port of the kingdom—or I would say of the world—that contains so much wealth, within the same extent of population, or which every where exhibits greater proofs of equally spread comfort, and the total absence of suffering or privation of any kind? I have not, during a much longer stay among you than Mr. Sadler ventured to make, seen a single individual in rags; not one whose countenance exhibited signs of hunger; not one who appeared houseless or destitute, and not one unemployed, or asking alms. Does not, indeed, Mr. Sadler himself more accurately describe the state of your town and population, when he says, " The ship-builders and merchants of Whitby have lived in other and better times, and are, as I understand, as a body, *wealthy in an unusual degree*, and can, therefore, sustain these reverses, or leave the business, though at great sacrifices, which subjects them to such loss." This is, I believe, the true state of the case: but it is utterly inconsistent with the lamentations poured out in other parts of the same oration, or the pretended commiseration for the unhappy and unemployed workmen, who are not here to enjoy the sympathy manifested in their behalf, but, like the seamen and soldiers whom the peace threw out of employment, or like manufacturers of gunpowder and cannon, have gradually dispersed themselves in those quarters, and turned their industry into those channels in which employment presented itself to them.

I may refer you, however, as a very striking proof of what the ship-builders of Whitby really desire, and really anticipate, in the opening of India and China, to the ten or twelve ships that are now actually building in your stirring and busy dock-yards, which even Mr. Sadler himself could not have failed to have seen were not idle and deserted, as he pretended to describe them; two of these lying on the stocks immediately opposite the window of the house in which Mr. Sadler himself resided, and one of a large and beautiful class, belonging to his host, destined expressly for the China Trade; both with their projecting prows apparently impatient to plunge into the liquid element, and stem their unfettered way towards the East; one of them with a bust of Lord Eldon at its head, as if about to lead the way; and, I confess, that when the venerable chief shall assemble his adherents, for the purpose of breaking down the restraints which now impede our commerce with the East, I shall be ready to hail him as a leader, and number myself among the most faithful of his followers. (*Loud cheers.*)

Mr. Sadler concludes as he began, by denouncing, what he calls " the modern system," and especially that part of it which seems to be pretty current, " the practice of *buying where you can buy cheapest.*" He considers this a fatal error: but whether he acts upon the opposite maxim in his own affairs of trade, does not appear. Any man who should follow Mr. Sadler's implied advice and buy where he could buy dearest, would have but a short career. And yet this is the system by which this friend to Monopoly, and enemy to Free Trade would pretend to enrich England, and impoverish the rest of the world! If Mr. Sadler will persist in talking of the Shipping Interest, he should, certainly, not address himself to the seamen and sea-ports of England, where the youngest cabin-boy might become his teacher. He might, perhaps, be heard uncontradicted on

> ' The barren plains
> Of Sericana, where Chineses drive,
> With sails and wind, their cany waggons light.'

For on this ' windy sea of land,' (as Milton most expressively calls it), he might ' wander up and down alone,' and waste his poison on the desert air. But there is not a ship-master, or a ' sea-boy, on the high and giddy mast,' that would not laugh his doctrine to scorn. (*Loud cheers.*)

Who, indeed, can there be, whether a seaman or not, that does not perceive the absurdity of a system which affects to foster the Shipping Interest by prohibiting all foreign commodities, and dictating to foreign nations the terms on which they should trade? Indeed, it appears to me that of all the absurdities that were ever yet set forth as political axioms, the most absurd is that of Mr. Sadler, who calls upon the Shipping Interest of England to support a system which shall confine the people of this country to the produce of their own soil and industry, to the exclusion of all foreign commodities,—a system which would render ships perfectly unnecessary. It would be the best thing that could happen to the Shipping Interest to see the very reverse—to have nothing *but* foreign produce consumed in England, and all our own produce consumed abroad, for, then, twice the number of ships that are now in existence would be required. (*Loud cheers.*).

I have drawn so largely on your patience, however, during the *five* hours that you have honoured me with your unbroken attention, that I should be most unreasonable indeed were I to ask you to extend it to me for a still longer period, tempting as is the occasion presented me by the fallacies so easy to be exposed. I have confined myself, however, in this notice of Mr. Sadler's speech, to that which, though it ought to have been the most essential, was really the least prominent portion of it, I mean his *allusions*, for he scarcely ventured beyond these, to the question in which his auditors were mainly, if not exclusively, interested,—the Shipping Question. As the honourable gentleman, however, took occasion to quote largely, and from authors of deservedly high repute, in favor of his peculiar views, making even Adam Smith to be an advocate for restrictions and monopolies; and invoking the shade of Bacon, as a hater of innovation; while Locke and Addison were pressed into the advocacy of views the most opposed to the general tenor of their writings; I ought not to close without protesting against such a profanation. If the authority of Adam Smith be of any worth in Mr. Sadler's estimation, what becomes of all the denunciations which the latter continually delights to pour forth against the political economists, of which Adam Smith is the prince and chief? If Bacon, whose writings abound with the constant suggestion of innovations and changes, be a philosopher, in Mr. Sadler's estimation, what does he think of that fine passage in which he speaks with due contempt of those who value usage and established institutions above all improvement, and says,—" A froward retention of custom is as turbulent a thing as innovation; and they that reverence too much old times are but a scorn to the new." Really, if the writings of the ancients are to be ransacked in support of measures, and with reference to circumstances, altogether beyond their power to anticipate, it is time to oppose to this delusion the testimony of history and experience on the broadest scale; and by shewing what *has* been done by an encouragement of unfettered intercourse between nations of antiquity, to encourage the hope of what may be done, by following out the same wise course, among the nations of modern times. (*Cheers.*)

After the details which I have given you in the course of these Lectures, of all the objects of interest or importance in Palestine, you will not, I am sure, deem it irrelevant if I show you, from the most ancient authority in existence, that the vast wealth acquired by Tyre and Sidon, which gave birth to Carthage, and which exceeded in opulence and splendour all the marts of the ancient world, was wholly by means of foreign commerce. There was no landed interest at either of these places, for the territory occupied by both was scarcely larger than the Isle of Wight; the commerce was extensive and free; and foreign commodities, of every kind and description, were to be found in abundance in both. Let me refer you only to the eloquent, yet minutely detailed account, given of its trade and its riches, by the prophet Ezekiel, where you will see that there was scarcely a country of the then known world with which Tyre did not traffic, and scarcely a nation or a people who did not furnish wares, and merchandize, and traders to its port. Of the opulence, natural and individual, acquired by this freedom of trade, what further need be urged than the fact, that of Tyre and Sidon it was deemed an appropriate and characteristic description to say that their merchants were princes, and their traders the nobles of the earth.

Nor, while Hiram, King of Tyre, was thus enriching Phœnicia by his wise and liberal policy, was Solomon, the royal monarch of Judea, uninfluenced by the example. His foundation of Tadmor, in the Desert, subsequently called Palmyra, was made wholly for the encouragement of foreign commerce; and whenever the advantages of such commerce may be doubted, let it be answered, that this, and this alone, was sufficient to plant in the heart of the wilderness or desert, for so the site of Tadmor was at the period of its foundation, a city, which by the mere operation of foreign trade, without either a landed or a manufacturing interest—for there was not a hundred acres of cultivable soil within a hundred miles of its walls, or a single commodity manufactured within its gates,—rose to a degree of opulence and splendour to which history affords no parallel : and its splendid ruins, the magnificent representations of which are familiar almost to every one, attest, beyond all power of contradiction, or possibility of doubt, the true source of that wealth by which Solomon, in all his glory, was surrounded—namely, the vast foreign commerce which was maintained throughout the Mediterranean by the fleets that crowded the harbours of Tyre and Sidon—the extensive foreign trade prosecuted from Ezion Geber, by the Red Sea, to Tarshish, Ophir, and the Isles—and the equally rich and distant commerce carried on from India by the Persian Gulf and the Euphrates to Palmyra, from whence the foreign commodities of all the Eastern world were imported into Judea, and spread again throughout Egypt, Asia Minor, and Greece, enriching each by its exchange for the surplus natural produce, or the industry, of the respective countries into which it found its way.

If a further instance were needed, Alexandria is at hand to furnish it: a city founded by the Macedonian Conqueror whose name it bears, on as barren and forbidding a soil as it is possible to imagine, with an arid desert on all sides round, and with nothing to recommend it but its port and favourable position for foreign trade. By the operation of this alone—for the commerce with India was soon brought to pass through that channel—it attained, in a comparatively short space of time, a degree of wealth and splendour almost appalling by its magnificence, and surpassingly colossal in its features, even in that most wonderful of all wonderful countries, Egypt. In Alexandria, a city, one of the streets of which alone was five miles in length, and two thousand feet in breadth, were, at one time, upwards of four hundred theatres, or places of public entertainment! and the fleets that crowded its harbours, and the foreign merchandize (for the trade was almost wholly foreign), that enriched its inhabitants, were almost upon the same scale of magnitude and splendour.

In later times still, the Island, or the barren Rock of Ormuz, in the Persian Gulf, equally with all the places I have yet named, without a landed interest, a mere speck in the extent of its surface, and destitute alike of soil, verdure, water, or any of the materials of agricultural wealth, became, by its foreign commerce, a place of such extraordinary opulence, that the descriptions given of it by the early voyagers, appear almost fabulous, from their extravagance ; yet the corroborating testimony of all the best authorities of the times leave no doubt of its wealth and grandeur being almost unequalled ; a circumstance which our own Milton, whose appropriate application of his vast learning is as much a subject of admiration as the sublime genius of his muse, emphatically embodies in his magnificent poem, where, in order to assemble together all the images of greatest grandeur that even *his* imagination could collect, to shew the overwhelming wealth of the Satanic glory, he says—

> ' High on a throne of royal state, which far
> Outshone the wealth of Ormuz, or of Ind,
> Or where the gorgeous East, with richest hand,
> Showers on her kings Barbaric pearl and gold,
> Satan exalted sat.'

Another instance, and I have done ; but this, too, shall be one in which the effect is purely one of foreign trade, unsupported by any landed interest, and as independent also of fetters and restraints as each that has gone before it. I might have spoken of Florence and Livorno, of the mighty republics of Genoa and Venice, but your own re-collections will supply the chasm, while I advert only to this last link in the great chain of causes and effects, as one formed in our own day,—I mean the little Island of Singapore. While the whole Eastern world, with its population of 400 millions, has remained stationary in some parts, and retrograded in others, under the blighting influence of monopoly and restriction, the little Island of Singapore, scarcely marked on any of our charts fifty years ago, and when first known, known only as a nest of pirates, and a den of wild beasts, was selected as a fitting spot for trying the experiment of Free Trade in the East ; and in the short space of three or four years only, population flocked to it from all the surrounding shores, a town sprung as if by some magician's wand ; its harbour was crowded with fleets, bearing the flags of every maritime nation on the globe ; its merchants extending their operations in every direction with success ; and its population every day augmenting in numbers, wealth, and happiness. But this was so severe a censure on the system of monopoly, which reigned every where else in the East, that it could not be suffered to endure ; and, accordingly, the East India Company used their influence to check this prosperity, and succeeded : so true is, it, as has been most emphatically said, that ' Monopoly is the fruitful source of error, oppression, and crime.' (*Cheers.*)

Need I say more of Mr. Sadler's views, than that they are directly opposed to that wise and liberal system which was the cause of all the wealth enjoyed by Tyre, Sidon, Palmyra, Alexandria, Florence, Genoa, Venice, Holland, and every other country that was ever yet distinguished for its opulence, in ancient or in modern times ; and that he would carry us back to those monopolies and restrictions, which have reduced Spain and Portugal, from the splendour of their ancient days, when the sun never set on their dominions, to the degraded and miserable condition in which they now lie prostrate at the feet of the nations, a bye-word and a scorn to them all.

Sirs, our greatest error is, not in encouraging the branches of commerce that are already free, but in obstructing the growth of those that are deprived of the pure atmosphere in which alone they can flourish. Commerce is a tree that delights not only in a goodly soil, in copious moisture, and a ripening sun, but needs, above all, full scope and play, to stretch forth its mighty branches, to wave them freely in the wind, and let the circumambient air play round its leaves in fresh and invigorating freedom. It will then so spread itself abroad, that the nations of the earth may all repose beneath its shade ; while its branches extend so far and wide, that in their turn they again become the roots of new and ample trunks, resembling, in the language of Milton, the Eastern tree :—

> — ' Such, as at this day to Indians known,
> In Malabar, or Deccan, spreads her arms,
> Branching so broad and long, that in the ground

The bending twigs take root, and daughters grow
About the mother tree, a pillared shade,
High, over-arched, and echoing walks between.'

Yes! the parent tree is already planted, the soil is rich, the waters that British industry is ready to pour around its roots are abundant, the climate is congenial to its growth; the blighting atmosphere of Monopoly alone impedes its progress. Let the legislature of England but permit the free intercourse of her sons with those Eastern daughters, who now await their coming, and both the mother country and the offspring shall rejoice at the union. Let those over-arched and echoing walks' reverberate with the spirit-stirring sounds of Freedom, nor ever cease their echo till Monopoly be banished from the earth, and her very name held in remembrance only as a curse, that once afflicted mankind, but which can never again return. (*Loud cheers*).

At the close of this speech, which terminated a Lecture on the Evils of the East India Monopoly, occupying nearly five hours and a half in the delivery, and which was listened to throughout by a crowded auditory, with intense attention, interrupted only by occasional bursts of applause, a vote of thanks to Mr. Buckingham was voted, seconded, and carried by acclamation.—*York Courant.*

REPORT OF THE ADDRESS

Delivered at the Grand Masonic Dinner at Glasgow, held in the Town Hall, on Tuesday, the 18th of August, 1829.

The following is an accurate report of the speech of Mr. Buckingham, at the grand dinner given by the public authorities of Glasgow, in the Town Hall, on Tuesday, the 18th instant, at the close of the splendid Masonic procession and honours on laying the foundation of the New Bridge across the Clyde, (at which not less than 150,000 spectators were present,) R. Dalglish, Esq. Preceptor of Hutcheson's Hospital, in the Chair, Lawrence Hill, Esq. Chamberlain to the Hospital, croupier. Among the company were the Lord Provost and Magistrates, Mr. Campbell of Blythswood, Sir Walter Stirling of Faskine, a gentleman who, sixty years ago, was present at laying the foundation stone of Jamaica Street Bridge, the Sheriff, Principal Macfarlane, Rev. Dr. M'Leod, J. S. Buckingham, Esq., Mr. Cunningham of Lainshaw, Mr. John Grant of Nuttal, Mr. Wallace of Kelly, Colonel Hastings and the officers of the guard of the 12th Lancers and 42 Regiment, William and Walter Stirling, Esqs. of London, Captain Gray, 57th Regiment, Mr. Ewing of Dunoon Castle, Robert Finlay, Esq., Mr. Wilson of Thornley, Robert Stevenson, Esq., engineer, James Dennistoun, Esq., &c. &c.

In introducing the health of a distinguished visitor, Mr. Buckingham, the Chairman passed a high eulogium on the value of the recent public labours of this gentleman, in endeavouring to call the attention of the whole country, and of Glasgow in particular, to the importance of a more extended intercourse with our Eastern possessions.

The mere mention of Mr. Buckingham's name drew forth the loudest demonstrations of applause, and his health was drank with all the honours in a most enthusiastic manner.

Mr. Buckingham rose to return thanks, and addressing the Chairman, spoke nearly to the following effect:—Mr. Preceptor, and gentlemen, or if I might be permitted to use any other terms, I would rather say, Friends, fellow-countrymen, and brothers,—for in each of these relationships have I mingled with you to-day : in the first, with individuals whom I had the happiness to know, years ago, on the other side of the globe: in the second, as having come among you for a great public object, which requires the union of every branch of the country; and, in the third, as a free and accepted Mason, joining hands with the brethren of the Order, and forming one of your splendid procession, clothed in the appropriate emblems of purity which so truly characterise the end and aim of that sacred institution. If I were called upon to say in which of these relationships I felt most closely allied to you, I should find it difficult to answer. Feeling as I do, in all its superior force, the powerful charm of friendship, I acknowledge openly the strength and durability of the social tie. But the link of national union, and the love of country, is neither less powerful nor less enduring, and therefore the patriotic claim must have its share. While, as a mason, I yield to none in the enthusiastic ardour with which I honour its precepts, and endeavour to observe its rules; and therefore I feel the fraternal bond between us to be as strong as either the social or the patriotic. Instead, however, of singling out any one of these, as that in which I would prefer to address you, it will be more in harmony with my own views and wishes, that I should be permitted to thank and to salute you in all. It was the object of my visit here to-day, to assist in paying honours, and not to receive them. In this cordial spirit I have been borne along by the flowing tide of conviviality which has already set in so strong among us, maintaining my full share in that open expression of joyous hilarity, which the assembly, the occasion, and the manner of its being conducted, are so well calculated to inspire. Since, however, instead of my being permitted to remain in the crowd, by which I here feel myself so agreeably pressed on all sides around, you have condescended to draw the attention of your guests to the humblest among them all, and to single me out by name, as worthy of your special commendation, I should neither do justice to you, Sir, who have so been pleased to honour me, nor to the generous hearts in which your flattering eulogium found so immediate and powerful an echo, any more than I should do justice to my own feelings, if I could content myself on such an occasion, by merely returning you my formal thanks. Not, however, that I mean to occupy your time or attention long. Much as I feel, I will not weary you with its expression. But I cannot be wholly silent, when so many motives combine to persuade me to another course.

Sirs, I may truly say, that if the duration of human life is to be estimated by the number of ideas that pass through the mind, and of sensations that affect the heart, to-day I have lived a year; for, from the first moment of my entering the sacred edifice in which we commenced the holy labours of the morning, up to the moment in which I am now addressing you, I have been literally oppressed with thoughts and feelings too varied and too large for utterance! If I were to devote an entire year to their detail, and were to write them with the rapidity of the most practised hand, I do not believe that I should complete my task within the period, or that any thing but a pen of lightning could follow such a tempest of thought.

Let me first, then, express my humble acknowledgments of deep and unaffected gratitude, to that learned, pious, and venerable minister of God, who, in the sacred temple in which the multitudinous host were congregated for devotion, poured forth such a strain of sound doctrine, pathetic appeal, and holy ardour, as must have touched the heart of the most apathetic among his hearers,—more especially when he so beautifully illustrated, by copious and appropriate references to the sublime authority before him, the most useful duty that man can perform toward his fellow-men, or the created dust to its Creator—that of spreading out the sea of knowledge, till it washes every habitable coast upon the globe—that of diffusing the light of education, science, and divine truth, until it embrace the people of every country, colour, creed, and clime. (*Loud Cheers.*) As a travelled Mason, more especially, I may say that every portion of the public worship, founded as it is upon the sacred volume, as well as every part of the sublime mysteries of our Order, have for me an additional charm : and I can never hear the one, nor mingle in the other, without emotions as agreeable as they are powerful, and which nothing but the particular associations from which they spring, could ever give birth to. If for instance, the Hill of Zion, or the Towers of Salem—the beauty of Jerusalem, or the glory of Lebanon, are spoken of—the rocks, the spires, the pinnacles, and the forests, instantly re-appear before me, for I retain the most vivid recollection of them all. If Nineveh or Babylon are alluded to, their desolate remains are as distinctly seen as they were while I trod them in reality; and when the temple of Solomon, the Garden of Eden, and other renowned edifices and sites are named, the Brotherhood will easily understand the additional charm with which these sounds fall upon my ear, since these too I have visited as a part of my long and distant pilgrimage.

In passing from the sacred edifice—where, I may say, the great Architect of the Universe appeared to have given to the very reverend and venerated individual who led our devotional exercises, an especial inspiration, befitting the solemnity of the occasion —and in going from thence into the crowded streets of this increased and increasing city—my sensations, though of a new order, were still powerful and pleasing. For who could see unmoved the twice ten thousand cheerful and happy countenances that beamed from every casement, lattice, roof, and terrace, in the streets through which we passed—here and there illuminated, if I may so speak, by brighter eyes and lovelier features than those composing the general mass? or who could witness, without something bordering on awe as well as admiration, the ten times ten thousand spectators that hemmed in the procession on either side, in such a manner as to make a solid platform of human heads, on which, as on the testudo of the ancients, an army might have mounted to the breach, had they been disposed to besiege and carry off in triumph the fair captives who were to be seen hanging out their banners upon every battlement? Yes! I repeat, that a feeling of awe was inspired in my mind by the sight of so much inert power, which an evil-minded leader could so soon rouse into action, and at the head of which he might spread terror through the land; but that awe was mingled with admiration, when I beheld our little rivulet of moving men, meandering, as it were, like an embroidered thread, through an immense surrounding mass—one single effort of which, had it been set in hostile motion, would have overpowered and annihilated the whole;—and yet, notwithstanding every apparent motive to excitement, when the marching centre was throughout its whole line of length covered with the external emblems of rank, of wealth, and power—when unarmed and undefended individuals bore about their persons a profusion of jewels, the most insignificant of which would have formed a treasure for life to any one of the spectators by which they passed—and when the civic baton was the only ensign of authority any where displayed, except in the mere guard of honour which brought up the rear;—notwithstanding, I repeat, all these outward and apparent motives to discontent, such was the influence of freedom, knowledge, and religion, upon the countless multitude—that a smile of joyous participation in all the glories of the pageant as it passed, sat upon every countenance, and not a hair of any man's head appeared to have been hurt, nor any feeling manifested among the old or young, amidst the myriads that thronged around the procession, but that of humility, content, and joy. Truly, indeed, has our sublime poet Milton said

'———————Peace hath its triumphs,
No less renowned than war.'

And this was one of them. Never, in the whole course of my experience—which has been more extended than my years would indicate, and into which an age of events has been crowded—never did I before witness such a mass of human energy so passively submissive, without subservience or fear; nor in all the gorgeous and festive pageants in which it has been my lot to take a part, do I remember any thing approaching to the perfect peace and good-will which everywhere prevailed on this occasion. Well, indeed, did the reverend expounder of the sacred text, who addressed us in the morning, choose for his theme this beautiful passage, which, as I before remarked, seems to have been pointed out to him by an especial inspiration—' And all thy children shall be *taught* of the Lord, and great shall be the *peace* of thy children.' Yes, Sirs, peace is everywhere the handmaid of knowledge and truth, and after witnessing its 'renowned triumph' to-day—where the well educated population of this busy town breathed not a murmur to disturb the serenity of the scene—let no one henceforth dare to say, as some oppressors of the human race still insult both the majesty of heaven and the dignity of men by saying—that the increased knowledge of the poorer classes tends to subvert the due order of society, that ignorance is essential to secure the subjection of the mass, and that education uproots loyalty and obedience. Never was any maxim more false, as well as more degrading: and it must be especially gratifying to the friends of knowledge to see, as we have seen to-day, a union of the sacred text, of sound theory, and extensive practice, all allied in one holy league against this monstrous prostitution of truth and nature. Away then with the scandalous sophism for ever! Let it be sent to brood again over that utter darkness, which alone could have engendered any thing so foul or so offensive. (*Loud cheers.*)

Passing from the procession itself to that which was its end and object, the laying the foundation stone of the additional bridge to be thrown across the Clyde, in order to connect and facilitate the intercourse between the opposite banks of this noble river, I could not but reflect that, if *you* were engaged in this smaller work, I too, and upon a somewhat more extended scale, aspired to be a Bridge-builder. That you conceive it an object of great importance, to facilitate the intercourse, of which the Bridge we have founded to-day is to be the medium, I have the best proof in the vast pains taken by you to commence it with all becoming splendour and solemnity. That it is believed the interests of the individuals living on either side of the stream will be improved by this intercourse, is equally certain, from the splendid donations which persons possessing property on its banks have given to aid the work. And that the city of Glasgow conceives it an object, in the accomplishment of which all its inhabitants have more or less an interest, may be inferred from the fact of its Corporation having given the munificent present of three thousand pounds, to assist the undertaking. Sirs, the world will applaud your wisdom, as well as your liberality, in this act ; and from it I, too, gather hope ; for if it be judicious to expend time, and labour, and money, to connect together the opposite banks of the Clyde, notwithstanding that two bridges already exist within a few hundred yards of each other for that purpose, will it not be an object equally worthy your attention to give me your support, when I say that my humble endeavour is to construct a Bridge which shall unite together the shores of England and those of her extensive and valuable possessions in India ? (*Immense cheering.*) I too, Sirs, wish to facilitate that intercourse, which, as our reverend teacher so impressively taught us, is but fufilling the divine command, and which, as you have shown us, is the best and most effectual means of connecting together divided parts of the same country by the strongest of all links, mutual and reciprocal interests. I ask the aid of all true Masons throughout the world (for we are a large family, and embrace all kindreds, tongues, and kingdoms) to assist me to construct the arches of this Anglo-Indian Bridge. It cannot fail to be a magnificent structure, be the designer who he may. The four hundred millions of Asiatics to whom it would open a new road, would form a splendid procession ; and as to the wealth of which this Bridge would soon become the bearer, I may, without exaggeration, say that it is perfectly inexhaustible. And yet the pile might be completed for less money than you have cheerfully consented to pay, to throw your smaller structure across the stream of the Clyde. To erect the Indian Bridge, nothing more is wanted than a removal of the dams and impediments that clog the approach to the opposite shore. Let these be taken away, which your voices may easily command, and nothing more is needed ; the Bridge will then build itself, provided we lay the foundation. This is all that I ask the Masons, the merchants, the patriots, the Christians of Britain to do ; and after what I have seen and heard to-day, I am most anxious that the people of Glasgow should lay the first stone. (*Loud cheers.*) They have already shown a promptitude which makes it unnecessary for me to say much to urge them on ; but this I will say, that if they do not make haste, the people of Liverpool, of Manchester, of Bristol, of Leeds, and of Birmingham, will be before them ; and in contending for the honour of priority in this matter, let them be assured that great and lasting will be the renown of those who take a lead in an enterprise, which, more than any other that history has yet recorded, will, in its accomplishment, bring countless blessings in its train. (*Continued cheering.*)

But, Sirs, I will not trespass too much on your indulgence ; and, yet, I cannot sit down without giving expression to another idea which was suggested to me, as we stood upon the banks of the Clyde, engaged in the solemn rites and mystic ceremonies of the day. The connection of the two shores has been spoken of as a union of interests. Let me call it then a *nuptial* union. You all remember that the Doge of Venice used annually to wed the Adriatic to his splendid city, ' seated on the waters,' and that one part of the ceremonial was to drop a ring into the blushing wave, by which to bind the bride and bridegroom fast in their embraces. In the nuptials of the opposite banks of the Clyde, the wholesome custom of Europe has been literally followed : the lovers have seen and known each other well, and for a fitting period ; and the full measure of their coquetry as well as courtship has been enjoyed before the consummation. But I would wed the Clyde itself, and to a noble family—aye, even to a whole family—for though I am no advocate of polygamy with mortals, yet since it is an Eastern bride that I would provide for your colder stream, with whom the Eastern fashion must be followed of wedding without previous courtship or acquaintance, I see nothing to prevent the nuptials being wholly Eastern, so that the Clyde may become polygamous on the occasion, and wed at once those splendid streams, the Tigris, the Euphrates, the Indus and the Ganges. (*Loud and reiterated cheering.*) Sirs, this would be a splendid marriage indeed ; for every single bride would bring her lord a truly regal dower ; and as to the progeny that would result, I fear to venture on so *prolific* a theme ; for in less than a single lunar year these Oriental ladies would bring their Scottish husbands a long line of descendants, enough to fill at least a dozen times over all the wards and class-rooms in Hutcheson's hospital or school. (*Loud laughter, mingled with great cheering.*) Lord Byron has said indeed—

'The cold in clime are cold in blood.'

but only let the Caledonian's veins be once swelled with the amorous embrace of these Eastern brides, and, my life upon the issue, he will never afterward be cold in blood, though his uncovered limbs were shivering on Ben Lomond, or

'Freezing on the hoary Caucasus.'

Sirs, I should tire even *your* patience, which I see is as courteous as it is excessive, if I were to indulge this current of thought that runs in full stream through my mind. I imagine the pithy lines of Hudibras to be breathed in whispers from other quarters,

'For brevity is always good,
Whether we are—or are not—understood.'

And profiting by so undoubted a truth, I beg to say, that whether what I have uttered be intelligible or not to those who hear me, I shall inflict no more of it upon the hospitable kindness that has so politely heard me through. Before I sit down, however, allow me to repeat how sincerely and deeply I feel the compliment you have paid me, in sending forth your commendations of my humble labours to the world. Sirs, I am too frank to flatter. It is a characteristic of my early profession to speak bluntly as well as freely. The sailors of every country that I am acquainted with, are too honest to be parasites, and the sailors of Britain especially. I have been banished for speaking too freely, but I have never yet been suspected of being too courteous in phrase. If this should give additional weight to any praises I may venture to express, let that weight be added now ; for I repeat, with all the candour of one who habitually wears his heart upon the outside of his bosom, and whose inmost thoughts dwell constantly upon his tongue, that I have never, in any one day, seen more to admire, nor in any one day had more exalted sources of pleasure, than in this in which I am now addressing you. (*Cheers.*) Let me then not sully this happiness, by 'bestowing my tediousness' upon you any longer, but conclude by proposing a toast, which I believe you will all drink with enthusiasm. 'The marriage of the Clyde with four Eastern wives—the Tigris, the Euphrates, the Indus, and the Ganges; and may no hostile power ever interpose to divorce the union.'

Mr. Buckingham was greeted at the close of this speech with the loudest and most enthusiastic plaudits, and personal congratulations from all quarters of the Hall ; and the toast was drank with three times three, amidst the most deafening acclamation.—*Glasgow Chronicle, August 20.*

REPORT OF THE SPEECH

Delivered on the Opening of the Royal Exchange, at Glasgow, on the Health of Mr. Buckingham being proposed, on the 3d of September, 1829.

Yesterday, the new Exchange Rooms in Queen Street were opened to the Public, and there was, as proposed at the laying of the foundation stone, a splendid dinner on the occasion, at which not less than 450 gentlemen were present, James Ewing, Esq. of Dunoon Castle in the Chair, Henry Monteith, Esq., Croupier. Among the company present we observed the Honourable the Lord Provost of Glasgow, the Earl of Glasgow, the Hon. Charles Douglas, Sir Walter Stirling, Mr. Campbell of Blythswood, Counts Rivedin and Brancaleoni, Principal MacFarlane, Mr. Brown of Hamilton, Baillie Gray and the other gentlemen of the Magistracy, J. S. Buckingham, Esq., Provost Boyd of Paisley, Mr. Hamilton the Architect of the Buildings, Major Middleton, 42d Regiment, Baillie Leitch of Greenock, the Reverend Doctor Laurie of Hillhouse, &c. &c. &c. The Hall was elegantly fitted up. In the centre, between the two ranges of columns, three tables were placed the whole length of the room, and within the columns, and between them and the wall, on each side, were other tables, all decorated with the choicest flowers from the Botanic Garden. The large window at the west end of the room, was decorated with festoons of flowers, and rare plants furnished from the same quarter. The room was lighted by five chandeliers of exquisite workmanship, by Messrs. Lang and Co. of this City, of six lights each, and, on the whole, the appearance of the room was highly beautiful. In the forenoon, under the direction of Mr. Allison, master of the Exchange, the room was thrown open for the public, who were admitted by the south door, and went round the room to the north door, at which they made their exit. Not fewer than 30,000 persons are calculated to have been admitted, and, under the excellent regulations of Captain Graham, not the slightest confusion occurred.

The Representative of the Dean of Guild and Merchants' House of Glasgow, Mr. DAGLISH, in returning thanks in behalf of that body, proposed the health of Mr. BUCKINGHAM, whose labours in the public cause, he eulogized in the highest terms, and felt that he represented only the universal sentiment of the mercantile interest of the kingdom, when he expressed his warmest wishes for the continued health and success of this gentleman in the arduous undertaking on which he had entered.

On the mention of Mr. BUCKINGHAM's name, the applause was even louder and more general than on the former occasion of its being proposed at the late Masonic dinner, and was continued for several minutes, reverberating from all sides of the building. When it had subsided, Mr. Buckingham rose, and the silence being such as to admit of every word being heard, no portion of his address was lost. He spoke very nearly as follows :—

Mr. Chairman and Gentlemen—There is a measure of applause which begets and quickens utterance of speech : there is a measure also which impedes, and even takes it away. This last you have bestowed on me so abundantly,—my cup may be said to be so filled to overflowing, that it is matter of wonder, even to myself, that I should be able—strong as is my desire—to give any expression whatever, even the most inadequate, to the feelings with which so large a measure of your approbation cannot fail to overpower me.—Believe me, however, when I say, most sincerely and unaffectedly, that faint and feeble as may be the language in which I offer you that assurance, the feelings that dictate it are of the most intense description, and that their very excess creates the embarrassment which a more moderate degree of consciousness or temperament would neither experience for itself nor imagine to exist in others.

When I had last the honour of sharing with you the festive pleasures of your hospitable board, I was unconscious that a renewal of such enjoyment was so near at hand. I had anticipated, indeed, that by this time I should have been in the sister island—*thinking*, no doubt, of Scotland, for who could have met so cordial a reception among you as I have done, and soon forget the scene of its occurrence ?—but no longer being an actual participator of the prolonged gratifications with which my brief sojourn among you has so abundantly been crowned. This accidental interruption of my progress I regarded at the moment as an evil ;—but it adds another to the thousand instances that crowd upon my recollection, in which a shadowy evil has become substantial good : for have I not reason to rejoice at any event which leads me to linger among you yet a little longer, and which tends to cement more firmly the friendships already so strongly entertained ? I do, indeed, rejoice that the opportunities of our social and festive intercourse have been so multiplied, and that they have not been

' Like angel's visits, few and far between.'

My only regret is, that we cannot more frequently enjoy those assemblings, so honourable to you, in the great public objects which bring ye together ; and so agreeable to me, in that happy union of the useful with the agreeable, which gives to every mortal pleasure its highest relish at the moment of its existence, and leaves behind the most refined remembrances, when the actual period of enjoyment itself has passed away. High, however, as this gratification is, there are not wanting those who would mar it if they dare. It was but a very short period before my entering the room, that I received from some envious individual an anonymous communication, endeavouring to cast odium on your splendid undertaking, and to dissuade me, if possible, from being present among you to-day. But that the hon. Chairman had already, with great force and eloquence, alluded to the dissension that was attempted to be introduced by those who considered that their own private interests in the remote quarters of the town would be injured by the erection of this more central, and therefore more convenient spot for assembling, I should not have adverted to this circumstance at all. Having, however, just mentioned it, I may add that, although the writer assumed a signature which he no doubt thought would give his epistle grace and favour in my estimation,—for he calls himself "A *Free* Trader,"—yet he has not approved himself worthy of his title—because to deserve that, he ought to be also "A *Fair* Trader." He is, however, little better than a smuggler—who tries to introduce his contraband opinions under the cover of a mask, and in the anonymous obscurity of night, without coming, like an upright merchant, and an honourable man, to tell us his objection with open countenance, and in the light of day. And what does he require?—that improvement in one quarter of your city should be arrested because it throws into shade the imperfections in another? If this, indeed, were to be admitted as legitimate reasoning, why, then, the progress of improvement throughout the world would be stayed; and the globe itself should cease to revolve around its own axis: for, according to such a blighting and destroying principle, the splendour of the day ought not to beam forth light, and life, and love, upon the one half of our orb, because the falling shadows of night would, in consequence of this, envelope the other. Who could entertain for a moment so monstrous a proposition? For myself, I confess that the highest degree of vengeance I should desire to inflict upon the mistaken individual who has ventured to intrude it upon my notice or upon yours, would be to have him descend among us from the splendid roof that resounds with the echoes of our enjoyment, and there to witness for himself how far above all standard of comparison is that divine delight which springs from the labour of aiding improvement and accelerating the wheels of human advancement, to that cold, and dull, and solitary feeling of malignant triumph which some minds are base enough to feel at every interruption to the onward march of knowledge and liberality, and of all the thousand blessings that follow in their train. Had he but have come among us, and seen the happy countenances that bespeak the heart's full joy, he would then have experienced other and loftier aspirations than those which dictated his malicious but happily harmless effusion. (*Cheers.*)

But let me turn to other and more agreeable reflections, of which the materials are as abounding as the viands of your sumptuous board, and have thronged upon me in my absence, like the clusters of the stars that stud the vault of heaven. For though I have been absent, I have not been very distant. The bosom and the banks of your beautiful stream have been my alternate spheres of action and repose; with the mountains of Ben-Lomond, and the waters of the Holy Lake, almost continually in sight. Nor let it surprise you that scenes so full of inspiration as these should have tempted me to indulge the double dream of bard and prophet; or that on looking around me, on the gay and fragrant wreaths of almost every plant and flower that opens its buds and petals to the sun—brought, no doubt, for the occasion, from the magnificent collection of your Botanic Garden, where I so recently passed an evening, in retracing, amid its exotic groves and shrubberies, the tropical regions, in which I had seen the treasures of the teeming earth in all their pristine vigour and proportions—if I perceive, as I *do* perceive, one favourite flower wanting to make the wreath complete. I say, Sirs, wonder not if in the ardour of my desire that this flower should form a part of every national decoration in all time to come, I give vent to an effusion which sprung spontaneously from my imagination, while hastening up this morning, from the confluence of your river with the sea, towards its source, riding, not on the "wings of the wind," but on one of those fiery arrows that shoot through air and water by a power to which the Clyde was the first to do homage—steam, and enjoying the triumph of science, not in subduing, but so regulating the elemental laws of Nature, as to make man more worthy the dignity of wearing the impress of his Maker, by wielding even the fiery element of destruction to purposes of benevolence, improvement, and enjoyment. Then it was that this prediction involuntarily escaped me—

> Where now the Clyde her downy Thistle weaves
> Around the Shannon's graceful Shamrock leaves—
> And where the Mersey, Thames, and Severn bring
> The blushing Rose, to grace the mystic ring—
> Soon shall the Ganges, o'er his ample tide,
> Waft the white Lotus, as a willing bride;
> Then will THE UNION be indeed divine,
> And the wide world do homage at its shrine.

After this brief but refreshing and invigorating absence—to what have I returned? To a banquet that a Persian Satrap might even designate as gorgeous—to an edifice, which in the chasteness of its proportions, and the richness of its ornaments, reminds me of those classic structures, amid the fallen ruins of which I have so often lingered in other lands—to a union of the Art of Greece, in the architectural skill that has reared the splendid pile, with the Science of Europe, here employed in the candelabras suspended from its ceiling, to give us light in a new element of aërial flame, and these again adorned with all the rare and curious productions of Nature, from every quarter of the globe, in the waving and palmy foliage of the Torrid Zone, growing up as if at the command of some magician's wand, in the same soil and climate with the cedar and the fir of the arctic and antarctic circle, mingling and blending into one the burning heats of the Arabian Desert, the frozen pinnacles of Nova Zembla, and the fertile fields of Italy and France. (*Loud Cheers.*)

Sirs, the last occasion on which we met together, was one of a most interesting description ; and yet, though clothed with all the pomp and splendour that your efforts could bestow—it was not in the least degree·more interesting or more important, either in a national, or, if I may use the phrase, in a domestic point of view, than this. Your object, then, was to facilitate the intercourse between two particular districts of your town. Your aim now is to unite not merely two, but every quarter of your populous and flourishing city, by forming a point of union, in which the wealth, intelligence, and enterprise of the whole community may find the combination of circumstances most favourable to their developement ; and in which, once at least between every rising and setting sun, the opportunity may be afforded to every frequenter of this Central Mart, to open up his stores of information, and to communicate his wants and wishes, as well as to receive from others the same free gift of their intelligence, and to hear the free expression of their desires, in that cordial and friendly reciprocity which, like the dew of heaven,

' ———————— is twice blest,
Blessed in him that gives—and that receives.'

The clear and convincing manner in which the innumerable and advantages of such a Public Institution have been already so fully detailed, would make it idle repetition for me to go again over the same well-trodden ground. But I must hazard a remark at least on one particular feature of such a "Gathering," as this will every day afford, which has not been sufficiently expatiated upon. It is the humanizing and refining tendency which such meetings have, to round off from the minds of men, those sharp angles of prejudice, which, under less favourable circumstances, are sure to project beyond the surface, and destroy both the simplicity and the beauty of the mental form. In all large cities and ports in every part of the world, where men meet so frequently and so freely as you will now do, taking rank, as you deserve, with the most distinguished among them all, the gusts and tempests of political passion subside into the tempered atmosphere of ordinary calm ; and even the leaders of hostile parties in the State, as well as their humbler followers, can differ in opinion on matters of public policy, and yet in private or social intercourse forget that they are ranged under opposite banners in the field. In the smaller towns, on the other hand, the mere absence of places of free and frequent resort, occasions each adherent of a separate creed in politics, as well as faith, first to greet coldly when accident throws them together—next to shun each other's recognition when they pass—and lastly to merge from coldness and silence into scarcely disguised hostility, and from thence to open war. This is the Upas tree that poisons social intercourse in almost all the smaller places of the kingdom, where some distinctive colour, badge, or epithet, will so divide even families as well as individuals by an impassable gulph—that the factions of the white rose and the red, and the wars of York and Lancaster are acted over again, by those who have every thing that characterised these factions, except their self-devotion and their dignity. By such a daily assembling as this Institution will afford, whatever remnant of this spirit may yet linger in your society will speedily disappear. As the rays of the glorious sun are never entirely withdrawn from the British dominions—his morning rays gilding the minarets of Delhi and the pagodas of Benares, before his setting beams have spent their last splendour on the Christian spires and steeples of Quebec—and as the waters of the Ganges and those of the St. Lawrence, receive equally, and at the same moment, his earliest and latest light—so may we hope here to see the East Indian and the West Indian, as they have been to night associated in our toasts, no longer rivals but friends—the African and the Hindoo—the swarthy negro and the fair Canadian, subjects of the same king, servants of the same master, worshippers of the same God, united in a patriotic as well as philanthropic bond, silken in its softness, but adamantine in its strength. Then, indeed, may we also hope to see such an amelioration in the condition of each, that both may become the harbingers to their fellow-men, in woods and deserts yet untrodden by a Christian foot, of those ' glad tidings' which the greatest monarchs have rejoiced to hear;—then may we hope to see, what cannot be accomplished until these pitiable distinctions that now divide mankind be blended into shade, the African and Hindoo themselves the introducers of Civilization into their respective regions, when, personifying this Universal Good, we may hope to see her thus advancing over all the darker spots of our still undelineated globe, and chasing away by her effulgence, the mists and shadows of ignorance ; thus—to tranfer from another subject the language of your own native poet, Campbell, whom I am proud to number among my friends—thus should we see Knowledge penetrating even the remotest wildernesses of Asia and of Africa—

' Led by her dusky guides—like morning brought by night.'

(Reiterated and prolonged cheers.)

But, Sirs, there is one great essential, without which, even this splendid edifice you have erected for this most useful purpose, would be unavailing—namely, *liberty* to meet and breathe your thoughts as freely as the air. This, indeed, you happily possess: and, therefore, it is that I the more readily appeal to you on behalf of those who have it not. Where? I can imagine a hundred whispers to ask;—and I will answer where. In that rich and beautiful, but injured and oppressed country, India—of which I have spoken so much before—but though I have spoken of it so fully, I believe I have never told you this:—At the very recent period when the East India Company, in the arrogance and insolence of irresponsible power, introduced a Stamp Tax into India, and contended for the legal right to tax every man, British, Foreigner, or Native, at their will and pleasure, a humble memorial was drawn up by the British Merchants, to be presented to the Bengal Government, praying the suspension of the law till reference could be made to the superior authorities at home ; and with a view to the general convenience, a meeting of the leading mercantile men, was called to take place in the Exchange Room at Calcutta. The number could not exceed 50, all men of the greatest eminence for wealth, talent, and character—the only object being to shape their Memorial, by conference and revision, so as to render it as acceptable to the Government as possible, consistently with the expression of their prayer. Will it be believed—and yet, however incredible, it is undeniably true—that the Government of Bengal absolutely prepared to send a troop of soldiers to disperse these assembled petitioners by the bayonet or the bullet, as the case might need ! when, doubts being suggested as to the legality of this, and the Advocate General for the time, being referred to, his answer was—that by the law of England, an individual taking away the life of any Englishman so assembled would be guilty of murder, and be responsible to the laws of his country for his crime ; an opinion which shook the *courage* of these Eastern despots, and the troops were countermanded. Thank heaven, Sirs, that you do not live under such an iron, or, should I not rather say, such a bloody rule as that: but in thanking heaven for yourselves, let me implore you to think of others who do, one among them, a leader too, on this occasion, as full of spirit as of intelligence, and of virtue as of both, I speak of Mr. James Young, a native of Glasgow, one of the sons of your late reverend Professor of Greek, in the University of your City, and member of a family well known in India for having furnished from its single stock, distinguished members of the civil, military, and mercantile bodies of that country. He is soon, I hope, to return to join the ranks of those opposed to the continuance of this execrable system; and Glasgow will herself then see that she may well be proud in having such a citizen and son.

Let it not be said, however, that we who have fought together in this same good fight—although it has been my lot to be cut down, covered with wounds, and trampled in the dust, while he has escaped with fortune and without a scar ; let it not be said that we, but more especially myself, are not impartial evidences on this subject. If you would hear only of the pains of hunger from those who never felt it, learn only of the pangs of death from those who never knew its torture, and suffer no man to speak of the horrors of the dungeon, because he himself had lingered out a long captivity in its loathsome cells, then must your evidence be *impartial* indeed. But, Sirs, the

English Poet exhibits a deeper knowledge of truth and human nature when he says, in reference to all the ills of life.

' He best can paint them who has felt them most.'—(*Much cheering.*)

Believe us, therefore, who have suffered, and the more so on that account; for we are the harbingers destined by fate to tell these tales of other lands, the pioneers to cut away the impeding obstacles to the general march; though ourselves, perhaps, be hewn down in clearing the path for others. But do not, on that account, discredit or discard the only testimony that can be of any worth, because acquired in the best of all possible schools, experience and actual service. Let me add, too, that the very circumstance of an unrestrained enjoyment here, will, when it reaches the eyes and ears of those who, in India, paint and pant in vain for equal liberties, tend only to make their sorrow and their indignation greater; for it will draw back all their recollections to their native land, till they are made to feel the full weight of their present degradation, by contrast with the freedom that they quitted with their homes. So true it is, in the language of a foreign poet, of whom I see the countenance of an intelligent countryman (Count Brancaleone) here beside me, and whose eye glistened with delight to be addressed in his native tongue,

———— ' Non e maggior dolore
Che ricordarsi del tempo felice
Nella miseria'———— ————

There can be no greater torment than the recollection of periods of happiness in the midst of misery. And this, I am sure, will be the feeling of our unhappy but worthy fellow-countrymen and fellow-subjects in India, when they read the accounts of our free and flowing festivities here.

Let me not, however, prolong this interruption of your interesting proceedings.—I feel powerfully, and, therefore, I express myself with corresponding warmth :—And this too, has given me a burst of momentary inspiration, which, the sight of the venerable patriot, at the right hand of the Chairman, Sir Walter Stirling, turns into a local channel, as his presence revives the recollection of the allusions which he made on the last occasion of meeting, to the quarterings or emblems of your City Arms. Remembering these, and desiring that under their auspices you should assemble all your forces, and unite them in one irresistible phalanx to overthrow the gigantic Monopoly of the East—and wrest from its withering grasp the Commerce that is your birth-right and your portion—though still unjustly withheld from you—I would say—

Oh ! for a Herald's voice, of mightiest power,
Amid the triumphs of this festive hour,
To make the war-cry o'er your mountains bound,
And every glen re-echo back the sound.
Seek ye for banners ?—Here in this bright field
Behold them—blazoned on your Civic shield.
The Bell—that bids ye wake the slumbering world,
The Bird—that bids ye fly, with sails unfurled,
The Fish—that bids ye sweep the trackless route,
The Tree—that bids ye pluck the ripened fruit,
All, all proclaim—the Bell, Bird, Fish, and Tree,
' Let Glasgow flourish'—and let Trade be free.

[This poetic reference to the Arms and the Motto of the City of Glasgow, produced a most electrifying effect; and when Mr. Buckingham resumed his seat, the thunders of applause were the loudest and most prolonged that were heard throughout the evening.] *Glasgow Chronicle, September 4th.*

ADDRESS

To the Ladies of Northumberland, on the Burning of Hindoo Widows—after the Ball at Newcastle, on Tuesday, the 17th of November, 1829.

Mothers, Wives, and Daughters !—For in all these hallowed and endearing relations, would I ask for a moment's attention of that sex whose ear was never yet deaf to the calls of humanity—whose eye never yet refused the tear of sympathy for the helpless orphan and the widow; I have myself, the happiness to be a husband

and a father; and feeling, therefore, the full force of the sacred relations in which we all stand towards parents, partners, and offspring, I believe that I shall not ask your attention in vain; more especially as I now address you, at the moment of my reaching home, after having been a participator in the gaieties to which you lent all your influence, and over which you spread all your blandishments, in the splendid Assembly-room of your chief city, surrounded by all the leading families of the county of Northumberland.

It would seem, at first sight, to be a doubtful eulogy to say, that the very excess of the delight which seemed to animate all hearts, and to diffuse an additional charm over every countenance, was itself the source of, to me at least, very deep and thrilling horrors. Yet, so it was. From the mazy labyrinth of the joyous dance, and from the full tide of harmony that poured its lengthened strain along, I was transported, in imagination, to the banks of the Ganges, where, at the very moment, perhaps, in which you were thus basking in the meridian splendour of enjoyment, the funeral pile was preparing, the flames were actually kindling, and discordant yells were drowning the cries of the murdered victims then expiring amid all the horrors of protracted orture on the altars of idolatrous immolation.

Whilst you read this sentence, I see your bosoms swell with sympathy; I see your eyes grow dim with pity; and I hear your anxious and quick-beating hearts ask, 'Who are these unhappy sufferers?' Shall I tell you? They are women—mothers— widows. Nay, they are among the highest born, the noblest, the most delicate, the most lovely, the most honourable, and most faithful of their sex.

The heraldric antiquity of the proudest house in England dwindles into insignificance before the venerable ancestry of the families of Hindoostan. The highest born among us can produce no roll of pedigree like theirs. The fairest form, the brightest eye, the softest lips that England may boast, do not surpass the splendid beauties which Asiatic courts contain. Even those among you the most renowned for grace and elegance, might admit as your compeers, in all that constitute your attractions, the lovely daughters of the East, the offspring of Kings and Emperors, whose gorgeous halls and palaces were once as lustrous and as splendid as your own. Shall I add another claim to the long list already enumerated? They are our fellow-subjects, and as much the inhabitants of the King of England's dominions as if their baronial castles stood upon the banks of the Tyne and the Tees. Of these faithful wives, fond mothers, highly born, lovely, and nursed in the lap of tenderest delicacy, the appalling number of more than Seven Thousand have been put to death, by the most frightful of all tortures, in the brief space of ten years! The fires that scorch their delicate frames, that crack their sinews, burst their eye-balls, sear their brains, and burn their hearts to cinders, are never extinguished! Between the rising and setting sun, two victims, on an average, perish daily! The smoke is for ever blackening the surrounding atmosphere! Do you ask where this most gloomy of all horrors prevails? Let your flesh creep with terror; let your cheeks be alternately flushed with indignation, and grow pallid with shame; and let your lips tremble with fear, while you pronounce the words—IN BRITISH INDIA! Yes! where you, perhaps, have husbands, fathers, brothers; if not, where you, at least, have a voice; for who, of any rank, is there in England that is destitute of influence over those who sit in her councils? And who is there possessed of influence that does not bend before your powerful sway?

As English Ladies, then, than whom none stand higher in the scale of excellence, let me conjure you by every tie that you regard as sacred, to think of this. Pause for a moment in your bright and gay career, to ask how many young and lovely widows have perished in the devouring flame, since we met together for enjoyment last!!! Think, while your happy lips are breathing forth the sounds of harmony and joy, how many Indian widows are giving forth their last faint shriek, in all the gasping agonies of death. Demand of your own hearts, whether, while they beat in bosoms formed for pity, as well as pleasure, they ought not to give one moment, at least, to think of those for whom the torture is preparing. And, whether the song, the dance, the pageant, or the revel, demand your attention next, let me beseech you to consider whether the song would not be sweeter, the dance more joyous, the pageant richer, and the revel gayer far, if you could cheer your hearts with the reflection, that before you abandoned yourselves to either, you had exerted that influence which you all possess, to extinguish the destroying flames that now wrap in their fiery embraces, SEVEN HUNDRED VICTIMS of your own sex and country, *every year*!!

I know that this reflection would afford you a pleasure of the most exquisite kind. And, believing this, let me confess that, at the very moment of your retiring from the ball, I was strongly tempted (and *feeling* thus, why should I scruple to *avow* it) to appeal to your assembled influence there upon the spot before you repaired to rest. My heart was almost bursting with the thought, and the words hung impatiently upon my tongue. Strong in the purity of my motive, I know I should not have faltered; but the possibility that some misconstruction might have been placed on that motive, and that the end might therefore be protracted, made me pause for re-consideration. I now repent, as I have done a thousand times before, that I did not follow the first virtuous impulse of an enthusiastic, but I hope, an honourable zeal, instead of suffering the cold dictates of prudential fear to awe me from my purpose. The only way in which I can show the sincerity of my repentance, and atone for the omission, is to address you now, before I lay my own head upon my pillow, and send it through the channel of the press; as your dispersion to your various homes renders this the only probable medium through which I can now reach your ears, and when I have done this; I shall not sleep less sweetly, nor dream of less happy days.

The gentlemen of Newcastle—your fathers, husbands, brothers—are at the present moment appealed to, and invited to direct their regards to India, to encourage what they may there find worthy, to arrest the further progress of that which they think should be stayed. Need I say how you can quicken the lagging resolutions, and kindle the latent spark? Whose tongue is so persuasive, whose eye so encouraging, whose praise so cheering as that of those we love?

> Oh! ne'er to *Man* has pitying Heaven,
> A power so blest, so glorious given;
> Say but a single word, and save
> Ten thousand mothers from a flaming grave;
> And tens of thousands from the source of woe
> That ever must to orphan'd children flow;
> Save from the flame the infant's place of rest,
> The couch by nature given—the mother's breast.
> Oh! bid the mother live, the babe caress her,
> And, sweeter still, its lisping accents bless her.
> INDIA, with tearful eye, and bended knee,
> LADIES of ENGLAND! pours her plaint to thee,
> Nor will NORTHUMBRIA'S DAUGHTERS bear the stain,
> That India poured her plaint to them in vain.

Sandyford, near Newcastle.   J. S. BUCKINGHAM.

NEW ARRANGEMENT OF THE LECTURES.

The following Explanation of the Plan, Object, and new Arrangement of the Lectures on the Countries of the Oriental World, which will be followed by a Syllabus of the Lectures themselves, will appropriately terminate this Review of the proceedings of the year.

THE near approach of the period fixed by law for the termination of the existing Charter of the East India Company, and the important interests involved in the decision to which the Legislature of the country may come on that occasion, appeared to me to render it of the highest importance, that every city and town in the kingdom should be duly impressed with the share which they really have in the issue of this great question. It was, therefore, with a view to awaken more rapidly and more powerfully, the attention of the country at large to this momentous topic, that, at the beginning of the year 1829, I first undertook a personal tour through the provincial portions of Great Britain, in order to follow up, by *viva voce* appeals to their inhabitants, the impression previously, but still imperfectly made by the books and papers already written on the same subject. The superiority of this method of informing the understandings, and engaging the feelings of mankind, to every other mode, and especially to that of written treatises, is universally admitted; and, although the undertaking has been attended by very considerable sacrifices on my own part, (without making which I could not have left my home and my occupations in order to carry it into effect,) yet when I reflected on the magnitude of the interests involved in the choice, I could not hesitate for a moment. If the sacrifices necessary for this purpose had been even ten times greater than they were, I should still have chosen to make them, from the conviction that by this personal Tour (which the relinquishment of all my most important engagements at home, could alone leave me at liberty to pursue), there is not merely a hope, but a certainty, of the India and China Trades being opened to the country, and a national benefit of millions obtained thereby; while, without such personal efforts, there is at least a strong probability that the existing Monopoly of the India Company would be renewed with very trifling relaxations, and much of the benefit to be reaped from its abolition postponed for perhaps another twenty years.

This opinion may appear to some so vain and groundless, that I may, I hope, be pardoned for stating the reasons which lead me to entertain it. They are these:—Throughout every part of the kingdom, I have found men of all classes from the highest to the lowest, so busily engrossed with the affairs and events by which they are immediately surrounded, that they have neither time nor inclination to attend to that which is remote. The humbler and middle classes of society have enough to do to struggle for subsistence; and the few hours they can spare from labour, they are glad to give to pleasurable recreation. The richer classes are as much engrossed with their peculiar pursuits as their inferiors; and have still less inclination to turn aside to the investigation of any subject not promising immediate individual profit or personal pleasure. The very ignorance that thus prevails on all subjects connected with India, its Government, or Commerce, is an additional reason why all public discussion or private conversation on such topics is carefully avoided. The histories of India and Indian transactions are long and tedious. The Parliamentary Reports and Proceedings connected with India, are too voluminous to be read by the generality of public men, and too expensive to be easily accessible to private individuals. A debate on an Indian question, whether in the Lords or Commons, receives therefore less attention than one on any other subject, and popular writers for the public press are careful not to weary their readers with what they believe to be uncongenial to their tastes.

But, though this reasonable unwillingness on the part of the conductors of the public press to write much about India, and the equally natural indisposition on the part of the people to read much on the same topic, still exist; yet this reluctance does not manifest itself in an equal degree on the part of either, when the same matter is presented to them in another shape. It is for this reason that though it is very difficult to prevail on any individual to give even a few shillings for a book, yet there is not the same unwillingness to pay an equal sum for the purchase of what he considers more animating and amusing—the oral information obtained at a public Lecture. And, supposing the book to be purchased, its perusal leaves a much fainter impression than hearing the same facts and arguments from the lips of a public speaker. Reading is also a solitary occupation, and the impression left by it dies away for want of sympathetic support, soon after the book is laid aside. But, when an assembly of several hundreds sit together in the same room, and any striking fact or powerful argument is adduced, which make a similar impression on the whole multitude, expressions of astonishment, or indignation, or applause, follow, and, like an electric spark, the feeling is communicated to all. The speaker is animated—the hearers re-echo the enthusiasm—the people become pledged in the sight and hearing of each other, to co-operate in one general cause—and the result is some immediate act, by which they execute, as it were, a common bond of union, to carry their determinations into execution, with spirit and effect.

It is in pursuance of this great object, that the following plan, which admits of progressive developement, has, after much consideration, been decided on as best calculated to attain the end in view: namely, to commence with a popular description of the several countries which lie between England and India, and which are those portions of the Oriental World through which any traveller going to India by land would be most likely to pass. For, important as the facts and arguments bearing on the questions of Indian Government and Indian Trade undoubtedly are, these alone would attract but very limited audiences, and especially if commenced abruptly, and without any preceding discourses. But, by the previous delineations of countries and manners, preliminary to, and in some degree connected with, the main object, and in a way that draws increasing audiences of all classes and of both sexes, the sympathies of the community are so gradually awakened, and so powerfully engaged, that, when the last of the Series comes to be delivered, the number of auditors is often five-fold; and their minds are so well prepared for the views to be maintained, that, in every instance that has yet occurred, the result has been the demonstration of unanimous and enthusiastic approbation of them, and the formation of East India Associations in every part of the country that I have yet visited for the purpose.

The result of my personal Tour has been everywhere indeed most gratifying; and the effect produced altogether unexampled. No Lectures, within the memory of any inhabitant, were ever attended by so many influential persons as those forming my Course in the several towns of England and Scotland ; in addition to which, the subject of the India Monopoly became by this means the topic of conversation in every party and every family. There was not a single newspaper in the country that did not contain articles exposing its evils ; and the public press and public mind of the kingdom were more strongly excited, more durably occupied, and more effectually enlisted against that Monopoly, than by any other means that could be devised, or than by the expenditure of £100,000 in money for that purpose. I can have no scruple in saying—because it is undeniably true—that all the progress made by the question in the past year, and it is very considerable, has arisen from my first visit to Liverpool in January last,—without which, no meeting, or petition, or deputation, would have gone from thence till the following year, if even then ; and neither Manchester, Leeds, Birmingham, nor Bristol, would have been roused, without the Lectures delivered in each ; for at first *all* of them were cold, and were only brought into united and vigorous action by the impression originally made by these personal labours : so that to this also may be attributed the pledges of Ministers given in answer to the numerous Deputies that went to London soon after the delivery of these Lectures in the towns named, in consequence of which the progress of the question was hastened at least a year in date.

The arrangement of these Lectures has been now so improved and modified as to admit of several short Courses, of three Lectures only in each ; but each complete in itself, and any portion of them capable of adaptation to the extent, population, and wealth of the inhabitants of the several towns in which they may be delivered, and so as to bring them, therefore, within the means of the middle, as well as of the upper classes, to attend. The divisions are as follow :—

FIRST COURSE.—EGYPT.

Lecture I.

1. Geographical Features of the Country—Boundaries, and Extent of Surface.
2. The River Nile—its Sources, Mouths, Inundation, and Deposits.
3. The Cataracts—The Delta—Lakes Mœris, Menzaleh, and Mareotis.
4. Canal across the Isthmus, connecting the Red Sea and Mediterranean.
5. Climate—Etesian Winds—The Khamseen or Simoom—Absence of Rain.
6. Mineral and Vegetable Productions, and state of Agriculture and Cultivation.
7. Egyptian Animals—The Buffalo, Crocodile, Hippopotamus, Hyena, and Stork.

Lecture II.

1. Ancient Cities, Temples, Pyramids, Labyrinths, Obelisks, Statues, and Tombs.
2. Alexandria—Canopus—Sais—Tanis—Bubastis—and Heliopolis.
3. Memphis—The Pyramids—The Sphynx—The Catacombs—and Mummies.
4. Lake Mœris—Its extent and object—The Labyrinth—Pyramids and Statues.
5. Antinoë—Hermopolis—Crocodilopolis—Tentyra—Eliethias—Silsilis—Esneh.
6. Edfou—Assouan—Temples of Thebes—Royal Tombs and Statue of Memnon.

Lecture III.

1. Chief Towns—Alexandria—Rosetta—Damietta—Boolac, and Grand Cairo.
2. Population—Arabs—Turks—Greeks—Armenians—Abyssinians—and Copts.
3. Religion—Mohammedan—Christian—Jewish—Priests of each.
4. Manners—Dress—Exercise—Amusements—Passions—Domestic Life.
5. Government—Caliphs—Soldans—Mamelukes—Beys—Present Pasha.
6. Commerce—Monopoly—Colonization—Trade with India and Europe.

SECOND COURSE.—PALESTINE.

Lecture I.

1. Extent and Boundaries of Syria and Palestine —Sea Coast, and Interior.
2. Mountains—Lebanon—Hermon—Sion—Olives—Tabor—Ebal, and Gerizzim.
3. Plains of Esdraelon and Galilee, and the fertile Vallies of Judea.
4. The River Jordan—Sources & Course of the Lycus, Adonis, and Orontes.
5. The Lake of Tiberias, Galilee, or Genassereth—and the Dead Sea.
6. Syria—Palestine—Heshbon—Bashan—Gilead—The Decapolis, and the Hauran.

Lecture II.

1. Ancient Cities of Tyre, Sidon, Jericho, Ammon, Sodom and Gomorrah.
2. Jerusalem—The Temple of Solomon—Calvary, and the Tomb of Christ.
3. Bethlehem—Nazareth—Capernaum—Tiberias—and Cesarea on the Coast.
4. The Decapolis—Gadara—Gamala—Bozra—and Geraza.
5. Singular Remains of ancient Cities in the Plains of the Auranites.
6. Splendid Temple of Baalbeck—and Superb Ruins of Palmyra.

Lecture III.

1. Chief Towns on the Coast—Gaza—Jaffa—Acre—Bairout—and Latakia.
2. Cities of the Interior—Jerusalem—Neapolis—Antioch—Aleppo—Damascus.
3. Population—Turks—Arabs—Druses—Jews—Christians, and Neseereeahs.
4. Manners—Marriages—Polygamy—Amusements—The Bath—Cemetries.
5. Singular Costume of Druse Females, Levantine Consuls, and Aleppo Ladies.

THIRD COURSE.
ARABIA, MESOPOTAMIA, AND PERSIA.

Lecture I.—Arabia.

1. Peninsular form, and Maritime boundaries of its Coasts.
2. Subdivisions—Arabia Deserta—Arabia Petræa—Arabia Felix.
3. The Red Sea—Its peculiarities—Coral Reefs, and Navigation.
4. The Arab Horse—the Ass—the Camel—the Dromedary—Locusts and Quails.
5. Antiquities—Ezion Geber—Written Mountains—Horeb and Sinai.
6. Suez—Jedda—Mocha—Sana—Muscat—Bussorah—Medina, and Mecca.
7. Manners of the Desert Tribes—Encampments—Caravans—Character.

Lecture II.—Mesopotamia.

1. Geographical Outline—The Euphrates and the Tigris—Taurus and Korneh.
2. Ancient Positions of Birtha—Haran—Amida—Thapsacus, and Nisibeen.
3. Ruins of Ur, Nineveh, and Babylon—Hanging Gardens, and Tower of Babel
4. Chief Towns—Orfah—Diarbekr—Mardin—Moosul—and Bagdad.
5. Population—Turcomans—Koords—Devil Worshippers, or Yezeedis.
6. General Political Condition of the Remoter Provinces of the Turkish Empire.

Lecture III.—Persia.

1. Form, Elevation, varied surface, and general character of the Country.
2. Rivers—Kara Soo—Choaspes—Zeinderood,—and fertile Vallies.
3. Subdivisions—Irak—Khorassan—Soosiana—Farsistan, and Mazanderaun.
4. Climate—Gardens—Fruits—Horses and Mules—Caravans.
5. Antiquities—Tauk-e-Bostan—Ecbatana—Shushan—Shapoor—Persepolis
6. Tabreez—Teheraun—Kermanshah—Hamadan—Shiraz, and Ispahan.
7. Population—Sheeahs—Armenians—Jews—Fire worshippers, or Guebres.
8. Ancient Wealth of Persia—Its Satrapies—and Trade by Balsora and Ormuz.

FOURTH COURSE.—INDIA.

Lecture I.

1. Vastness of extent, and gigantic scale of its Geography.
2. The Himalaya Mountains—The Ghauts—and the Nilgherries.
3. The Indus—Ganges—Burumpooter—Jumna—Nerbuddah—Kistna—Godavery.
4. The Coasts of Orissa—Coromandel—Guzerat—and Malabar.
5. Provinces—Hindoostan—Bengal—Rajesthana—and the Deccan.
6. Climate—Mineral, Vegetable, and Animal Productions of the Country.

Lecture II.

1. Antiquities—Salsette—Elephanta—Ellora—Oojein—Taje Muhal—Dacca.
2. Cities-Delhi--Agra--Lucknow—Benares—Dacca—Poonah--Surat--Hyderabad.
3. Principal Foreign Settlements—Goa—Pondicherry—and Serampore.
4. Chief English Towns or Presidencies—Bombay—Madras—and Calcutta.

Lecture III.

1. Religions—Hindoos—Mohamedans—Christians—Parsee—and Pariahs.
2. Manners—Dress—Food—Languages—Marriages—Nautches—Music.
3. Character—Superstition—Duplicity—Docility—Timidity—Fidelity.
4. Government—Native Rulers—English Stewards—Financial System.
5. Character, Manners, and Habits of the leading English Families in India.

FIFTH COURSE.
EVILS OF THE EAST INDIA MONOPOLY.

Lecture I.—The India Company.

1. Events that first led to the formation of an English East India Company.
2. Avowed object of the Legislature in granting the original Charter.
3. Means by which the Territorial acquisitions in India have been obtained.
4. Repeated renewals of their Charter at fixed periods, and on what grounds.
5. Limitation of Dividends by Parliament—Its object and effect.
6. Constitution of the East India Company theoretically imperfect.
7. Miscellaneous materials of which the Proprietors are composed.
8. Radical System—Annual Parliaments, Universal Suffrage, & Election by ballot.
9. Announcements of the Directors, and manner of their election.
10. Total absence of all interest in the general welfare of the Country.
11. Patronage the only end, aim, and reward of all their labours.
12. Refined methods of bribery, without violating the letter of the law.
13. Practical consequences of mismanagement—Enormous increase of Debt.
14. Motive for still increasing rather than diminishing the burthen.
15. Absence of all improvement in the condition of the Indian Estate.
16. Wretchedness of the population from excessive taxation.
17. Superstitions of the Natives encouraged, and made a source of gain.

Lecture II.—Commerce with China.

1. Early Attempt of the East India Company to obtain Settlements in China.
2. Trade in Tea, originally insignificant, but now greatly augmented.
3. Profits on this, the sole present source of gain to the India Company.
4. Consequent jealousy against any portion of it being enjoyed by others.
5. Effect of this Monopoly, to inflict a heavy tax on one of the necessaries of life.
6. Profits not so great to the Company as to the Free Trader, from Extravagance.
7. Present Stagnation of Trade in England, arising from over-production.
8. Vast population of China, and active and consuming character of the people.
9. Reduction in the price of Tea would lead to increased consumption here.
10. Manufactured goods of every kind and description would be received in payment.
11. Trade now carried on by the Americans from China to the Eastern Archipelago.
12. Merchants, Manufacturers, Shipowners, and all other classes injured by this.
13. Reasons assigned by the India Company in favour of their China Monopoly.
14. Assumed necessity of existence, and claim of large gains to repair losses.
15. Imputed inferiority of character in English seamen to that of Foreigners.
16. Apprehension for the health of his Majesty's subjects, and for the Revenue.
18. Consequences of the Monopoly to degrade the English flag and character.

Lecture III.—Colonization of India.

1. Contrast between the state of America, New South Wales, and India.
2. Reasons why English settlers have produced such opposite effects.
3. Enumeration of the difficulties under which the English in India labour.
4. The arguments used by the East India Company against Colonization.
5. Pretences on which they defer any interferences with Native Superstitions.
6. Examples of successful interference in abolishing Human Sacrifices in India.
7. Prevalence of a desire among the Natives to possess British Manufactures.
8. Proclamation for the seizure of Englishmen found trading in the interior.
9. Miserable pretence of advances towards a more liberal system.
10. Duty of all classes to unite in opposing the renewal of the Charter.

G

SIXTH AND LAST COURSE.
WHAT IS TO BE DONE WITH INDIA?

LECTURE I.—FUTURE GOVERNMENT OF THE COUNTRY.

1. Declaration of the Sovereignty of India in the King of Great Britain.
2. Appointment of a Viceroy, with full powers and responsibility.
3. Assistance of a Representative Council of English and Natives.
4. Declaration of Proprietary Right in the Soil to belong to Individuals only.
5. Sources of future Revenue, in taxes on property, income, or rank.
6. Inconvenience and Injustice of indirect taxes on commodities.
7. Organization of the Indian Army—order of service and promotion.
8. Efficiency of Regiments, and provision for a Staff Corps.
9. Constitution of the Civil Service, to include Revenue and Diplomatic officers.
10. Establishment of a separate Judicial branch of public servants.
11. Defects of the present system of administering Justice.
12. Formation of a perfect Code, suited to all the religions of the world.
13. Introduction of the English Language as the universal public or official tongue.
14. Establishment of Public Schools for the education of all our Indian subjects.
15. Economy and efficiency of Instruction as a security for loyalty, happiness, and peace.

LECTURE II.—QUALIFICATIONS OF PUBLIC FUNCTIONARIES.

1. The Question of India Patronage as at present exercised, considered.
2. Consequences of transferring it to the Minister or the Crown.
3. Lord Grenville's proposed mode of selecting Candidates for office.
4. Beneficial effect of such a stimulus on England as well as on India.
5. Public Examination of Candidates reported as qualified.
6. Subsequent Education to be pursued by each, from sixteen to twenty.
7. Final Examination at twenty, previous to receiving appointment.
8. Employment of two years in finishing Education, by Travel in Britain.
9. Completion of probation, by a journey of two years on the Continent of Europe.
10. Journey to India, through Turkey, Asia Minor, and Persia, by land.
11. Superior advantages of this mode of preparation over that now in use.
12. Objections as to time and expense of process, answered.
13. Age of arrival and entry on public duties in India, twenty-five.
14. Standard of selection to first appointments,—fitness and merit.
15. Advantages to be given to the husbands of English wives, and why?
16. Subsequent promotion, by gradation in the line of service.
17. No removal from the Service but by verdict of a Jury.
18. Rewards for meritorious conduct, by landed estates in India.

LECTURE III.—BENEFICIAL EFFECTS OF THE NEW SYSTEM.

1. Simplification of the Political System, and integrity of rule.
2. Exercise of public opinion on the conduct of public men.
3. Speedy Administration of Justice in an intelligible form.
4. Extended cultivation of immense tracts of land, now lying waste.
5. Improvement of cotton, sugar, silk, and every other article of Indian produce.
6. Discovery of new articles of Commerce, mineral and vegetable.
7. Steam communication on the rivers, especially in towing.
8. Building of Inns, Dwellings, Bridges, Canals, and other public works.
9. Daily spread of European taste, by the influence of example.
10. Organization of Militias and Magistracies for internal police.
11. Establishment of Scientific Societies, Public Journals, and Schools of Art.
12. Increased wealth of the country, by increase of intelligence.
13. Augmented consumption of every description of English goods.
14. Communications from India with all the Asiatic continent.
15. Opening of China, Japan, and the Eastern Archipelago to civilization.
16. Employment for our increasing surplus educated classes of society.
17. Duties of Mother Countries to their Colonial Offspring.

The intention is to give any one or more of these Short Courses in every town, making the stay in each to depend entirely on the degree of interest evinced on the first visit; and to admit of an attendance on these being brought within the reach of all the educated classes of the kingdom, especially of the more respectable among the middle ranks of society, and to avoid the necessity of any purchase of Tickets pledging an attendance on the whole, the terms have been reduced to HALF-A-CROWN for each separate Admission, (which is only half the original rate of charge), as being better adapted to the means of the great majority of the reading and enquiring portion of society.

This price will be uniformly adhered to in large Assembly Rooms, Music Halls, or other places not admitting separation of ranks; but in the event of the Lectures being delivered in a Theatre, which may sometimes be deemed desirable, the prices of admission to the separate divisions of the House will be exactly those which are established by usage in the town itself.

Having been repeatedly invited by the public Authorities and Institutions of several of the principal towns in England, to communicate these particulars to them as a guide for their information, which has generally been accompanied also by a desire to know the best method of proceeding, and the number of Subscribers which would be deemed sufficient to warrant the delivery of a Course in any of the cities or towns of the kingdom, I beg to suggest to such persons as may feel an interest in this matter, the placing a board in each of the Public News Rooms and Booksellers' shops of the towns in which they reside, for the reception of such names as may be obtained, and having the List circulated to private individuals and families if necessary; and whenever the names subscribed may be sufficient to insure an audience of 200 persons for *one* Short Course of Three Lectures only, I shall be happy to visit such towns, and risk the issue beyond that number on my own account. The necessity for some security or guarantee of numbers, arises from two causes: first the importance, for the sake of the public good, of giving a preference to those towns in which the largest numbers can be addressed at one time; and secondly, the necessity of preventing loss, by obtaining sufficient to cover the actual expense.

I can sincerely say that I should rejoice to be in a condition to make this question of expense a matter of no importance to myself. But the world are well aware of the manner in which I have been despoiled of the accumulated fortune which years of labour had been passed in acquiring; and as the East India Company, who might have restored the plunder committed on me by their servants abroad, but who have rejected every appeal made to them for redress, have now a still more powerful motive to wish for my destruction, and to assist in trampling me in the dust, I have only my own energies, and the support of the British Public to rely on, for carrying my object into effect;— and cannot, therefore, if I would, charge myself with all the burthen of its cost.

London, Jan. 1, 1830.   J. S. BUCKINGHAM.

PLAN

FOR THE

FUTURE GOVERNMENT

OF

INDIA.

BY

JAMES SILK BUCKINGHAM.

LONDON:

PARTRIDGE & OAKEY, 34, PATERNOSTER ROW;

AND 70, EDGWARE ROAD.

1853.

Price One Shilling.

PLAN

FOR THE

FUTURE GOVERNMENT OF INDIA.

INDIA, its people, its resources, and its government, has occupied a larger share of my attention than any other topic, for a period of nearly forty years. In the year 1813, I first left England for Turkey; and after traversing a large portion of the Oriental world, and making its peculiarities and condition the subject of careful research and investigation; after accomplishing two successive journeys overland to India, the first by way of Egypt, the Red Sea, and Arabia; the second by way of Palestine, Messopotamia, Assyria, and Persia; and ultimately visiting Bombay, Ceylon, Madras, and Calcutta, including most of the stations and settlements on the coasts of Malabar, Ceylon, and Coromandel, constantly in close intercourse with the natives of all ranks and classes; I became a resident of Calcutta in 1818, and was occupied from that year till 1823, as editor of the first daily journal published in India, *The Calcutta Journal*, and the only one not conducted by an actual servant of the Government. From 1824 to 1829, my whole time was devoted to the study and exposition of Indian affairs, in the editorship of *The Oriental Herald*, published in London; and from that period to this (with the single exception of three years travelling in America), I have never relaxed in my interest in, and attention to, Indian affairs, in Parliament and out of it, as the inhabitants of every town of any

B

size in England, Scotland, and Ireland, can bear witness, by the delivery of public addresses in each, on India and its government. I may add that, within the same period of time, I have read attentively all the works that have been published on India, from Sir John Malcolm, Sir Thomas Munro, the Honourable Mountstuart Elphinstone, Mr. James Mill, Mr. Rickards, Mr. Thornton, General Briggs, and others of the earlier period, down to Mr. Campbell, Mr. Prinsep, Mr. Chapman, Mr. Norton, Mr Sullivan, Mr. Cameron, Mr. Kaye, and the writers of more recent date, as well as every speech delivered in either House of Parliament on the subject of India, and such portions of the evidence as have yet been made public by the Committees of the Lords and Commons.

I make this statement only for the purpose of showing that the conclusions at which I have arrived, are not the result of any crude or hasty conceptions, such as might be expected from a President of the Board of Control, who admits that up to the period of his taking office, he was wholly ignorant of India and its affairs, never having devoted his time or attention to the subject; yet who, in the short space of about six months after thus taking office, in the complete state of ignorance avowed, nevertheless undertakes an elaborate defence of the existing system of rule in India, in a speech of five hours duration, and in exposition of the principal features of a new bill for the government of India, which, in this short space of time, he professes himself perfectly competent to draw up and present to the legislature of the country for their acceptance.

The result is just what might have been expected. The Bill appears to satisfy no party, except its author, and perhaps the Cabinet and his colleagues, who, if it had been even much worse, (though that is hardly conceivable) would have felt themselves bound, by the etiquette of official life, to defend the abortive offspring of one of their own body. The East India Company complain of it in the bitterest terms, as destructive of their ancient privileges. The proprietors of East India Stock denounce it, as perilling their dividends, and taking away their hopes of benefit from patronage. The Conservatives condemn it by the speech of Mr. Disraeli, by the motion of

Lord Stanley, and the amendments of others of their party. The Liberals repudiate it, by the speeches of Mr. Hume, Mr. Bright, Mr. Cobden, and many others; and even Mr. Macaulay, with all his eloquence, is compelled to limit his eulogy to one or two provisions out of a large number, of which he can say nothing in praise, and therefore judiciously ignores them altogether; while the public at large, as far as can be gathered from the expression of their sentiments, through public meetings and the press, are as little disposed to approve the Bill as any of its opponents in either House of Parliament.

In the course of the debate in the Commons it was urged as a reproach to those who disapproved the Bill, that they had produced no other or better plan themselves: to which they replied, by quoting the well-known remark of Sir Robert Peel, that " it was time enough for a physician to prescribe when he should be called in." To answer this challenge, therefore, in default of a more official champion, I venture to supply this deficiency, by proposing a plan; and if my countrymen give me credit for possessing an average amount of capacity for such a task, they cannot doubt, after the preliminary recital of my experience, that I have had at least abundant means of forming an accurate judgment, any more than they can doubt my perfect freedom and independence, as being no longer actively engaged in public life, and having, therefore, nothing to hope and nothing to fear from those in power, whether at the India House or in the Cabinet.

I proceed, therefore, to develop the principal features of the plan for the future Government of India, which, after the maturest consideration, appears to me most likely to accomplish the chief end of all good government, " the happiness of the people governed;" and, collaterally with this, to benefit, to the greatest extent, the people of this country by the speedy development of the resources of India, the extension of our commerce with its inhabitants, and the attachment of all ranks and classes of our fellow subjects in that vast and varied empire to the British rule, from a conviction of its strength, mildness, equity, and justice.

Sovereignty of the Crown.

THE foundation stone of the new superstructure, should be the
entire disuse of the name and authority of " The East India
Company," which, being incorporated as a Trading Association, really ceased to have any legitimate existence, when its
trading powers were annihilated, by the Charter Act of 1833,—
and the substitution of the name and authority of " the Crown
of England," to which, as much as all other portions of the
British Empire, India now undoubtedly belongs.   The fiction
of a Sovereign authority in the Company, is now too thinly
veiled, to pass current even with the natives of India.   They
know that the Crown of England appoints the Governor-
General and Commander-in-Chief; that the Royal Navy and
Royal Army take precedence in India of the Company's
marine and Company's troops; that the Supreme Courts of
Justice at each of the Presidencies, administer justice in the
Queen's name, and that the Judges of these Courts are wholly
independent of the Company's authority.   They have, for ages,
been accustomed to regard the honours conferred by the
Monarch as far higher than any which the Company could
bestow ; and they know that " the Monarchy " is an enduring
feature of the British Constitution ; while " the Company " is
a body of private individuals, whose power is overruled by
that of the Minister of the day ; and even its nominal authority
granted or farmed out to it, on a lease for twenty years only.
For these, and other reasons, this fiction of the Company's
name being used as the governing power of India, ought to be
at once discontinued; as we have already discontinued the
equally false and flimsy fiction of " the Great Mogul " being
the Sovereign of India, and the Company merely his stewards ;
though the poor old man was all the while a state prisoner at
Delhi, and could not go beyond his capital without permission,
while a petty allowance was granted to him for his maintenance, and all the surplus of his revenues remitted to England
for the benefit of the Company, and the proprietors of East
India Stock.

As a first step, therefore, let the Queen be declared by the Bill, and proclaimed in every city, town, and district in all India, as the actual Sovereign of that portion of the country now subject to British rule.

———

Formation of a Home Government.

A VERY general idea seems to prevail, that it would be impossible for an Indian Minister to execute the duties of his office, as Secretary of State for Indian affairs, without a Consultative Council, composed chiefly of persons who had resided in India for a certain number of years; and considerable difficulty seems to have been felt, as to how such a Council should be formed, whether by election, and if so, by whom, or by nomination, or by a mixture of both. But it may be well first to settle the previous question, " Is such a Consultative Council indispensable, or even necessary at all?" I am clearly of opinion that it is not.

The Secretary of State for Foreign Affairs conducts all the correspondence and communications with as great a variety of countries and people, and of as varied languages, religions, manners, and customs, as all India, without a Consultative Council of the nature deemed necessary for that country; and the statesman filling this post, is presumed to understand thoroughly the conflicting interests and diversified political systems of each—including those of France, Russia, Austria, Prussia, Norway, Denmark, Sweden, the smaller States of Germany, Holland, Belgium, Switzerland, Spain, Portugal, Tuscany, the Papal States, the two Sicilies, Greece, Turkey, Egypt, Persia, and China—Northern, Southern, and Central America, from Mexico to Cape Horn, with all their numerous empires, states, and republics—having correspondence with some fifty ambassadors and ministers of different degrees, and hundreds of Consuls and Vice-Consuls spread over these various regions. Yet it has never been proposed or suggested that the Secretary for Foreign Affairs should be assisted by a Consultative Council, formed chiefly of persons who had resided a given number of years in any or all of these distant lands.

In like manner, the Secretary of State for the Colonies presides over and directs the business of his department—which embraces legislation for, and communication with, as great an extent and variety of countries, as all India presents, and with considerable differences also of religion, language, local laws, and customs in each:—including Upper and Lower Canada, where the religion is chiefly Roman Catholic and the language French, Nova Scotia, New Brunswick, and Newfoundland, where Protestants prevail; the West Indies, where, as in Trinidad, the language and customs are Spanish; Guiana, where they are Dutch; Gibraltar and Malta, where they are Spanish, Italian, and Phœnician, or African Arabic; the Ionian Islands and Cerigo, where they are Greek; the Cape of Good Hope, where they are Dutch; the Mauritius, where they are French; the Island of Ceylon, where the people are Buddhists and Mohammedans, and the language Singalese; Hong-Kong and Shangai, where the native population are Chinese; and onward to the Southern Colonies of Australia, Van Dieman's Land, and New Zealand; offering in the whole as great a diversity of people and interests as all India presents. Yet no Consultative Council has ever been proposed to aid the Colonial Minister, formed of individuals who were personally acquainted, by actual residence, with all these varied countries, subject to his supervision and control.

Why, then, require such a body to aid the minister for *India?* or, if necessary and proper for him, why not have such a body for the Foreign and Colonial Minister also? If it would be good for one, it would be equally so for the others: if it is not required for these two, neither is it needful for the one.

The truth is, that the permanent staff of all the Public Departments, who are brought up in them from their first entry as clerks, and rise by length of service and capacity, to the highest positions which the service admits, possess all the knowledge of details which any Consultative Council could furnish; and hence it is, that though the Secretary at War may know nothing of the army at his first filling that post (which was the case probably with Mr. Sidney Herbert); though the President of the Board of Control may know still less, if possible, of India, on taking office (which was the case with Sir John Hobhouse, Mr. Herries, and Sir Charles Wood); they are assisted by the Office Staff, who possess all the information of which they themselves are so ignorant; and by time and labour (if, indeed, they are supposed to remain long enough), they thus get to know sufficient to enable them to form a sound opinion on the matters submitted to their decision. Even the Public Secretaries of these Departments, who are changed with their superiors on every change of ministry, are often in the same happy state of ignorance. Mr. John Parker and Mr. Henry Ward, when made Secretaries of the Admiralty, were both completely ignorant of naval or maritime affairs. Mr. Emerson Tennant, Mr. Robert Gordon, and Mr. James Wilson, when made Secretaries to the India Board, were equally ignorant of Indian affairs: and these also had to rely entirely on the permanent staff of the office for all the detailed information they required.

But the most remarkable proofs that can be cited, that local knowledge of India is not deemed requisite to qualify persons for being appointed to the direction of its affairs, is to be found in the fact that neither in the appointment of the Governor-General who exercises supreme power in India, nor in the election of India Directors who exercise supreme power over the Governor-General, and can recal him if they see fit, nor in the nomination of a President of the Board of Control, who really exercises supreme power over the Directors, and can send any order he pleases to the Governors of India, either without consulting the Directors at all, or in spite of their unanimous protest or remonstrance; in neither of these cases is any knowledge of India or Indian affairs deemed requisite. Hence Lord Hastings, Lord Amherst, Lord Auckland, and Lord Dalhousie were all appointed without any practical knowledge of or acquaintance with India; and all of them engaged in unnecessary and expensive wars: hence Mr. Masterman, Mr. Astell, Mr. Ellice, Mr. Smith, and many others who never set foot in India were elected as Directors; and the most recent

election of all was that of Mr. Majoribanks,—a young gentleman of no experience of public affairs, either in India, in
England, or elsewhere—his only claim being that he was the
son of a leading partner in Coutts's Bank, and a son-in-law of
Sir James Hogg, then Chairman of the Court,—and this, too,
at a time when a gentleman of long experience in India, who
presented to the public the highest testimonials of two successive Governors-General as to his fitness for the office, was
obliged to withdraw his solid claims before the empty pretensions of his young and inexperienced competitor.

After these examples, it will be seen that the qualification of
a " practical knowledge of India and its affairs " has never
been deemed necessary for the highest of all offices in its
government; and that the pretence of the necessity of a Consultative Council for the Indian Minister is merely an endeavour
to delude the public with a specious reason for still keeping up
the Company, as an advising Board, or forming it into a Council with the slight modification of adding a few Directors
nominated by the Minister, and rendering it even a less independent body than it is at present: in short, keeping up the
fiction of what is falsely called " a double Government ; " as,
after all, the real governing power is single—being vested in
the Indian Minister alone—though all the expense and delay
of a double Government is retained.

One certain and inseparable evil of this so called " double
government" and " divided power," is, that neither party is
willing to admit its responsibility ; and it becomes almost impossible to fix it on the right person. If there be any wrong
to be complained of, or any act deserving censure, the President
of the Board of Control fixes it on the Court of Directors, by
whom it is bandied back to the Board of Control ; when sometimes
both unite to charge the blame on the Government in India,
and this again retorts the charge on the Home authorities ; till
the public and the Parliament, wearied out with this protracted
war of words, get tired of the subject, and the guilty parties
are never known or made in any way responsible to the Parliament or the public.

For all these reasons, and many more that might be urged,

my conviction is, that it would be best to dispense entirely with the agency either of a Court of Directors or Consultative Council, and place the whole responsibility of the Indian Government in the hands of an Indian Minister of State, with an adequate, permanent, official staff, in the same way as the Foreign and Colonial Ministers now conduct their respective departments.

By this means, all the expenses of the East India House, of Haileybury, of Addiscombe, and of every other portion of the machinery of the East India Company, would be saved ; and the service rendered far more effective by concentration in few hands, than as now divided among so many.

But, in such a change, the Indian Minister should be put on exactly the same footing, as to rank and salary, as the other Ministers of the Crown ; and when a Cabinet was formed, the member of it best fitted, by his previous studies and experience, for the office, should be selected to fill it, instead of its being given to the one who might not be thought fit for any other department, and therefore be content with a smaller salary, which is often the rule of choice at present. He should be divested at the same time of all patronage beyond that of his immediate official staff; and this should apply only to first appointments in the lowest grade; the promotion beyond this being by length of service, except in cases where special aptitude for special duties might require the selection of some particular individual of the office for higher occupation, for which others of his standing might be deemed less fit.

Representation of India in Parliament.

THIS naturally leads to the consideration of how to render the talents and experience of men who have passed a large portion of their lives in India, or devoted much of their time to the study of its affairs, most usefully available. I think this could be best done by their being sent into Parliament as representatives of *India*. As a beginning, it might perhaps be sufficient to restrict the representation to the five Presidencies, namely, Bengal, Madras, Bombay, Agra, and the Punjaub. An intelligent and independent constituency could be formed out of the British residents in each of these, including the Civil and Military service, the officers of the Army and Navy, the British settlers, as merchants or planters, and the professional classes, as clergymen and ministers of religion, legal and medical men, engineers, and others. Five members might be assigned to each Presidency. The candidates need not be present in India, as they would, in all probability, be selected from those who had returned to England after having distinguished themselves in the civil, military, mercantile, or professional classes in that country, and be chosen for their high reputation. The votes might be communicated to the Returning Officer, at the chief town of the Presidency, in writing, so as to save personal attendance (as was proposed by me in the sketch of a Reform Bill for England, so long ago as 1837, and which has recently been proposed in the House of Lords by the Earl of Shaftesbury, and will no doubt be ultimately adopted), and all the expense and trouble of polling, under proper guarantees, of course, against fraud, of which, however, from the nature of the constituency, and their scattered residences, there would be little danger, as none of the foul agencies of canvassing, treating, bribery, or intimidation, so disgracefully rife in England, could there have place. There need be no limitation to the number of candidates, but the five who obtained the greatest number of suffrages would be elected.

If the distance of India should be urged as an objection to this, it may be answered, that the choice of the Indian Members would be known as speedily now as that of the Members for the Orkneys could be half a century ago ; and the delay of a few weeks in the formation of each new Parliament, would be of no great importance. Nor could any one truly say that this number of members would be too great for the representation of India. When London and its suburbs send twelve members for a population of 2,000,000 of inhabitants, twenty-five members for 150,000,000, could hardly be complained of as disproportionately large.

By such a system as this, the able men from India, who will not now go through the degradation of a five or six years' canvass, and an expenditure of some thousands of pounds, to be elected by a body whose suffrages confer no honour, since they have not the slightest relation to the merit of the individual chosen, would be almost sure to be sent to Parliament by such a British Indian constituency as that described ; and we should then see men of the same high character as Sir John Malcolm, Sir Thomas Munroe, Sir Henry Russell, Sir Henry Strachey, Sir Charles Metcalfe, Sir Francis Macnaghton, Sir Edward West, Sir Charles Forbes, Sir Herbert Maddock, Mr. Holt Mackenzie, Sir Charles Trevelyan, Mr. Sullivan, Mr. Wilberforce Bird, Mr. Mountstuart Elphinstone, Sir Erskine Perry, and a host of other Indian worthies, civil and military, legal and mercantile, filling the seats for India in the House of Commons,—where their Indian knowledge and experience would be of infinite service to the Indian Minister, and to the nation at large ; and, being publicly given on their own individual responsibility, would be of far more value than if they were sitting in private conclave as a Consultative Council, offering advice which might not be adopted, and of which the world would know nothing, till the occasion on which it might have been useful was passed away, and all its utility was at an end.

It is impossible to overrate the benefits which would result from the light to be thrown on Indian affairs by twenty-five such representatives as these, independent alike of the Crown, and the Court of Directors ; having no patronage of appointments to sway their opinions or their votes ; and only the honest convictions of their own independent judgments for their guide.

If the existing body of East India Directors should be thought by those most competent to judge (namely, the British Indian constituencies just described), to possess within themselves " all the talents" necessary for the business of Indian legislation, there could be no possible objection to their choosing the whole body of twenty-four, and one over, as their representatives, in which case they might find a noble field for the exercise of that public spirit and disinterestd devotion to Indian welfare, which they all so zealously profess when they become candidates for a seat in the Direction; and then, instead of being compelled, as they now are, to send out dispatches, signed with their own names, and delivered as their own acts, though they have protested against their contents in the strongest terms (a condition of such prostrate humiliation, that one wonders how any man, with a spark of self-respect, could stoop so low as to become the unwilling instrument of another's pleasure, and against his own convictions), they would then be able to beard the Indian Minister in his place in Parliament, and, by convicting him of ignorance or injustice, shame him into doing right, by carrying the House with them, or in their favour. The very circumstance, indeed, of five and twenty such well-informed, independent men being in the House, to detect, expose, and denounce whatever they deemed wrong in Indian affairs, would operate as a most powerful check against any Indian Minister daring to sanction any act, or course of proceeding which he felt himself unable to defend.

The Home Government for India would be thus incorporated with the general Government of the country, by being considered merely as an additional Department of State; and, being aided and checked by the presence of British Indian representatives in Parliament, with whom, of course, the ultimate adoption and ratification of all measures for India would rest, as they do in point of fact, it would be carried on as part of the general business of the empire, in the same manner as the business of the Home and Foreign Departments, the Colonial, the Naval, and the Military is executed at present.

To effect this change, no new Bill, or Act of Parliament would be necessary; the present Act or Charter of the East India Company would quietly expire in April, 1854; and the Company and its proprietary body die a natural death, as far as their connection with or control over India and its affairs are concerned. Nor could they have the smallest right to complain of this; as the period fixed for the duration of their privileges has been known to them for the last twenty years; and their stock and dividends being guaranteed to them till twenty years even beyond that period (1874), any opposition on their part to the Government resuming the power thus leased out to them for a specific time, would be as unreasonable as that of a tenant whose lease had expired, and who should complain of his landlord because he was unwilling to renew it. As a matter of courtesy, the Minister of the day might pay them the compliment of communicating with them on the subject, before their lease should actually expire, so as to prepare them for the change ; but their consent or concurrence is in no degree necessary ; and their formal protests and complaints at the India House, and in the Court of Proprietors of East India Stock, are at once useless and ridiculous. They accepted their lease on the known conditions of its expiring in 1854; and were, therefore, consenting parties to their own dissolution, as a political body, when that period should arrive.

Whether, like the South Sea Company, which has held together for upwards of a century after the bubble on which they were founded had burst, the East India Company should choose to remain still as a trading association without trade, or a political association without power, might be safely left to themselves ; but their votes being no longer required, for the election of Directors, or, if required, there being no patronage to give them in exchange, they would speedily relinquish all further care about the matter.

Appointment of a Viceroy.

The Queen's Sovereignty being proclaimed over all India, the next step would be the selection and appointment of a fit and proper person to represent " The Crown," in this part of its dominions, and for whom the title of " Viceroy " would be most intelligible, and most appropriate : for, if Ireland deserves such a distinction, India would possess an equally powerful claim to it ; and with the natives of that country, of every rank and class, it would convey the desired impression of regal and monarchical authority.

Hitherto, the choice of the Governor General, as well as the power of recalling him, has rested with the East India Company; but the Crown possessing a veto of approbation or rejection, the farce has been gone through by the "double government," of making it appear on all occasions that the Company were the real choosers of the person to be sent out; whereas, in point of fact, the choice originates with the Crown, or the Minister of the day; and the course pursued is simply this :—the Cabinet instructs the President of the Board of Control to inform the East India Directors that my Lord this, or the Marquis of that, is the person of whom they approve as the Governor-General to be appointed; and the Directors, knowing that it is useless for them to name any other, as the Crown would put a veto on their choice, are obliged to consent, and give the appointment, often against their own predelictions and convictions, as they cannot help themselves. The second farce performed, is at the public dinner which is always given by the Directors to all the Governors sent out to India, whether they approve of the choice or not. At this banquet, the President of the Board of Control, and the other members of the Cabinet who may have forced the unwelcome Governor on the Directors as a protegée of their own, are usually present and must often smile when they hear the fulsome eulogies of the Chairman of the Court, whose official duty it is to preside at such entertainments, bestowed on the very Governors against whose appointment they have the strongest objection, but which they dare not, nevertheless, refuse to ratify.

Hitherto, also, the Ministers of the day have been actuated by very different motives, in the selection of their Governors for India. Lord Moira, it is now well known, was sent out at the request of the Prince Regent, to enable him to repair a shattered fortune, ruined chiefly by advances to that profligate prince for the most unworthy purposes; though the embarrassments of the noble lord were so great, that all his allowances as Governor-General and Commander in Chief were insufficient to pay even the interest of his debts; and, on his return from India, his carriage and horses, the only visible property he had, were seized by his creditors, and he died at last in debt and exile, as Governor of Malta. His successor, Lord Amherst was selected by Mr. Canning, from personal rather than public motives; and when he plunged the country into the first Burmese war, and exhausted the Indian Treasury, Mr. Canning admitted in the House of Commons that though he was deemed sufficient for the task of ruling such an empire in a state of peace, the contingency of war had not been calculated on. Sir William A'Court, afterwards Lord Heytesbury, was chosen by Sir Robert Peel, as being one of his political party; but though approved by the Court of Directors, he was recalled by the Whigs just on the point of his embarkation, and Lord Auckland, one of their family compact, though highly objectionable to the India Directors, as being thought deficient in ability, was sent out instead, chiefly, it is believed, because he was poor as a nobleman, and India was a fine field for repairing or making a fortune. The Marquis of Tweeddale at Madras, Lord Falkland at Bombay, and other Governors that might be named, owed their appointments entirely to their political connections with the Government of the day, the question of their fitness weighing only as a feather in the balance, compared with political and family considerations. And the "double government," as it is called, is such a screen to transactions of this kind, as to veil the real nature of them almost entirely from the public view.

Under the new system of rule for India, this will require a complete reform. The Viceroy should be chosen on no other ground than his perfect qualification for the duties of that high and responsible office. Instead of appointing needy noblemen, political partizans, or family connections, the ablest Indian officer that could be found, should be selected for that post; and, when selected, clothed with all the attributes of rank and power that should make him, in the eyes of the native princes and people, as well as in those of the English residents, whether in the public service or in private life, a becoming Representative of Majesty in the East. As a check upon the choice of the Cabinet, it should be required to be ratified by a vote of the House of Commons, a vote of the House of Lords, and the approbation of the Sovereign; and, on the return of the Viceroy, from a successful administration of Indian affairs, during

c

his three, five, or seven years' term, he should, if successful, be admitted to the House of Peers with a degree of rank corresponding to his merits; or, in the event of falling short in the performance of his duties, or being guilty of mal-administration during his term of office, be subject to impeachment and censure, by votes of both Houses of Parliament; for the same bodies that can publicly vote their thanks to those who behave well, should have equal power to pronounce their public censure on those who do ill.

Under such a system as this, we should see such men as Sir Charles Metcalfe, Mr. Lawrence, Mr. Bird, Mr. Thomason, Sir Frederick Currie, Mr. Elphinstone, and similar Indian celebrities chosen as Governors-General, and *their* intimate acquaintance with India and its affairs, in all their vast variety, would prevent them being made the tools (as is now too often the case with the raw and uninformed men who go out to fill the office) of designing persons, who are too apt to mislead them to serve their own purposes, and then escape from the responsibility of their own advice. We give peerages and pensions too, to leaders who win successful battles—though the bravery of their troops has often more to do in obtaining the victory than the skill of their commanders. Surely, the highest honours that the nation can bestow would be as well deserved by those who should govern a vast province well; and if any men deserved a Roman triumph at the people's hands, it would be those who, like Lord William Bentinck, left India better than he found it, and introduced more improvements—financial, political, and moral—than any of his predecessors—without oppression, and without a war!

Assistance of a Legislative Council.

Though, for the reasons before assigned, no Consultative Council would be necessary in *England*, where the Indian Minister would have his experienced official staff for all matters of detail: and his five-and-twenty Indian Representatives in the

House of Commons, whose advice and opinions he might at all times obtain: while the assistance and concurrence of both Houses of Parliament would be available for the consideration and revision of any legislative measures which he might deem requisite for the better direction of Indian affairs ;—yet, in *India*, where no such aids would exist, and where, after all, the chief business of the actual government must originate and be carried into execution, it would be important to have a *Legislative*, and not merely a Consultative Council—possessed both of authority to advise with the Viceroy, and power to co-operate with him, on nearly equal terms, in conducting the business of the country, by passing such laws and regulations as might from time to time be deemed requisite for the improvement of the revenue and judicial services, and every other branch of the Indian Administration.

Such a Council might be formed of ten English and ten native members—sufficiently numerous to admit of the wholesome diversity of experience and opinions, and sufficiently few to concentrate responsibility; the Viceroy being President of the Council, and having a casting vote: and twelve members besides the President forming a quorum.

The Council should not be nominated by the Crown, as they might then be formed of mere political partizans of the reigning party in power; nor be nominated by the Viceroy himself, as they might then be too subservient to his views. But they should be elected by the five Presidencies already named, two English and two Native members from each.

The same English constituency, as that already indicated for the choice of the twenty-five Members of Parliament, five from each Presidency, might be available for election of the English Members of the Indian Legislative Council; and a Native constituency could be easily formed for the election of the Native Members, out of all Natives holding offices, under the British Government, and not being mere subordinates or clerks.

The mode of election might be the same as that prescribed for the English Members of Parliament for India, the names of the voters being sent in writing to the returning officer appointed for that purpose, at the chief seat of Government, and the two highest on the list of candidates from each Presidency being declared to be elected.

The duration of their term of office might be made concurrent with the reign of the Viceroy; vacancies by death or resignation, during that period, to be supplied by new elections in the same manner.

The three English Judges of the Supreme Court of Judicature at the seat of Government, might be, ex-officio, Members of this Legislative Council, as their knowledge of the principles of jurisprudence, their legal experience, and the weight of their character for learning, independence, and integrity, by which, the occupants of the English Bench are almost uniformly characterized, would be a guarantee against crude and hasty legislation, and greatly add to the public confidence in the measures receiving their sanction.

The result of such an arrangement would probably be this; that the English Members of the Council, elected as described, would be the *élite* of the Civil, Military, Legal, or Mercantile classes, of the several Presidencies, best known by character and reputation to their fellow countrymen; and that the Native Members would include the most eminent of their respective classes for wealth, knowledge, and popularly high character, and many such are easy to be found in all the Presidencies, including Hindoos, Mohammedans, and Parsees—thoroughly well acquainted with the resources, wants, and interests of the country, and requiring only a field for the exercise of their talents.

Of the high qualifications of some of the principal Natives of India, for the most difficult duties of government, those best know who have lived most amongst them; but if any should doubt this, let them take the examples of the Rajah of Mysore, as described by Bishop Heber, in his interesting Tour in India—of Rammohun Roy, and Dwarkanuth Tagore, both of whom visited this country and are almost as well known in England as in India. Indeed, it may be affirmed, that considering the circumstances under which they were placed, three men of greater talents than these, were never produced in the same age in any country of

Europe; while, as to the Natives of the generation just preceding them (not to go back to the Akbars, the Shah Jehans, and other remarkable men of earlier date), we have the testimony of the Duke of Wellington, whose Indian dispatches abound with instances of the highest praise bestowed on the natives, who acted with him, for their capacity, intelligence, and trustworthiness, in all affairs of public business. He speaks with admiration of the manner in which the Regent of Mysore, Poorneah, administered the Province under his care, after having been prime minister to Hyder Ali, and Tippoo Sahib, and governing Mysore during eleven years; the Great Duke is equally eloquent on the diplomatic talents and services of Govind Rao, and of the unimpeachable integrity of Bisnapunt, all native Indians who had acted with, and assisted him in his Indian campaigns; and to one of whom, Poorneah, the illustrious Englishman made a present of his picture, " in testimony of the high sense which he entertained of the admirable administration of the affairs of his kingdom."

Such men still exist in India, though a few generations more of our depressing policy might go far to extinguish the race. But, let them be once admitted to a participation with us in the government of their own country, and the very hope of such a distinction will give birth to many more. Nor need we fear that the policy, which won for Alexander of Macedon the rapid and easy subjugation of the East, and made the Romans welcome conquerors of provinces—namely, that of admitting the natives of the conquered countries to the free and full participation of Macedonian and Roman rights and privileges—will produce any other feelings in the native breast than those of pride and satisfaction at being at length associated with us in devising the best means for making their common country prosperous and happy.

Admissions to the Indian Service.

Having provided for the Home Government of India by an Indian Minister and staff, and the presence of Representatives

of India in the Imperial Parliament; and having equally provided for the choice of a Viceroy and Legislative Council in
India itself, to whom should be entrusted the largest powers to
frame and enact laws and regulations for the administration of
affairs in India—subject only to such general principles as
might be laid down for their guidance, but without the useless
delay and expense of perpetual references to the home authorities on all trifling occasions—the next important point to be
considered would perhaps be the conditions of admission to the
Indian service.

It is no doubt desirable to prevent this being made a matter
of patronage or favour, either of the minister of the day, or of
any other body; and for this purpose, nothing can be better
than to make it the reward of the highest merit, in open com-
petition to all the youths of the empire, both here and in India,
—in short open to all British subjects, whether in the mother
country, the colonies, or India itself, without distinction of
colour, race, or creed. It may be quite true, that great abili-
ties in youth are not invariably the guarantee for high moral
character and official aptitude in later life; but, as a general
rule, it may be safely admitted, that where such early proofs of
ability are given, the chances of subsequent excellence are far
greater than where they are not; and therefore it is the safest
rule that can be followed.

As to the mode of carrying this system of open competition
into actual operation, it is not very difficult to devise. Every
year an average number of appointments to the Indian service
will become vacant, by deaths, retirements, and resignations.
This being ascertained, an equal or greater number of candidates for such appointments will be invited. The age of admission might be fixed at not less than twenty. The education
might be conducted wherever the parents thought fit,—by
private tutors, at public schools, at the universities, or all in
succession. A Board of five Examiners being formed, one
appointed by each of the Universities of Oxford, Cambridge,
London, Dublin, and Edinburgh, a period would be fixed in
each year, when all who were within the proper age, and who
deemed themselves qualified (whether born in England, the

colonies, or India—whether Christian, Hindoo, or Mahomedan),
would present themselves for examination. If fifty, for
example, were the number required, the fifty highest on the
list would obtain the nomination, and the remainder might be
remanded for the next year if they saw fit to try again, or seek
some other profession. To give due reward to merit according
to its proper degree, the highest on the list—the senior
wrangler, as we might call him—should be allowed to choose
the Presidency which he would prefer, and the branch of the
service he would like best; and the remainder should have
the same choice, as far as the vacancies would admit, in regular
succession, till all the nominations were completed.

After thus receiving their public admission into the Indian
service, the special education required for the particular branch
or line of duty chosen, should be entered on by the aspirants. If
it were the diplomatic, then the history of India, its courts, laws,
and customs, with the Persian language and literature should
be studied—this being the court and diplomatic language of
India. If it were the legal or judicial, then the science of
jurisprudence, the rules of evidence, the Hindoo and Mohammedan laws, and the vernacular of the Presidency chosen,
should be pursued. If it were the revenue branch, then the
science of political economy, agriculture, natural history,
botany, civil engineering, and the construction of public works
of irrigation, drainage, &c., would be fitting subjects of investigation. If it were the military, then the special topics of information requisite to qualify them for the proper duties to be
discharged, would be the object of their study. For all this,
two years of time might be allowed; and at the end of that
period, a special examination by competent persons might be
made, and if passed satisfactorily, the appointment to the service should be confirmed; but if not, the candidate might be
remanded for another year, or lose his first position.

This would bring the aspirant to his twenty-second year,
when he would be yet too young to be placed in any of the
important posts which the Indian service would require him
to fill. Another year might therefore be most advantageously
passed by him in visiting personally the chief marts of industry in

England, Scotland, and Ireland, and making himself thoroughly acquainted with his own country. After that, let him make his way to India by land, visiting in his journey the principal capitals of Europe, on his way to Constantinople, and from thence going onward by such route as he and his companions (as it might be advantageous to travel in groups of five or ten together) might prefer—through Asia Minor and Syria, to Egypt, and thence by the Red Sea ; through Mesopotamia *via* Bagdad and Bussorah, and thence by the Persian Gulf; or through Circassia, Georgia, and Persia, and thence by Affghanistan to the Punjaub, and down through the Indian peninsula to the seat of the Supreme Government, there to receive the necessary orders and authority for repairing to his proper post.

One of the greatest disadvantages of the present system is that both the civil and military servants of the Company arrive in India too young—while mere boys indeed, in experience as well as years — with constitutions weakened by luxurious ease, and in danger of still greater injury by the sudden effects of great change of climate, and free, not to say intemperate living, during their stay at the Presidencies, before they are deemed fit to be sent on their duties into the interior. Another evil of this sudden change from a society composed wholly of Europeans, to one in which they are surrounded chiefly by dark-skinned Asiatics—greatly their inferiors in rank, emolument, and position—is to beget in them a supercilious contempt for a race so different from their own, and whom they seem to think they are specially appointed to overrule and command ; and this haughtiness of disposition towards the natives is daily fostered by the examples and customs by which they are surrounded.

A course of two years' supplementary professional study, after passing their first examination at twenty, and another year employed in visiting the chief marts of their own country, would mature both their minds and manners, and bring them to the age of twenty-three before they left England ; and, allowing a full year, which might be most advantageously occupied in their overland journey to India, by either of the various practicable routes indicated, or others that might be opened, (and the greater the number the better), travelling, as they might do, in parties of five or ten persons in a group, under the charge of a more experienced civil or military servant returning to India after leave of absence in England ; and being excited by emulation and previous study to examine and record, in their own manner, every object of interest on the way, according to the bent of their peculiar taste or aptitude, they would not only be advanced another year in age—being twenty-four on reaching India—but they would have been advanced ten years at least in the knowledge of the various countries they had traversed, the people with whom they had mingled, the varied and useful information they had received, and the sharpening the intellect and maturing the judgment by daily and hourly exercise.

They would moreover have, in the course of such a journey, the best opportunity that could be presented of turning their book-knowledge of languages to practical use, and would be perfected in the art of speaking and writing at least the four principal languages of the Continent—French, German, Spanish, and Italian—all opening new stores of literary and scientific reading to them in their leisure hours, and fitting them for conversation and correspondence in each. At the same time, from the moment of their arriving at Constantinople, and during all their journey from thence to India, they would improve their acquaintance with the Turkish, Arabic, and Persian tongues—of more value to them than those of all Europe, for facilitating the acquisition of Hindoostanee, and the other vernaculars of India, into many of which the Arabic and Persian enter so largely. Above all, such a journey would progressively *Orientalize* them, by making them every day more and more reconciled to the darker skins, and different creeds and manners of the people of the East: so that, by the time they reached their journey's end, they would become so acclimatized in feeling, as well as in health, as to look upon the natives of India with far more sympathy and respect than if they had suddenly landed among them from an English steamer, with all their national prejudices in full vigour.

Such journies as these would improve and strengthen the physical constitutions of all who should perform them. The daily exercise, on horseback, or on foot, with an occasional march on a dromedary or a camel; the bivouac in the fine open air of the desert or the plain; the constant vigilance necessary to be exercised at every hour; the rough but wholesome fare of the village or the tented tribes; the escape from all the frivolities of fashionable life in London, and the late hours and overheated rooms either of study or gaiety;—all these would so knit the frame, harden the muscles, strengthen the natural emotions, and purify the mind of the travellers from twenty-three to twenty-four, that this single year of their career would perhaps be one of the most useful, and most truly pleasurable of all their lives: and would do more to make them manly and robust in body and mind, than almost any other course of training that could be prescribed.

If the expense of such a preparation as this—namely, two years' professional study after the first examination, one year in examining the most important portions of England, Scotland, and Ireland, and one year in travelling overland through Europe to India, making four years in all—should be objected to as a heavy burthen on their parents, it might be answered that the expense would not be so great as maintaining a youth, designed for the Church, for three years, at either Oxford or Cambridge; nor half as great as keeping a young Barrister, or Physician, after he had left the University, till he could maintain himself by his practice; or paying the extra expenses, after the education was complete, of an under-paid Midshipman in the Navy, or an Ensign in the Guards, till they could subsist on their pay; nor lastly, nothing near so great as the sums *sometimes* paid for the purchase of Indian Writerships at the present time, which *some* Directors have been legally convicted of receiving, and other more careful ones may probably never yet have been found out.

To the local Government of each Presidency would, of course, be allotted the task of subjecting the young officers, civil and military, to their final examination; and then appointing them, within the departments for which they had been specially prepared, as the wants of the service and their own special aptitudes might suggest.

That the Indian service should be only accessible by the same channel to all, would, I think, be indispensable : and promotion in each might then be dependent on seniority as a rule, with power on the part of the local Government to advance any individuals who might prove themselves to be possessed of very superior talents for any special duty for which they might be required. To make either of the branches of the service open to persons of maturer age, appointed either from England, or by the Governors in India, would be attended with the certain evil of great jobbing in the exercise of political patronage, and the intrusion of unfit and unqualified persons. In short, patronage of every kind should be as carefully excluded as possible, as it is neither safe to intrust it to Directors, Presidents, Ministers, or Governors. The required education and training, length of service, and fidelity in the discharge of duty, should be the only claims admitted; and no dismissal from either branch should be allowed, without the sentence of a competent court, and after a full and fair trial and conviction.

Transfer of the Indian Army and Marine.

If the sovereignty of the Crown be proclaimed, every branch of the public service would at once become royal or national of course ; and the Company's name being extinct, the disparaging distinction which has hitherto been kept up, of King's and Company's troops and King's and Company's ships of war, would immediately cease. All our greatest military commanders have spoken in terms of the highest commendation of the Indian Sepoy regiments; and it is well known in India—though kept as much as possible out of view in England—that the Native soldiers have stood their ground and advanced to the attack of forts, when English soldiers have either hesitated or turned back. The whole Army and Navy of India should therefore be incorporated with the Army and Navy of the Crown : and placed on a footing of perfect equality as to pay, rank, and honours of every kind.

At the same time, considering that the Native Indian troops are better adapted to the climate than English ones, the distinction of European and Native regiments might still be maintained, and the speciality of the Indian service still continued, as the Officers of Regiments formed wholly of Natives and destined for permanent service in the country require, no doubt, peculiar information and experience to qualify them for their duties; and this, the previous system of education and training already marked out for all branches of the Indian service, would accordingly furnish.

While serving together in India the pay and emoluments of Officers, whether of English or Native Regiments or Ships of War, should be alike; and the present scale is not at all too liberal for either. One reform, however, might be advantageously adopted for both, which would be the *entire abolition of prize-money, head-money, gun-money,* and every other kind of *plunder*. The temptation which these offer to foment quarrels that might otherwise be easily settled without recourse to arms; —the monstrous disproportion in the share of the plunder awarded to the Commander-in-chief, whose life is rarely risked in the battle, and that awarded to the private soldiers and the non-commissioned officers who bear the chief brunt of the danger;—the wrongs inflicted on the innocent people, who had no share whatever in causing the dispute, by the capture of their ships, cattle, and other descriptions of property;—all these give to modern warfare the character of mercenary and buccaneering adventure.

The speeches put into the mouth of the Queen by her ministers, perpetually deprecate war as one of the greatest of evils. The Cabinet professes the greatest anxiety to maintain peace with all nations. The India Directors are continually sending out despatches, deprecating war and increase of territory as the things most especially to be avoided, and the Governors-General reiterate and re-echo the same strain. Nevertheless, in spite of all this, the greatest temptation to war is suffered to remain in full force. Sir James Brooke and his followers get £20,000 for massacring so many hundred of Dyaks—Sir Charles Napier gets £70,000 as his share of the plunder of the Sikhs in Scinde—and even Her Majesty herself does not refuse to receive, as a present from the army, the Koh-i-noor diamond, plundered from its conquered possessor—while admiring crowds gather round it in the Great Exhibition, without reflecting for a moment on the legalized system of plunder and prize money through which it was obtained.

The boast of the officers of the army and navy almost universally is—that they serve their country purely for the love of it; and " honour and patriotism " are their constantly professed motives in arming themselves for the fight. The time seems to have arrived when this boast should be tested as to its sincerity: and the opportunity of the change now required in the organization of the Indian army and navy, seems favourable for the experiment. Let all officers of every grade, as well as the men, be liberally paid; and let retiring pensions after certain length of service be liberally allowed. But from henceforth, let there be no division of plunder, spoil, or prize money, for any; so that every temptation to the provocation of unnecessary wars shall be removed : and conquest, thus divested of its chief reward to the conqueror, and chief punishment to the conquered, would be much less an object of ambition than at present. Such a change would do more to stop the thirst for new acquisitions of territories than all the eulogies of peace uttered by royal or ministerial lips, and all the homilies sent out from the India House for a century.

First duties of the Legislative Council in India.

The three most important duties of the Legislative Council in India would be—1. To revise and adjust the System of Revenue—2. To expedite and purify the Administration of Justice, and 3. To take the amplest practicable means for promoting the Education of the People.

Revision of the Revenue System.

As respects the Revenue, nothing can be worse than the present systems—whether of the Zemindaree, or Razotwar, or Village Settlement, as all of them are based on the false and barbarous Mohammedan principle, that the lives and property of all the conquered people belong entirely and exclusively to the conquerors; that they have therefore a lawful right *to seize the whole of the land as their own,* to annihilate private property in the soil altogether, and to permit its cultivation only on payment of one-half the gross produce of every estate, without contributing any aid towards its cultivation;—when they have done that, to tax every possible article of property besides, such as houses, shops, fruit-bearing trees, carts, ploughs, harrows, and implements of trade of every kind;—and all these having been found insufficient, then to take the monopolies of opium and salt into their own hands, and make a profit of 1000 percent. on the former, to smuggle, against the laws, into a friendly state, and help to demoralize and destroy thousands every year by its use; and to tax the latter, one of the most indispensable necessaries to the rice-feeding Indians, at several hundreds per cent., so as to deprive many of the use of it altogether, and to lead to its adulteration by a mixture of dirt and ashes, for the sake of increasing the quantity at the expense of its quality. In addition to all which, the Government has recently multiplied the licences of houses for the sale of ardent spirits, and are thus fast making one of the most temperate of nations, the inhabitants of which scarcely even touched intoxicating drinks till the English taught them the habit, into a nation of drunkards.

The revision required for this would be at once to raise large loans on the security of the State, which could be easily obtained at five per cent., and expend them in digging tanks and wells for water,—opening canals for irrigation, as in Egypt and old Assyria, where canals branched off from the Nile, and others united the Tigris and Euphrates, and watered all Mesopotamia, flooding the country with fertility. That this would be a profitable outlay is proved from the fact, that ten,

fifteen, and twenty per cent. of profit has been the result of the
few experiments of this kind already tried in India.   The
whole of the lands should then be sold, by public competition, to
the Natives or others, who desired to become purchasers—giving,
in all cases, the preference to the actual occupants, so as to
make the soil the property of individuals. The proceeds of such
sales should be wholly expended in internal improvements ; the
result of which would be, that in a very few years, an increased
revenue might be derived from increased production, and the
rate of assessment be speedily reduced from one half to one
fourth of the gross produce, the former being a ratio which is
so excessive as to ruin the richest country under heaven.

By ceasing to make wars of acquisition or aggression, and
merely defending their own frontier, so as never to go beyond
their own territory, the surplus revenue from the improved
land and increased area brought under cultivation would
furnish a fund still further to extend internal improvements,—
to deepen rivers, to open roads, to build bridges ; and these
perpetually operating as cause and effect, would give every
year increased beneficial results, till all other taxes, duties, and
imposts, save that on land alone—and this, perhaps, reduced to
a fifth of its produce—might be abolished, and increased wealth
and decreasing taxation go hand in hand together.

Formation of a Code of Laws.

The necessity and utility of this great work was acknowledged twenty years ago : it was, indeed, commenced by
Mr. Macaulay, and followed up nominally by Mr. Cameron
and others.   But the India Directors and the Board of Control,
by procrastination, dissimulation, and obstruction, prevented
its execution : so that twenty years have elapsed—an enormous
sum of money has been spent on the persons and machinery
provided for this purpose, amounting to many thousand pounds :
and yet literally nothing definitive has been done.*
It is pretended, indeed, that with such a variety of reli-

* " Cameron's Address to Parliament."   Longman and Co.

gions, languages, laws, and customs, as India contains, no
Code could be made to suit them all.   This, however, could
hardly be true, even if all these peculiarities of religion, law,
and custom, were to be left untouched; but no one who
desired the welfare of India could wish for this.   All the good
parts of these existing peculiarities might be retained, and all
the bad ones rooted out.   We profess ourselves to be most
scrupulously careful not to *interfere* with the religions and
customs of the Native Indians.   Would that we had been only
half as scrupulously careful not to invade their country, depose
their Native sovereigns, empty their public treasures, plunder
their private properties, take away the lives of those who
resisted our power, and subject all classes to the most grinding
system of taxation that the world ever witnessed!   After all
this unscrupulous tyranny and cruelty, it is the most hypo-
critical pretence, and nothing more, to affect great scruples as
to making any *inroads* upon their established customs.   We
have broken in upon all their rights and privileges, wherever
it was *profitable* for us to do so: and we have only ab-
stained where we thought no gain was to be derived from their
abolition.

Nevertheless, from time to time, there have arisen firm and
benevolent individuals, who, in spite of these pretended
scruples on the part of the India Company, and in direct
opposition in many instances to their instructions and authority,
have destroyed some of the most cherished customs of the
Natives, and that without the slightest danger to the safety of
the State. Mr. Jonathan Duncan and Colonel Walker effectually
put an end to the horrid practice of some high caste tribes murdering all their female infants at the birth, which these tribes held as
a religious custom.   Lord Wellesley prohibited the practice of
mothers throwing their children into the Ganges to be devoured
by sharks, which was also a religious custom.   Lord William
Bentinck, in opposition to the principal Indian authorities,
framed a law for abolishing Suttee, or the burning alive of
Hindoo widows, and this was one of their most cherished religious rites.   And lastly, Thuggee, or the practice of murdering
ravellers by gangs, of professed worshippers of Doorga, was

rooted out by Col. Sleeman: and this was a peculiarly religious custom, for the goddess Doorga, or her priests, had always a large share of the plunder to propitiate her protection.

Whatever positive crimes against human nature, or customs revolting to humanity and justice, may still remain among the Indians, may with equal ease be extirpated. What is wanted, is a due sense of right and wrong, to perceive what is evil and what is good, and moral courage to destroy the one and uphold the other. We have plenty of courage to slaughter our enemies, and, if need be, even our friends, the moment they turn against us; but we have not courage, forsooth, to suppress immoral customs, lest we should be unduly "interfering with Native prejudices?" Such is our weakness and inconsistency.

A Code for India, therefore, may easily be made as universal in its application to all the varieties of religion and custom in Asia,—as the Code Napoleon has been found equally adapted to all parts of Europe. In England we have not one set of laws, either criminal or civil, for the Christians, and another for the Jews, one for the Greek church, and one for the Mormons, one for the Mohammedan who may sojourn among us, and one for the North American Indian who may visit our shores. All are equally amenable to our civil and criminal law, our government, and our police.

In India it might be the same. The broad lines of demarcation, as to the laws of property and its due protection, might be clearly drawn—subject to all such peculiarities of inheritance and descent as might have in them no positive injustice or immorality:—as in England we have the law of gavel-kind in Kent, freehold, copyhold, and leasehold everywhere—laws of promogeniture and entail for landed property, and equal distribution or devise by will for personal property. The laws relating to crimes against the person, and crimes against property—from murder down to petty theft—are pretty nearly the same in all countries—as these are matters on which almost every sane man entertains similar views, by the innate sense of right and wrong, and the dictates of conscience which every one must more or less experience. Let, therefore, the Code be as simple, clear, brief, and intelligible as language can make

D

it, on all the great principles and chief landmarks of civil and criminal law; and let there be added to it an equally simple, clear, brief, and intelligible system of procedure, that all may understand it. And when made as perfect as a year of co-operative labour and joint revision in India could make it, let it obtain the sanction of the Crown, as our Colonial laws do at present, and then be proclaimed as the acknowledged Code, over all India, printed in every language written or spoken by the people there, and a copy deposited in every public office, from the Supreme Court down to the humblest Police Station, that all may have an opportunity to read and understand the law by which their conduct is in future to be regulated :—a provision which in the country is neglected, though common justice demands that if men are punished for the infraction of the laws, the very first requisite is, that they shall know what these laws are,—which, in England, at least, not one in a hundred can tell, without applying to a lawyer.

Proceedings of Legal Courts.

If a reform be required in the laws themselves, so equally is it necessary in the mode of their administration. That justice should be accessible to all, without fee and without expense, is a maxim often professed, but never yet reduced to practice. The new Government for India would furnish an admirable opportunity to introduce this wholesome innovation. At present, all law proceedings in India are loaded with heavy taxes to the Government in the shape of stamps, with fees to pleaders and attorneys, besides costs of witnesses and other charges, making it almost impossible for a poor man ever to become a successful suitor, or to obtain legal redress for the most grievous wrong. But it is especially for the protection of the poor and the ignorant that law and justice are wanted. The wealthy and the intelligent can generally protect themselves—or, at all events, can pay for such protection; but why should the poor man not have justice as well as the rich, since to him it is so much more important? It was well said by Mr. Bentham, and the sentiment is now becoming very general, " that of all the taxes which the wit or cruelty of man ever devised, taxes on justice are the most odious and indefensible." It is surely misfortune enough for a man to become entangled in a law suit, and to have to sustain the certain loss of much time, much quiet of mind, and the probable loss of a great deal of property besides; but to add to this, heavy expenses, to enable him to obtain justice, is a violation of all principles of equity.

Mr. Mill observes, in his History of India, that it would be quite as reasonable to fix a standard of height, as one of money, for regulating the claims to justice; quite as equitable to say that no man, unless he is six feet high, shall be permitted to enter a court of law, as to say that no man, unless he has a certain sum of money in his pocket, shall be allowed to commence legal proceedings for redress of any wrong he may have suffered : yet in practice, law and justice are perfectly inaccessible to the destitute poor. It was once said in the House of Commons, that " the English courts of law were equally open to all,"—to which Horne Tooke replied, " And so is the London Tavern; but both are open to no purpose, except they who enter them have money in their purses."

At the same time it is no doubt wise to prevent as much as possible all unnecessary litigation; and to punish with appropriate penalties those who seek to injure others; as well as to encourage all to seek justice who may deem their claims right, and enable them to do so without cost.

For this purpose, let there be well-qualified Judges, English or Indian, in sufficient number to have one or more within every fifty miles of distance—and still better, if a Court of Justice could never be more than ten miles off—this being a good day's journey in an Indian climate for a man on foot. To each Court let there be attached properly trained and qualified persons, as examiners of witnesses and documents, and sifters of evidence. Let it be their duty to prepare a statement of the facts proved by such means; and let a panchyet, or jury of five (one of the oldest institutions of India), be summoned on the spot, without previous selection or picking. Let the Courts be open to the public, and a competent reporter be attached to each.

Let the statement of facts be read in open court, before the Judge; let him declare the law upon the subject, and point out the Articles and Sections of the Code in which it is laid down, or at least the general principle applicable to the particular case; and after his charge to the Jury, let the majority of the whole, three out of five, deliver the verdict.

Here, the only persons to be paid, namely, the Judge, Examiners of Evidence, and Reporter, would be paid by the State. The Panchyet would act gratuitously, or on a mere nominal pay, as our Juries do in England : and as all their salaries would come from the revenues of the Province, neither stamps, fees, attornies, or counsel would be required. By this system, no one would have an interest in the procrastination of the proceedings, for the sake of the fees to be multiplied ; no one would have an interest in leaving any loop-hole open for a new trial ; but all parties would be free from that most powerful of all temptations to prolonged and uncertain litigation for pecuniary gain, as there would be nothing to reward them in the shape of costs or fees of any kind : and even the fine or penalty which might justly be imposed on the litigating party who should be proved to be in the wrong, should not go into the funds of the Court, but be paid over to the party declared to be in the right, as compensation for his loss of time and trouble, in defending himself against a proceeding for which it had been proved there was no just ground.

If such a legal and judicial system as this be contrasted with that which prevails in India now, where cases are fifteen and even twenty years under adjudication, being tried over and over again in different Courts, fifteen or twenty times, and incurring such heavy expenses in stamps, fees, and costs, to the litigants, as sometimes to ruin both parties, and reduce even wealthy men to beggary (of which some appalling instances are given in the pamphlet by Nourozjee Ferdoonjee, a Parsee officer in the Supreme Court at Bombay,* and the work of Mr. Norton, on the Administration of Justice in South India)†, the

* Published by J. Chapman, 142, Strand.
† Published by Stevens and Norton, Lincoln's-inn.

difference will be seen to be as great as between light and darkness—between simplicity and complexity—and between economy and extravagance—the one calculated to promote truth and justice, the other perjury and iniquity in its vilest forms.

Education of the People.

Of the importance of Education, as a means of producing wealth and happiness, it is unnecessary to say a word. All civilized nations seem now agreed in this: that where it is intended to rule over a people with justice, and to make the public weal, rather than private benefit, the ultimate object of all government—Education must be regarded as a general blessing, by its enabling the people the better to perceive and pursue their own advantage, and by this means to increase the general fund of wealth: while it enables them the more clearly to see the nature of the laws and government under which they live; and if these are equitable, to bind them more firmly in attachment to their country and its rulers. The welfare of the people of India being then admitted, by the professions of all parties, to be the first object which its Government should keep in view, the Education of the whole people, to the greatest practicable extent, becomes one of its most important duties.

Of the capacity of the Asiatics to receive instruction in every branch of learning known to Europeans, there can now be no more doubt than of the intellectual aptitude of the Egyptians or the Greeks—the one an African, the other an Asiatic people —to say nothing of the Jews of Palestine, the Assyrians and Babylonians, the Medes and Persians, and the ancient Indians themselves, whose learning and civilization astonished their Macedonian conquerors and the Philosophers of Athens, when England was a land of barbarians. The main question now is, What should be taught—and how to teach it?

The first kind of information which the present race of Indians, and the great bulk of the people most need, is the *useful*—the ornamental may follow after. But, in all the attempts hitherto made, their teachers have begun at the wrong end. Years devoted to Sanscrit, a dead and obsolete language for all practical purposes, are time thrown away; nor is it hardly more usefully bestowed in teaching the youths of India to read Milton and Shakespeare—whose beauties they must find it difficult to comprehend, and which might well give place to humbler beginnings. Something like the following, perhaps, might be the order of their studies:—

1. Reading and writing the English language correctly.
2. Arithmetic in all its branches.
3. Physiology, and the Laws of Health.
4. Geometry, Surveying, and Drawing.
5. Agriculture, Gardening, and Botany.
6. Geology and Natural History.
7. Chemistry and its practical applications.
8. Architecture and Civil Engineering.
9. The new Code of Laws for India.
10. Geography, History, and Astronomy.
11. Political Economy and the Laws of Commerce.
12. Natural Theology and Moral Philosophy.

This would appear to be the natural order in which the subjects might be most advantageously taught, with reference to their respective importance or utility, and the constantly improving capacity, which increasing age and augmented knowledge would give the Natives to comprehend and enjoy them; leaving their respective religious educations to be conducted by their own religious teachers, apart from the school—the only mode by which persons of such different faiths could ever be educated together.

Schools of the humblest kind, for children, for youths, and for adults, might be opened in every town and village of any size in India; and one teacher of each sex would be sufficient for the first three subjects at least—as both sexes should be taught thus far, though separately. The education for each might then be carried on by other teachers, as far in the list as the circumstances of leisure and position in life of the pupils would allow; some leaving off at No. 3, as all should proceed thus far, and others proceeding a step or two further : only the more fortunate, as to leisure and means, proceeding to the end.

To the poor, the education should be gratuitous ; to all others, at the most moderate rate, barely sufficient to cover the expense of materials, in books, objects, &c. ; but as the monitorial system of teaching originated in India, and is often called the Madras system—the one mostly now known as the Lancasterian, or Bell and Lancaster's—so the elder and better instructed pupils would teach the younger as far as they could go, and the cost would be trifling. Village schools abound in India already among the natives, and almost all the Indian servants of the British residents can write in their vernacular—whether Bengallee, Hindostanee, or Tamul. All that would be necessary, therefore, would be to place, in connection with such schools, and to multiply them when necessary, two competent teachers of the English language, to begin: so that their mother tongue and the tongue of their rulers would be the only language indispensable for the pupils to study ; and through these, all the useful information to be acquired by their further studies under other teachers, could easily be conveyed.

No outlay that the Government could make, in thus placing the means of useful education within the reach of all the people of India, would be more speedily or more abundantly remunerated than this, in the increased intelligence and skill of its millions of subjects,—in improved agriculture, manufactures, and every other branch of human industry,—and in the consequent increase of wealth, and means of consumption for British imports of every kind, of which there could not fail to be soon an immense demand ; as well as of Indian produce, cotton especially, by the British manufacturers in return ; and this would seal the death-blow of American slavery, more effectually than any other means that could be named.

Improved Means of Communication.

There is perhaps no better test by which to judge of the real interest taken by a Government in the prosperity of its

people, or of the real advance in civilization made by the people
themselves, than the state of the roads and means of internal
communication between one portion of the country and another.
We all know the wisdom and magnificence of the Romans in
this respect.   Not only had they the finest roads in the world
(many of which exist to the present day), leading from the
Capitol to every part of Italy; but, in their remotest and least
productive provinces, this great duty was never neglected.
Our own island of Britain, when it was chiefly covered with
forests and marshes, and had a mere handful of inhabitants
compared with the millions of India, was traversed in every
direction by their splendid highways; and even the farthest
East bears witness to their munificence in this respect.   In the
small territory of the Decapolis, which the Romans founded
after their conquest of Palestine, the merest speck of land,
lying east of the river Jordan and the lake Tiberias, there now
remain, within a square of less than 100 miles of length and
breadth, a greater number of public works, in roads, bridges,
aqueducts, temples, theatres, circuses, amphitheatres, nauma-
chia, baths, hippodromes, &c., than the English would leave
behind them in all India, a territory of 1,500 miles in length
and breadth, if they were to quit it to-morrow; and even the
Hindoo and Mohammedan rulers of India, our immediate predecessors, have left remains of their great works of this description in roads, bridges, canals, caravanseries, &c., which might
well put us to shame at our negligence.   In an article from the
Bombay Gazette of May 21, 1853, re-printed in the *Times* of
June 28, is the following paragraph :—

" The question of roads is really the question of the day for
India, which is ripe for agitation, and crying for it.   It is
allowed on all hands that the want of these is the great bar to
our commerce with central India.   But it is in vain to expect
that such roads will be made so long as a reference to the
Supreme Government at Calcutta is required for every particular
road or work which the local authorities may recommend.   It
is within our knowledge that on the most important line of
communication in western India, from Indore to Agra, the construction of a few miles of new road was stopped for upwards

of a year because the sum sanctioned by the Supreme Government was exhausted before the completion of the work, and the old road was, meanwhile, left without repairs and almost impassable! In passing it, carts were smashed, and bullocks died from exhaustion in numbers sufficient to rend the hearts of the brute beasts themselves, not to speak of the interests of commerce,—delaying whole trains of carts, or droves of pack bullocks, sometimes for days. Everywhere we want roads. It is the continued and crying want of the country. Every one admits the evil, though so little is done towards its abatement. We are further of opinion that the sinking of wells and the construction of tanks along the roads made is indispensable; assignments of land ought to be granted for the purpose of drawing water from those tanks and wells, and keeping constantly full cisterns or reservoirs, from which men and cattle could drink without labour in the course of their long and fatiguing journies during the hot season. *The former rulers of the country established such supplies* of fresh water at the principal villages; and in a country where the drought and heat in the fair season are so great, this considerate regard for the supply of a necessary of life, if formerly required, is so much more so now, when the men and oxen employed are so much greater."

The want of good roads for the speedy and cheap conveyance of cotton from the interior to the coast, appears to be the only reason why we cannot get our supplies of that article as good and cheap from India as from the United States of America. It is indeed alleged, and generally believed, that it could be furnished cheaper; and as to quality, we know that the finest muslins existing in the world are made in India itself, from Indian cotton, so that both cheapness and excellence would be combined. As before remarked, this would give the death-blow to American Slavery, by compelling the Slaveholders to give freedom to those from whose labour they could no longer derive the profit necessary to maintain them. This alone, if we were in earnest in our abhorrence of Slavery as a nation, and were not content merely to weep over the story of their wrongs, and hurl denunciations on those who inflict them, but ready to act as

well as talk, and make sacrifices if necessary, to ensure their
freedom, ought to be sufficient motive to urge the immediate
construction of good roads. But it would bring within our
reach many other articles of Indian produce besides cotton;
and when we consider that the river Ganges receives through
its course of 1,200 miles, from its entry on the plains to its
exit in the sea, no less than eleven tributary streams, several
of them equal to the Rhine, and few less than the Thames,* it
is easy to see what important auxiliaries good roads would be
to these natural channels for the transport of produce from the
interior to the coast.

An enormous quantity of flax might be had from India, were
there good roads for its cheap transport to the seaports. But
for the want of these it is left to rot and decay. About 200,000
tons of flax seed or linseed were exported from India in 1852,
of which the stalk is suffered to perish; though, if made use of in
the proper way, it would produce 25,000 tons of flax, at £30 a
ton at the lowest (some descriptions of flax selling at £160 per
ton); but, taking it at the lowest average, this quantity of lost
or wasted stalks would produce £750,000 per annum, and give
profitable employment to a vast number of natives in its manufacture, as well as profitable freights to British shipping,
and for every cargo of flax imported from India (none being
yet imported) a cargo of British manufactures would be exported to that country in return.

Flax is now chiefly imported from Russia, as well as linseed,
and the quantities of both are enormous. In 1852, no less than
70,113 tons of flax, and 796,000 tons of linseed, were imported
into England (chiefly from Russia) the value of which is com-
puted at £6,000,000 sterling, all of which might be produced
in India. The payments to Russia are chiefly in cash, instead
of manufactures; and the cash is often advanced by the English
merchants, through their agents in Petersburgh, to the cul-
tivators, in October, to help them to sow their seed—though
the harvest is not realized till the summer of the following year.

The exports of British manufactures to Russia are yearly

* Report of General Macleod and Col. Forbes, of the Bengal Engineers.

diminishing, while those to India are yearly increasing since the opening of the trade. In 1834, the last year of the expiring charter, the whole of the exports from Britain to India and Ceylon amounted to £2,500,000 in value; but in 1850, they had increased to £8,000,000, and are now considerably more; though not a twentieth part of what they might be, were the country wisely ruled, and its millions of inhabitants placed in a condition to be able to consume our manufactures like the people of other countries.

As a proof of the backwardness of India, and the miserable condition of its people, as compared with those of Europe, the following contrast may be given. The principal countries of Europe pay their respective governments a revenue of about 300 millions a year, while the people themselves, under most of these governments, are at least in the enjoyment of a large share of physical comforts; and when all their taxes are paid they have still abundant wealth remaining. The whole of the British dominions in India, equal in extent to the principal countries of Europe, Russia alone excepted, and much greater in fertility and natural resources than any or all of them, pays with the greatest difficulty, not *one tenth* the amount of revenue yielded by these countries, its highest produce of late years being twenty-eight millions sterling. The Emperor Baber, in the reign of our Elizabeth, raised from Bengal alone (hardly one-fifth part of India) nearly as much as we raise from the whole country, and still left the people wealthy, while we have drained them to the very dregs; so that, according to the testimony of Sir Thomas Munro, it is a frequent saying among the natives, that " the Company leave them their skins only."

Another contrast is this. Bengal is about the same size as Great Britain, each containing about 30 millions of cultivated acres. Great Britain raises, without impoverishing its population, a revenue of 50 millions sterling. Bengal with difficulty wrings from its population a revenue of less than 10 millions sterling. In England, the average value of the gross produce is £5 an acre. In Bengal not more than £1 an acre. In Great Britain the gross produce averages above £37 10s. 0d. per each individual employed in agriculture. In Bengal the average is only £1 7s. 0d. per head for each individual so employed; while even in the West Indies, the amount of produce exported (exclusive of that consumed in the country) exceeds £12 per head for man, woman, and child, white and black!

Lastly—The contrast is even still greater in the amount of the imports into India, as compared with those of other countries. The average annual imports of the different countries of Europe, of British productions (each of these manufacturing largely themselves) is about five shillings per head of their whole population; of America it is about fifteen shillings per head; of Australia, before the gold diggings were opened, about thirty shillings per head; and of British India, it is less than a single shilling per head!

If the cause of this difference be asked, the only answer that can be truly given is this, that India is worse governed than all the other countries named, that its resources are neglected, and the chief part of its revenues, small as they are in comparison with the means of the country, are wasted in extravagant establishments in India, in remittances of interest to India Stock-holders at home, in equally extravagant establishments in England, and, above all, in unnecessary and expensive wars; while the system of the land tax, by which the chief portion of the revenue is raised, is characterized by the great political economist of the day, Mr. Maculloch, in these terms, " The land tax in India is oppressive in amount, and the system under which it is assessed is subversive of the security of property, and of all industry. Supposing that the authors of this system had set about devising a scheme for paralyzing enterprise, and creating an insuperable obstacle to all improvement, they could not have hit upon one better fitted to accomplish such objects than the one they have established."

In consequence of this poverty of the people, and want of roads of communication, frequent and devastating famines occur, which carry off thousands at a time. For though rice and other grain may be abundant in some provinces, while it is deficient in others, there are no granaries of a portion of the surplus of one year, reserved for the possible deficiency of the next, the wretched peasants are too poor for this; nor are there any roads to convey speedily and cheaply the bounty of the soil in one province, to supply the wants of another—the short produce of which has mainly arisen from the neglect of the Government, to furnish and keep up those works of irrigation, tanks, and wells, which the Native rulers of India maintained in the interior. It has thus often happened, that while thousands have been dying of starvation in Upper Hindostan—for want of rice and other grain—whole cargoes of both have been sent from Calcutta to the Mauritius and Bourbon, to feed the French and English negro slaves in the sugar plantations there.

Debt, too, constantly increasing debt, is another of the consequences of this state of things. Every time the India charter has been renewed, the existence of the pending debt was urged as a reason why the Company should be allowed more time to pay it off; but every termination of the time allowed, showed the debt to be still further increased, when of course a fresh demand was made for a still longer period to pay it off. The result has been, as any person of the least penetration might have foreseen, that the more they were in debt, the more time they wanted to redeem it; and the more time was given to them the deeper they got in debt! so that there would be no end to such a process but bankruptcy and repudiation. The late Sir Robert Peel, in his speech in Parliament, on the 21st of June, 1842, thus adverts to this subject:—

"In 1835, the expenditure of India was £15,700,000; in 1841, it was £19,300,000, and is still increasing; in 1835, there was a surplus of revenue *above* expenditure of £1,500,000; in 1841, there was a deficiency of revenue *below* expenditure of £2,400,000, and this is still increasing. Already the Affghan and Chinese wars have added £15,000,000 to the Indian debt, which was £40,000,000 before; and if the the revenue continues to fail, both principal and interest will nave to be paid by this country."

The debt now exceeds £50,000,000, independently of the unknown expenses of the present Burmese war: and if England has at last to pay the whole, the sooner it takes the management of this rack-rented and half-ruined Estate out of the hands of its present incapable and spend-thrift managers, the less will be the future accumulations of debt; and the sooner we shall be able to arrest the downward progress of India, by first raising the revenue through improving the country and developing its resources, then paying off all its existing burthens, and carrying it forward in a career of prosperity worthy of so great and, if well-administered, so valuable a possession. Let a single example only of the famines so frequent in India, be given from the *Bombay Times*, that the English reader may form some conception of their horrors :—

"We have famines occurring almost decennially, some of which, within our time, have swept their millions away. In 1833, 50,000 persons perished in the month of September, in Lucknow; at Cawnpoor, 1,200 died of want, the £500,000 was subscribed by the bountiful to relieve the destitute. In Guntoor, 150,000 human beings, 74,000 bullocks, 159,000 milch cattle, and 300,900 sheep and goats died of starvation. Fifty thousand people perished at Marwar : and in the North-west Provinces, 500,000 human lives, are supposed to have been lost. The living preyed upon the dead ; mothers devoured their children, and the human imagination could scarcely picture the scenes of horror that pervaded the land. In twenty months' time 1,500,000 persons must have died of hunger, or of its immediate consequences. The direct pecuniary loss occasioned to Government, by this single visitation, exceeded £5,000,000 sterling—a sum which would have gone far to avert the calamity from which it arose, had it been expended in constructing thoroughfares, to connect the interior with the sea-coast; or districts where scarcity prevailed, with those where human food was to be had in abundance ; or on canals to bear forth to the soil, thirsty and barren for want of moisture, the unbounded supplies our rivers carry to the Ocean."

Dr. Spry, of the Bengal Medical Staff, in his work entitled "Modern India," published in 1837, gives his testimony as an eye witness to the horrors of these frequent famines in India. "I have seen," he says, "hundreds of the famishing poor traversing the jungles of Bundlecund, searching for wild berries to satisfy the cravings of hunger. Many, worn down by exhaustion or disease, die by the roadside; while mothers, to preserve their offspring from starvation, sell or give them to any rich man they may meet." (Vol. i. p. 297.) On this, the author of " Colonization and Christianity," William Howitt, in the section relating to the English in India, has these forcible remarks :—

" These are the scenes and transactions in our great Indian empire—that splendid empire which has poured out such floods of wealth into this country ; in which such princely presents of diamonds and gold have been heaped on our adventurers; from the gleanings of which so many happy families in England ' live at home at ease,' and in the enjoyment of every earthly luxury and refinement. For every palace built by returned nabobs from India, for every investment by fortunate adventurers in India stock, for every cup of wine and delicious viand tasted by families of Indian growth among us, how many of these Indians themselves are now picking berries in the wild jungles, sweltering at the thankless plough only to suffer fresh extortions, or snatching, with the bony fingers of famine, the bloated grains from the manure of the highways of their native country !

" Yet, amidst all this poverty and wretchedness, behold such contrasts as the following: Even so recently as 1827, we find some tolerably regal instances of regal gifts to our Indian representatives. Lord and Lady Amherst, on a tour through the provinces, arrived at Agra. Lady Amherst received a visit from the wife of Hindoo Rao, and her ladies. They proceeded to invest Lady Amherst with the presents sent for her by the Byza Bhye. They put on her a turban, richly adorned with the most costly diamonds, a superb diamond necklace, earrings, anklets, bracelets, and amulets of the same, valued at £30,000 sterling ! A complete set of gold ornaments, and another of silver, was then presented. Miss Amherst was then presented with a pearl necklace valued at £500, and other ornaments of equal beauty and costliness. Other ladies had splendid presents, the whole value of the gifts amounting to £50,000 sterling !

"In the evening came Lord Amherst's turn. On visiting the Rao, his hat was carried out and brought back on a tray covered. The Rao uncovered it, and placed it on his lordship's head, overlaid with the most splendid diamonds. His lordship was then invested with other jewels to the reputed amount of £20,000 sterling! Presents followed to the members of his suite. Lady Amherst took this opportunity of retiring to the tents of the Hindoo ladies, where presents were again given: and a bag of 1,000 rupees to her ladyship's female servants and 500 rupees to her interpreters."

These are the "gold and diamond diggings" which the appointment of a Governor-General opens to the successful occupant of this lucrative post: and thus it is that political and family interests and intrigues are so rife on every vacancy to obtain this rich prize, whether fit or unfit for the duties of his high and important station.

To revert, however, to the frequent occurrence of famines, with all their horrors, it may be asserted that nothing will tend to secure the country from a repetition of these dreadful calamities so much as new roads; but especially railroads : for which many portions of India are so well adapted; and on this subject, the present Government of India has all the requisite information, but wants the public spirit and zeal for the welfare of the country to act upon it as they ought to do.

In the Court of Proprietors of East India Stock, held at the India House in London, in June, 1847, the Chairman of the East India Company made this assertion,—"As to cotton in Bengal, it was more important to have railways for that article than in any other part of India; because the cotton produced on the Nerbudda lost twelve months from the time it was gathered until it was exported. It was liable, during that period, to great deterioration, as well as to heavy charges for warehousing and transport"—and he might have added, that twelve months' interest of money, borrowed perhaps by the cultivator at twenty to thirty per cent., was also swallowed up by the delay.

Railways, it is true, have been talked of, and projected, even in India, for more than twenty years (since 1832); but like everything else in the way of improvement, they have scarcely made the least progress during all that time. When a new territory is to be annexed, a suspected Rajah to be deposed, and his treasures seized, a new tax to be exacted, or any immediate object of gain to be achieved, there is no lack of promptness or energy in the Indian Government, either at home or abroad. But when such innovations as opening canals, digging tanks, forming a new code of laws, or introducing railroads, are proposed, then it is that the energy is wanting, and procrastination, " the thief of time," retards as long as possible the execution of them. It may be well, however, to give a short account of the several Indian railways at present proposed.

The East Indian Railway proposes a line from Calcutta to Rajmahal, on the Ganges—a distance of 200 miles, including a short branch to the collieries of Burdwan, a distance of 120 miles from Calcutta; and some progress (a few miles only) has been made in this. From thence, the Steam Navigation of the Ganges is good to Allahabad, passing by Boglipoor, Monghir, Patna, Dinapoor, Buxar, Ghazeepoor, Benares, and Mirzapore to Allahabad, at the junction of the Jumna and the Ganges, where the river navigation on each of these two streams becomes slow and difficult, from various impediments and want of water.

The Upper Indian Railway proposes to commence their road at this point, Allahabad, and proceed in a north-westerly direction between the two rivers, Jumna and Ganges, along the Plain of the Dooab, touching at Futtehpoor and Cawnpore, one of the largest Military Stations in India, on to Agra, on the Jumna, the capital of a new Presidency, and a most important city. From thence it will proceed by Muttra, another large Military Station, and Pulwa, to the imperial city of Delhi, having, on its right, short distances for branches to Lucknow, Furruckabad, Sikundra, Coel, Allyghur, and Meerut—all important places; and, on the left to Kalpy, Etawa, Gwalior, and Bhurtpore, also considerable stations.

The whole distance from Allahabad to Delhi is 400 miles, over a level tract, presenting no engineering difficulties whatever; on the contrary, affording facilities for economical con-

E

struction, such as perhaps no equal extent of country in any part of India can parallel. When this line shall be completed, another continuous one may be easily extended from Delhi, still in a north-westerly direction, to Kurnaul, Loodianah, Lahore, Jelum, Attock, and Peshawur, across the level plains of the Punjaub, to the very frontiers of Affghanistan; with a branch from Kurnaul to Simla, the Retreat of the Governor-General and Staff, at the entrance into the Himalya.

The *Delhi Gazette* states that the average cost of land carriage, in that quarter, is 30 rupees per ton for 100 miles. By railway, at the ordinary rate of 3d. per mile, the cost would be 13 rupees; showing a saving of 130 per cent. in the charge. Mirzapore is one of the greatest depôts in India for cotton. It is conveyed to that city at present on the backs of bullocks, carrying 160lbs. weight each, at an average speed of seven miles a day, in fair weather only! in the rains, the route is impracticable, and at a cost of about 5s. for each 100 miles! Taking the average distances from which the cotton is brought to Mirzapore at 500 miles, each pound of cotton costs in its transit by land more than 2½d. But after this, it has to be conveyed by water to Calcutta, at a cost of at least a penny per pound more, making the carriage of this bulky article nearly 4d. per lb., the original cost being less than 2d, and rendering it, therefore, quite impossible for it to compete with either American, Brazilian, or any other cottons, from countries in which greater facilities of inland carriage exist.

In *Herepath's Journal*, a high authority in railway matters, it is shown, from carefully considered data, that the existing traffic between Allahabad and Delhi (not allowing for any increase), would produce a profit of 150 per cent; taking even the lowest price now paid, namely 4d. per ton per mile; and conveying it at a moderate speed, would accomplish in half an hour the distance it now takes a whole day to achieve! If passengers were carried at 3d. a mile, the numbers now passing to and fro on that route (without allowing for any increase), would yield another 12 per cent. profit at least. But, even supposing that instead of 4d. per ton per mile for goods, and 3d. per mile for passengers, both were reduced to a single penny for each, and allowing the working expenses of the line to be 50 per cent. on its cost, the return would yield a profit of 50 per cent. on the capital sunk. The insurance of merchandize and property from Agra to Allahabad, in consequence of the danger and difficulty of the navigation, is as high as from Calcutta to England—the distance in the one case being 300, and in the other 15,000 miles!

The Bombay line is proposed to go from Bombay northwards, along the coast to Surat—then to ascend the Thul Ghaut at Mokree, and so on through and among the hills, by Domawutty, near Nagpore, to Allahabad—a work which, from the engineering difficulties of the hill country, and the general absence of large towns, population, and routes of inland trade through which it would have to pass, will probably never be accomplished; and could never be made to yield an adequate profit. The first twenty-four miles was opened in April last, yet none of the great authorities were present on the occasion, so little interest do they feel in such undertakings.

The Madras Railway, which proposed to go from Madras to Arcot, and on to Bangalore, in a westerly direction, for a distance of 200 miles, is open to the same objection. Its first 100 miles across the level country, like the first 100 miles of the Bombay line along the west, will be easy enough, but the remainder will, from the hilly nature of the country, be full of difficulties; while both are equally wanting in the essential elements of large towns, a thickly peopled district, and an established commercial route. Yet on these unpromising lines the East India Company have guaranteed a dividend of four and a-half per cent., for ninety-nine years—while the best line yet struck out, and the most important in every respect, as well as the most easy to be accomplished, namely, the Upper Indian Railway, has, up to this time, received little or no encouragement from them.

As a contrast between the manner in which public undertakings of national importance and utility are taken up and carried through in free countries and in despotic ones, let the following facts be compared.

So long ago as 1832, the construction of a railway from

Madras to Bangalore was projected; and in 1836 a line was actually surveyed by an officer of the Madras engineers, and resolved upon. About the same period, 1833, railroads first began to attract attention in the United States of America. But mark the difference—twenty years have elapsed since then, during which not a single railway has yet been opened in India beyond an extent of 24 miles; while in the United States, in the same period of time, more than 10,000 miles of railroad have been completed and are in full operation, and at least 10,000 miles more are in course of actual construction! From Boston, in the north, to Mobile, in the south, there is a continued line of 1,600 miles in length in daily use, and across the new State of Illinois, hardly yet reclaimed from the Indian hunting grounds, a line of 680 miles is in progress ; for which the Congress has granted 2,700,000 acres of public land. Yet the physical difficulties in the United States are greater than on any of the proposed lines in India, as the Philadelphia and Pittsburgh, and the Baltimore and Ohio lines are carried over the Alleghanny mountains at an height of 3,000 feet; and while in Europe there are undertakings on foot for tunnelling through the Alps, and carrying railways over the Danube, sending sub-marine telegraphs across oceans and seas—the Government of India are dozing and dreaming over their much smaller projects, not one of which, even the easiest of construction, has yet been carried into practical operation beyond the insignificant distance stated.

Tribunal for Redress of Grievances.

One of the greatest evils of the East India Company's rule has been the exemption which they have hitherto been allowed to enjoy from responsibility to the jurisdiction of English Courts of Justice, for the most flagrant wrongs committed by their servants and under their authority in India. Cases are perpetually occurring in which such wrongs are inflicted ; and by a rule of their own establishing, no memorial even, com-

plaining of the wrong or seeking redress, can ever be sent home
to the Court of Directors, without its being transmitted *open*,
through the local Government that has inflicted the wrong!
The consequence is, that in some cases, the memorial never
reaches the Court at all, and there is no power of calling any
one to account for this, either in India or in England. If sent,
it is sure to be accompanied with such comments and explana-
tions by the authority complained against, as to destroy all its
force, while the complainant is not present to rebut them, and
knows nothing even of their nature or existence. Added to this,
the Company have a rule of their own, equally convenient to
them and to their servants, that whatever is done by their authorities in India towards others, must be defended, however
unjustifiable it may be: because to open the door to redress of
grievances, would lead to endless complaints, and the shortest
way, therefore, is to strangle them in the cradle.

Many native Indians, on learning this, have innocently come
to England themselves to seek redress, and have applied in person to the Court of Directors. They have been generally received with the greatest politeness, and sometimes flattered into
submission by personal attentions and splendid hospitalities;
but in default of this, they are told that the Directors can listen
to no complaints except they are transmitted through the usual
channels (meaning the local authorities in India, the very
parties complained against). In their despair, the complainants
appeal to the Board of Control, misled by the name to suppose that this is a Board to control, or correct the Directors
when wrong, and by its overruling authority to compel redress
when they refuse it; little dreaming that as the President of
the Board has, by courtesy, as large a share of the Indian
patronage as the Chairman and Deputy Chairman of the Company, and twice the amount of the ordinary members, he continually identifies his interest with theirs, and however he may
compel them to sign despatches of their own, every line of
which they disapprove, yet in any case in which they wrong an
individual, the President is as sure to defend the Company in
Parliament, as if the patronage they allow him by courtesy
were regarded by him as a retaining fee to counsel.

The President therefore refers the complainant back again to the Court of Directors; and these have but one answer, which is, to refer him again to the local government in India. In his last effort for justice he gets some nine Proprietors of East India Stock, who feel for his wrongs, to summon a court of their body at the India House for the discussion of his case. In due time they assemble with solemn form. The Directors themselves muster in full force, and sit within the bar as the dignitaries of the Court; though, in point of fact, they are the very parties whose acts are complained of, and who are therefore on their trial. The farce proceeds, by some independent member detailing the grievance at length,—when a resolution for its redress is proposed and duly seconded. But as the proprietors are nearly all subservient to the Directors, to whose patronage they are constantly looking for rewards and therefore dare not offend them; and as the Directors know that they can command their votes, they listen with the greatest complacency to the tale of wrongs detailed, permitting the speeches to go on till nearly all present are tired out; and then moving, as an amendment, "the previous question" or "that the Court do now adjourn," which, being proposed by the Directors themselves as the easiest way of getting rid of the disagreeable subject, is sure to be carried by a large majority. The meeting is then dispersed; and the unhappy complainant is as much surprised as mortified to find that all this talk has ended in nothing; and that the redress he came to England to seek in person is just as far distant as ever!

This is not an imaginary picture. Four such cases of as flagrant wrong as ever was committed by the most despotic government on earth are now existing,—the injured parties or their Indian representatives being actually now in England seeking in vain for redress. The one is the case of the Nabob of the Carnatic; the other, the heir of the Rajah of Sattarah; the third, certain Parsee merchants of Bombay; and the fourth, the Rajah of Coorg, whose daughter has been recently baptized as a Christian under the sponsorship of her Majesty the Queen, but who has nevertheless been deprived of his private property by the Indian authorities, for which he can get no

redress; and when he asks the India Company to grant him a
prolonged leave of absence, that he may remain a little longer
with his daughter who is to be left in this country, and whom
he may never therefore see again, he is ordered *forthwith* to return to India, without the redress he came home to seek, under
pain of their severe displeasure!

Under the Imperial Government of India, such events as these
should never be permitted to take place without redress. And
to render this more secure, some public declaration should be
made, that all parties in India, rulers as well as subjects,
should be amenable to British Courts of Justice, both in that
country and in this; as her Majesty and the highest authorities
in the realm are in England. Or, if it be thought that the
peculiarities of such cases would require a Special Tribunal
for the Redress of Grievances, let one be established and
furnished with all the necessary powers to hear evidence—
examine witnesses—and enforce their judgment by the same
process as the ordinary Courts of Law and Equity in the land,
so that the maxim, "that there can be no wrong without a
remedy," may no longer be a standing lie, as it has hitherto
been frequently proved even in England, and still more frequently in India, but be made a solemn truth, and acted upon
accordingly.

Finances of the Company.

The original Capital of the East India Company, as a Trading Association was £6,000,000 sterling; and in the early
periods of their Commerce they divided as much as 200 per
cent profit, which dwindled by slow degrees and progressive
stages to 150—then to 100—and lastly to 80 per cent; and if
they had confined themselves to trading only, without forming
territorial conquests, enjoying as they did an exclusive monopoly
of the commerce with India and China, and all the other
countries forming the richest half of the globe, lying between
the Cape of Good Hope and Cape Horn, and including more
than half the population of the world, they would in all probabi-

lity, have continued to realize at least 50 per cent as their lowest
dividend, as long as their exclusive Charter lasted. But, in an
evil hour, they were tempted by the ambition of territorial
acquisitions; and as this required the erection of forts, the
organization of troops, and all the other expensive apparatus of
war, their trading profits soon became absorbed in the cost of
territorial government. Every new acquisition, notwithstanding the richness of the territory, and the large amount of
plunder often yielded by the conquest, in addition to its annual
produce, brought new and heavier charges, so that the Company's debt continually increased; and after two hundred
years of exclusive enjoyment of the greatest commercial privileges ever granted to, or enjoyed by, any mercantile association
since the world began, they have left off their trade with an
avowed debt of £50,000,000, and an accumulating one of at
least £10,000,000 more; or ten times the amount of their
original capital, with which they commenced their trade !

If this had been the career of any other mercantile association, it would of course have been declared bankrupt, and the
shareholders in its stock would have been without the slightest
claim to any further participation of capital or interest from
such a shipwrecked concern. But, from the favour which, by
means that may be more easily conceived than safely described,
the Company's directors have always succeeded in commanding
from crowned heads, ministers, and members of both houses of
Parliament, many of whom are large holders of their stock, and
many, also, large participators in their patronage for the relatives
of their families and friends, they have not only escaped the
fate which would have awaited any other Company not having
such powerful allies, but they have been actually guaranteed,
by the act of the Legislature itself, not merely the re-imburse-
ment of their original capital of £6,000,000 sterling (which
itself would have been sufficiently extravagant), but the payment
of double its amount, namely, £12,000,000 sterling. And while
other subjects of the Crown are well content to receive an
interest of four or five per cent. on their invested capital,—the
latter having been, till very lately, the maximum allowed by law
in all mortgages and loans, and three per cent. being the maxi-

mum of the public funds,—the stockholders of this favoured Company have been guaranteed by the Legislature an interest of ten and a half per cent., till 1847, when their double capital of £12,000,000 sterling is to be paid off!

Never, certainly, in the history of the world, was such liberal reward given to those who had mismanaged their affairs ; never were neglect, extravagance, and private advantage pursued at the expense of public loss, so honoured as in their case.

Notwithstanding all this, so little of hostility have I to the Directors or Proprietors of India Stock, that I would keep faith with them—though they have so often broken faith with others. I would respect their property, ill-gotten and unjustly augmented as it may have been, though they have so often recklessly and unjustifiably destroyed the property of others: and, for the sake of India and its future prosperity, I would even go further than they themselves claim, and instead of making their dividends depend in any way whatever on the future revenues of India, as they now do, I would at once recommend that on the declaration of the Sovereignty of the Crown, and the proclamation of the Queen over all her Eastern dominions, the whole of their doubled capital of £12,000,000 should be taken as part of the Imperial National Debt, just as we did when we paid £20,000,000 to purchase the emancipation of the Negro Slaves in our dominions ; and if the welfare of 3,000,000 of negroes was worth twenty millions to secure, the welfare of 150,000,000 of Indians would be worth £12,000,000 to advance. The interest of this sum, at 3 per cent., should henceforth be paid out of the revenues of Great Britain, as all our other charges for the maintenance of the national establishments and interest of national loans are now done. By thus leaving the whole of the revenues of India to support its own expenses of government, instead of remitting any portion to England, for dividends or any other purpose, we might devote the whole of the surplus which would then remain to the internal improvement of the country.

By such a change as this, a few years only would cover the vast interior of India with roads, bridges, canals, tanks, reservoirs, post-houses or halting stations, railroads, and all the other improvements of modern times. And when these had produced, as they would be sure soon to do, the enormous profits arising from increased irrigation, extended cultivation, turning waste lands into fertile fields, draining unhealthy tracts, improving their salubrity, and thus doubling the produce of India in all its rich varieties of tropical wealth: then, whatever surplus could be raised should go to the moral and social improvement of the people, by increased establishments for education, the founding of hospitals and asylums for the afflicted of every class, improvement of their dwellings, and amelioration of their condition, which would bind them to us in gratitude by the strongest of all ties—the conviction that any change of rulers would deteriorate their condition; so that, by interest as well as sentiment, they would become loyal and contented subjects.

As the country improved, with increasing resources, and ampler means, the burthens of necessary taxation would be the more easily borne; and this might be gradually lightened by the same process as takes place every year in England. The Indian Minister of Finance would produce his Budget for the year—before the Legislative and Representative Council of India—and if a clear surplus were shown to exist, when all the improvements adverted to above, had been effected, it would then be his duty to propose, and that of the Legislature to effect, a diminution of the rate of assessment on the land—which, as it is the simplest, the easiest, and on the whole, perhaps, the most universally equitable source of taxation, as all the chief elements of wealth spring from it, either from below or above its surface, (the objection to it in India lying in its extravagant amount rather than in its nature), we might live to see this land-tax reduced to an assessment of such moderate dimensions that one-tenth of its produce might be enough to keep up all the establishments of the country in full vigour—and leave the people in affluence and content.

Duties of the Mother Country.

There is a phrase in constant use, when speaking of the Parent State and her distant Possessions, by which the former is called the " Mother Country," and the latter are regarded as her " Offspring." These designations are at once appropriate, and pregnant with expression ;—as the relationships in which each stands to the other cannot be more distinctly, or advantageously stated than by these relative terms ; while the very conditions of affinity which they imply, at once point out their specific and reciprocal duties to each other. It may be asked, perhaps, in what do these consist ? And the answer to this question, if carried out in detail, would faithfully describe the very best line of policy for both that could possibly be pursued.

The duties of a good mother to her children, hardly require to be laid down minutely, as the instincts of natural affection not only point them out to every reasonable and conscientious parent, but make their discharge so pleasurable as to require no stimulus for their performance, beyond the delight which their daily exercise affords. They succeed each other in something like the following order :—

1. To provide for the more perfect development of all the physical powers, in the promotion of bodily health, by a sufficiency of the most wholesome food, a full supply of the purest air, abundant but appropriate apparel, freedom of limbs, moderate exercise or labour, and adequate repose.

2. To watch the first dawnings of the infant mind, and bring the intellectual faculties into as early and as active exercise as may be found to be compatible with perfect health and progressive physical growth, but no more; and, in directing and guiding its enquiries, to limit these as much as possible, to objects and topics of the first necessity, and greatest utility, as the foundation of all its subsequent pursuits in life.

3. To train the moral feelings, and adapt the daily habits in harmony with them, so as to produce, not merely a right con-

ception of the moral and social duties of each to all, by the law of kindness, love, truth, justice, and benevolence; but to make the exercise of these virtues as pleasurable to the mind and heart, as healthy and agreeable exercise is to the senses, so as to produce the most practicable combination of a sound mind in a sound body, the union necessary to perfect excellence in either sex.

4. To teach the use of such arts and labours as may enable all to earn an independent subsistence by their own exertions, whether in agriculture, manufactures, mining, engineering, commerce, trade, handicraft, or the learned and liberal professions, and to qualify all as speedily as possible to render themselves wholly independent of further parential aid.

5. When the period of mature age shall be attained, to offer friendly counsel and advice, as to the most appropriate time and form of separation from parental authority and control, by creating a separate establishment of their own; and assisting, if need be, with funds as well as influence, to make that establishment prosperous, permanent, and enduring.

6. And lastly, to continue, as long as both shall exsist, the same friendly relations after separation from the parental home, as existed while the rising youth were sheltered by its roof, and, whenever required, to be ready to assist, by every practicable means, the offspring to which they originally gave birth, to sympathize with their misfortunes, to rejoice in their prosperity, and to glory in their reputation and success.

If these are the duties of parents to their children—and who will venture to doubt it?—such also are the duties which Mother Countries owe to their Colonial Offspring. How imperfectly they have been performed, the pages of Spanish, Portuguese, Dutch, French, and English history unhappily will prove; yet how practicable it is to pursue a superior policy to that which these countries have observed, the earlier pages of Phœnecian, Greek, and Roman history abundantly testify. In both, there were no doubt great defects, but those of the ancients were mere light specks compared to the huge dark blots of the moderns.

Our own increased intelligence and our professed admiration

of the Christian code of morals, which we so earnestly proclaim it to be our wish to uphold, by giving bishops and arch-
bishops to our colonies to teach to others, if not to practise
themselves, the precepts of that code, leave us without the excuse which the ancients might fairly have offered, for any deficiencies of their earlier day, before the Gospel of Truth and
Love had dawned upon mankind.

Hitherto, we have ruled all our distant possessions with no
higher object than to make them yield as much of profit as
possible to the mother country; a barbarism as cruel as that of
an American Slave-owner making his own offspring toil with
the rest of his slaves for their master. We hold this to be a
deadly sin, on the west of the Atlantic; and justly denounce it
as a crime against human nature. But we have practised it
ourselves without any expression of horror in our own possessions in the Eastern hemisphere; as if difference of latitude or
longitude, could alter the nature and character of deeds, and
make that which is criminal in one region of the earth innocent
and honourable in another.

We can denounce the conquest of Spain, Portugal, Holland,
and Italy, by Napoleon, and rejoice at his overthrow, as a
plunderer of other lands; we can condemn the Bourbons for
their conquest and occupation of Algiers; we deprecate the
French for their attempt to regain the ancient boundary of the
Rhine, and to recover Belgium, Holland, and Italy, which they
once held but have since lost; we have no language too severe
by which to denounce the ambition of Russia to possess itself of
Turkey and supplant the Crescent by the Cross; yet we have
nothing but praise and self-gratulation to bestow on our own
countrymen for the equally criminal conquest of India, and we
glory in having achieved ourselves what we loudly condemn in
others.

At the same moment, too, that we are still boasting of our
love of peace, and deservedly honouring our Queen and her
Consort for the establishment of the Great Exhibition of 1851,
as the "Temple of Peace," to teach all nations the practice as
well as doctrine of universal brotherhood,—we are engaged in
an attempt to make new conquests of Burmah, Ava, and

Pegu, in the East; and summoning the *élite* of the nation to raise a large subscription for the purpose of setting up, in the Metropolis, as a "Memorial of this Universal Peace-proclaiming Exhibition of 1851," the equestrian statue of Richard Cœur de Lion, one of the greatest invaders and marauders that Europe ever produced; who began life by rebelling against his father, while yet a mere boy—who carried on a horrible war against his elder brother, in which neither party gave quarter—who renewed the war against his own parent, and besieged him in his Castle of Chalon, during which siege his father died;—who, after his capture of Acre, in the Crusades, refused to receive a ransom for the prisoners he had taken, and murdered 5,000 of them in cold blood, while his soldiers were celebrating the religious fête of the Assumption of the Blessed Virgin; who subsequently hung a whole garrison of Christians in France, even after they had offered to surrender, and soon after died of a wound in the Castle of Chalon, after a nominal reign of ten years over England as its monarch, though he had never spent a single year of all these ten within his own dominions; a man characterized by the three great vices of " pride, avarice, and voluptuousness," and whose whole life was a career of blood and murder!   Such are the men whom our chief nobility have met and subscribed largely (to the extent of several thousand pounds) to honour—700 years after his ignominious death—by setting up his statue in the capital of their own country, where thousands are pining in want, ignorance, intemperance, prostitution, and profligacy and crime, for which it is difficult to raise funds to carry forward the necessary agencies for their reformation!

If we needed more statues for the adornment of the Metropolis, in addition to those of the Kings, Princes, Dukes, Admirals, and Generals, which form the majority of the present number; and especially if we wished such statues to commemorate an Exhibition intended to promote " Peace and good will among men;" we might surely make a better choice than this of " Cœur de Lion," as we have yet no public statue in any of our squares or parks to our most successful navigator, Cooke—our most adventurous traveller, Bruce—our purest founders of Colonies, Oglethorpe and Penn—our greatest astronomer, Newton—our chief philanthropists, Howard, Clarkson, and Wilberforce—not one of our loftiest and most religious poets, Milton and Young—our most uncorrupted patriots, Marvell, Sidney, and Hampden—our most philosophic statesman and orator, Burke—or our great social reformers, Lord Ashley, and Father Mathew—each of whom are worth a hundred "Cœur de Lions" for their own merits and deeds, and still more for the beneficial examples of their lives, patterns worthy of exciting the emulation and imitation of mankind, and having much more in harmony with the " Great Exhibition of the Temple of Peace," than the ferocious blood-spiller, who had no greater virtue than that of the brute beast whose name is incorporated with his own, as if to be " lion-hearted," of which millions are to be found among the most ignorant and vicious of mankind, was to possess all the virtues that could elevate and adorn humanity, and like Charity, "cover a multitude of sins." Alas! for the wisdom of the nineteenth century !

To return, however, to India. We have hitherto governed it as a Foreign Despot, intent chiefly on the object of wringing from its wretched inhabitants all they could be made to yield us as a nation, in the shape of gain. We have overshot the mark, like the "vaulted ambition," which, leaping too high, loses its seat, and " falls on the other side." We have merely enriched some hundreds of families and individuals, but have burthened the millions of India and of England with a heavy and constantly increasing loss. Let us henceforth rule India and all our Colonies, as a Mother-Country should govern her Offspring, thinking first only of *their* welfare and prosperity, and in that, making our chief glory and reward to consist. If we do this, they will prove to us great blessings, and sources of wealth and strength. If we do not, they will, on the contrary, prove heavy curses, and become sources of poverty, weakness and disgrace; till at length, separating from the Parent state in anger and disgust, they will grow up, as America has done, to be rivals rather than allies, and with bitter recollections of their former treatment, which it will take whole generations to obliterate.

But it is time to draw to a close. I have confined myself in this short Tract, to the broadest Outlines only of a Plan for the Future Government of India, as the details would require much larger space; and indeed, the great principles of the Government being once settled, the details might be easily adapted to them as required.

I desire only that this Plan should be carefully considered, and impartially compared with the existing systems by which India has been hitherto ruled, or the Plan propounded by Sir Charles Wood and the Cabinet of Lord Aberdeen for its "improved administration," and I have no doubt to which the preponderating amount of approbation by the great bulk of the people both in India and in England will be given.

I am not so inexperienced in public life, however, as to suppose that it will be adopted by this or any other Cabinet. The " pride of office " is too great for that. It would be high treason against the Majesty of Government to suppose that any Individual, whatever the nature of his studies or extent of his experience, could produce a better Plan than that of a united Cabinet. And as its adoption would be a public homage to its superiority, it is never likely to be given. Nor is the House of Commons entirely free from the same " pride of dignity and power ;" and therefore it is that the chances of success for any measure in that nominally deliberative, but really party-bound body, is in an inverse ratio to the extent of the reforms it proposes. The slighter the improvement proposed to be accomplished, the greater the chance of its ready adoption ; but the larger the views, and the more searching the reforms it advocates, the fewer the number of those willing to give it their support.

There is a satisfaction, however, in setting up even a higher standard than is immediately attainable, and living to see a gradual recognition of its justice, and a step-by-step advance towards its adoption in practice. This pleasure I have before enjoyed, in many instances that might be named. This pleasure I may hardly live to realize in the present instance, though my children may share it when I am no more, and, in this anticipation, I commit my Plan to the judgment of posterity, if condemned as Utopian by my contemporaries.

For EU product safety concerns, contact us at Calle de José Abascal, 56–1°,
28003 Madrid, Spain or eugpsr@cambridge.org.